Besseres Englisch

Ellen Henrichs

Besseres Englisch

Grammatik und Übungen für die Klassen 5 bis 10

FALKEN

Zu diesem Buch gibt es ein Software-Lernprogramm unter dem Titel »The Grammar Master«, mit dem die wichtigsten Übungen vertiefend gelernt werden können (Disk. 5¼" für IBM-PC und Kompatible, Bestell-Nr. 7030).

Die Trainingssektionen beziehen sich auf die Kapitel

- The Tenses
- Conditional Clauses
- Reported Speech
- The Adjective: Comparison
- The Adverb

Das Programm beinhaltet einen Eingangstest. Damit kann jeder seinen Wissensstand überprüfen. Am Ende des Programms finden Sie einen Abschlußtest, der Ihnen Ihren Lernerfolg zeigt.

Außerdem ist lieferbar: »Vokabeltrainer Englisch« (für C 64/C 128 PC, Nr. 7001; Disk. 5¼" für IBM-PC und Kompatible, Nr. 7034).

Weitere interessante FALKEN Titel finden Sie auf Seite 143/144.

Unser Beitrag zum Umweltschutz:
Papier aus chlorfrei gebleichtem Zellstoff

ISBN 3 8068 0745 0

Nachauflagenredaktion: Dr. Werner Brand

Satz: LibroSatz, Kriftel bei Frankfurt
Druck: Neuwieder Verlagsgesellschaft mbH, Neuwied

08074585X161 514 131 211 10

Inhalt

Einleitung

Vorwort

„Besseres Englisch" ist gedacht als Nachschlage- und Übungsbuch für Schüler der Unter- und Mittelstufe weiterführender Schulen (Klassen 5–10), die im Bereich der Grammatik Schwierigkeiten haben. Aber auch Schülern der Oberstufe wird es nützen bei der Wiederholung und Auffrischung im Hinblick auf Kursarbeiten.
Dieses Buch ist so konzipiert, daß Schüler selbständig (oder auch zusammen mit ihren Eltern oder ihrem Nachhilfelehrer) Kapitel auswählen, die ihnen persönlich Schwierigkeiten bereiten, die jeweiligen Erklärungen durcharbeiten, um dann die entsprechenden Übungen zu lösen und – eventuell mit Hilfe des Lösungsanhangs – korrigieren.
„Besseres Englisch" stellt also eine Kombination von Mindestgrammatik und Übungsbuch dar. Es ist sowohl lehrbuchbegleitend als auch lehrbuchunabhängig einzusetzen. Bei frühzeitiger Anwendung hilft es, Lücken erst gar nicht entstehen zu lassen. Bei bereits bestehenden Lücken garantiert intensive Arbeit mit dem Buch deren schrittweise Beseitigung.
Die Auswahl der Kapitel orientierte sich am Schulalltag, d. h., es wurden solche Bereiche ausgewählt, die erfahrungsgemäß deutschen Schülern besondere Schwierigkeiten bereiten und Fehlerschwerpunkte in Klassenarbeiten, Tests usw. bilden.
Um zu gewährleisten, daß das Verständnis zum Teil recht schwieriger Phänomene der englischen Sprache nicht bereits an der Sprachbarriere scheitert, wurden die Regeln in verständlichem Deutsch formuliert, wobei jedoch darauf geachtet wurde, daß zusätzlich die in den Schulbüchern gebrauchten englischen Fachausdrücke angewendet werden.
Die einzelnen Übungen (unterteilt in A-Übungen = leichtere und B-Übungen = schwierigere) sind abwechslungsreich gestaltet und entsprechen in Form und Schwierigkeitsgrad Übungen in Klassenarbeiten.

Hinweise für Schüler und Eltern

Die englische Grammatik bereitet vielen Schülern vor allem wegen der Überlagerungen mit der deutschen Muttersprache oft Schwierigkeiten, die dann in Klassenarbeiten, Tests usw. besonders gravierend zu Tage treten. Besondere Schwierigkeiten bereiten die englischen Zeiten (tenses); aus diesem Grund ist ihnen in diesem Buch besonders viel Platz eingeräumt. Sicheres Beherrschen der Zeiten ist Grundlage für gutes Englisch. Der Schüler sollte sich also besonders intensiv mit den entsprechenden Kapiteln befassen und auch auf die im Englischen gebräuchlichen zusammengezogenen Zeitformen achten (z. B. he is not – he isn't,

I shall (will) come – I'll come, I shall (will) not come – I shan't (won't) come, I should (would) come – I'd come, I should (would) not come – I shouldn't (wouldn't) come usw.). Folgende Vorgehensweise für die Arbeit mit dem vorliegenden Buch sei vorgeschlagen:

1. Auswahl eines Kapitels, das dem Schüler persönlich Schwierigkeiten bereitet,
2. intensives Durcharbeiten des Regelteils (die Regeln nachvollziehen, eventuell durch Bilden eigener Beispiele; nicht einfach nur lesen!),
3. Lösung der Übungsaufgaben (schriftlich!),
4. Nachschlagen im Lösungsanhang,
5. Markieren falscher Sätze,
6. gegebenenfalls erneutes Lesen von Regeln und nochmaliges Schreiben vormals falscher Sätze.

Der Schüler sollte sich immer nur mit einem Kapitel befassen. Erst wenn dieses verstanden ist, sollte ein neues in Angriff genommen werden. Späteres Wiederholen nicht vergessen!
Ein Wort an den Schüler: Das alles klingt zwar nach schrecklich viel Arbeit, aber es lohnt sich! Viel Glück und Erfolg also beim Arbeiten.

The Tenses – die Zeiten

Die Bedeutung der englischen Zeiten

Die englischen Zeiten (tenses) bilden eines der wichtigsten Kapitel der englischen Grammatik. Jeder Satz beinhaltet eine oder mehrere Verbformen und damit eine oder mehrere Fehlerquellen. Bei der Korrektur von Klassenarbeiten, Hausaufgaben usw. stellt man immer wieder fest, daß der Gebrauch der 'tenses' eine der Hauptfehlerursachen darstellt. Aus diesem Grund sollte diesem Kapitel besondere Aufmerksamkeit geschenkt werden.
Dem deutschen Schüler bereiten die englischen Zeiten oft Schwierigkeiten. Gründe dafür sind:

1. Die englischen Zeiten werden zum Teil anders gebildet als die entsprechenden deutschen.
2. Die englischen Zeiten werden zum Teil anders verwendet als die entsprechenden deutschen.
3. Es gibt im Englischen Zeiten, die es im Deutschen nicht gibt und umgekehrt.

Für den Schüler bedeutet dies, daß er sich von seinem deutschen Sprachgefühl lösen muß und sich nicht durch Übersetzen in die Irre führen lassen darf. Um nur ein Beispiel zu geben:

Gestern habe ich einen Brief geschrieben.
Yesterday I wrote a letter.

Wie im Deutschen benötigt man auch im Englischen drei Verbformen zur Bildung aller Zeiten. Diese Verbformen werden Stammformen genannt:

1. Verbform: Infinitive – Infinitiv
2. Verbform: Past Tense Form – Imperfekt
3. Verbform: Past Participle – Partizip Perfekt

Deutsches Beispiel:
1. schreiben
2. schrieb
3. geschrieben

Die englische Sprache verfügt über regelmäßige (regular) und unregelmäßige (irregular) Verben. Regelmäßige Verben bilden die 2. und 3. Stammform durch Anhängen von '-ed' an den Infinitiv;
z. B.:
1. to work, 2. worked, 3. worked.

Unregelmäßige Verben lassen keine solche Gesetzmäßigkeit erkennen. Man muß die Formen, die man im Anhang eines jeden guten Wörter- oder Schulbuches findet, lernen;
z. B.:
1. to go, 2. went, 3. gone.

Tabellarische Übersicht über die englischen Zeiten Active Voice – Aktiv

Die englische Sprache verfügt über acht Aktivzeiten und die entsprechenden Verlaufsformen. Anders als im deutschen Sprachgebrauch werden die Zeiten im Englischen wesentlich genauer angewandt. Jede Zeit hat ihren ganz speziellen Anwendungsbereich, und jede Abweichung davon wäre ein Grammatikfehler. Es gilt also, sich die Antworten auf folgende Fragen genau einzuprägen:

1. Wie wird die Zeit gebildet?
2. Wann wird sie angewandt? (Signalwörter helfen, die Regel zu behalten.)
3. Was ist anders als im Deutschen?

Die Zeiten (tenses)	Bildungsweise	Beispielformen
Präsens (Present Tense Simple*)	1. Verbform bei 3. Person Singular: + -s	I work he works
Präsens Verlaufsform (Present Tense Continuous**)	Präsens von 'to be' (am/are/is) + 1. Verbform + -ing	I am working you are working he, she, it is working we, you, they are working
Imperfekt/Präteritum (Past Tense Simple*)	2. Verbform	I worked/went he worked/went
Imperfekt Verlaufsform (Past Tense Continuous**)	Imperfekt von 'to be' (was/were) + 1. Verbform + -ing	I was working you were working he, she, it was working we, you, they were working
Perfekt (Present Perfect Simple*)	have + 3. Verbform bei 3. Person Singular: has	I have worked/have gone he has worked/has gone
Perfekt Verlaufsform (Present Perfect Continuous**)	have + been + 1. Verbform + -ing bei 3. Person Singular: has	I have been working he has been working

* Die Nicht-Verlaufsformen haben oft die Zusatzbezeichnung 'Simple'.
** Statt 'Continuous' findet man auch die Bezeichnung 'Progressive' oder '-ing-Form'.

Die Zeiten (tenses)	Bildungsweise	Beispielformen
Plusquamperfekt (Past Perfect Simple*)	had + 3. Verbform	I had worked/had gone he had worked/had gone
Plusquamperfekt Verlaufsform (Past Perfect Continuous**)	had + been + 1. Verbform + -ing	I had been working he had been working
Futur I (will – Future*)	will + 1. Verbform (bei 'I' und 'we' statt 'will' auch 'shall')	I will work he will work
Futur I (going to – Future*)	Präsens von 'to be' (am/are/is) + going to + 1. Verbform	I am going to work he is going to work
Futur I Verlaufsform (Future Continuous**)	will + be + 1. Verbform + -ing	I will be working he will be working
Futur II (Future Perfect Simple*)	will + have + 3. Verbform	I will have worked/gone he will have worked/gone
Futur II Verlaufsform (Future Perfect Continuous**)	will + have + been + 1. Verbform + -ing	I will have been working he will have been working

Die Zeiten (tenses)	Bildungsweise	Beispielformen
Konditional I (Conditional I Simple*)	would + 1. Verbform (bei 'I' und 'we' statt 'would' auch 'should')	I would work he would work
Konditional I Verlaufsform (Conditional I Continuous**)	would + be + 1. Verbform + -ing	I would be working he would be working
Konditional II (Conditional II Simple*)	would + have + 3. Verbform	I would have worked/ would have gone he would have worked would have gone
Konditional II Verlaufsform (Conditional II Continuous**)	would + have + been + 1. Verbform + ing	I would have been working he would have been working

* Die Nicht-Verlaufsformen haben oft die Zusatzbezeichnung 'Simple'.
** Statt 'Continuous' findet man auch die Bezeichnung 'Progressive' oder '-ing-Form'.

Present Tense Simple – Präsens

	+	–	?
Bildungsweise	1. Verbform; bei 3. Person Singular* + -s	don't + 1. Verbform doesn't + 1. Verbform	do + 1. Verbform does + 1. Verbform
Beispielformen	I work he works	I don't work he doesn't work	do I work does he work

* bei Verben, die im Infinitiv auf -o oder Zischlaut enden, wird noch ein -e- vor das -s geschoben; z. B.: do – does, watch – watches.

Anwendung:

Present Tense Simple steht

- wie das deutsche Präsens bei regelmäßig wiederholten oder gewohnheitsmäßigen Handlungen;
  z. B.: Every Saturday he washes his car.
  Signalwörter
  every, usually, often, sometimes, always, seldom, never usw.
- bei allgemeingültigen Feststellungen;
  z. B.: London lies on the Thames.
- wenn mehrere Handlungen nacheinander passieren;
  z. B.: He pays for his petrol, then jumps into his car and drives away.
- bei Verben mit statischer Bedeutung, die keine Verlaufsform haben, wie to be, to love, to hate, to like, to understand, to think (denken), to remember, to forget, to notice, to realize, to sound, to hear, to see, to smell (riechen nach), to seem, to mean, to doubt, to prefer, to want, to wish, to belong usw.;
  z. B.: I love ice-cream.

A-Übungen (Exercises)

Put the verbs in brackets () into the correct Present Tense form. Mind the 3rd person singular -s!
(Setze die Verben in Klammern in die richtige Präsensform! Achte auf das -s in der 3. Person Singular!)

1. Peter and Mary (to go) to school every morning.
2. Mary (to read) a book every month.
3. I (to like) lemonade.
4. The children often (to watch) TV.
5. Mrs. Cooper (to clean) the window every week.
6. The boys sometimes (to listen to) pop music.
7. Mr. Miller seldom (to work) before 9 o'clock.

8. The tree (to stand) behind our house.
9. He (to open) the book, (to read) a few lines and then (to sleep) in his arm-chair.
10. In the evening they (to play) cards or (to write) letters.

B-Übungen (Exercises)

Put the verbs in brackets () into the correct Present Tense form.
(Setze die Verben in Klammern in die richtige Präsensform!)

1. The girls (not/to like) too much homework.
2. (to play) you cricket?
3. Mr. Miller (not/to go) to pubs.
4. (to stay) he at home every evening?
5. He sometimes (not/to spend) the evening at home.
6. Mrs. Miller (not/to work).
7. (to read) Peter books in the evening?
8. No, he (not/to like) reading.
9. (to speak) Mary French?
10. No, she (not/to speak) French, she only (to speak) English.

Present Tense Continuous – Präsens Verlaufsform

Bildungsweise: Präsens von 'to be' = sein (am/are/is) + 1. Verbform + -ing Präsens von 'to be': I am (am not) you are (aren't) he, she, it is (isn't)		we are (aren't) you are (aren't) they are (aren't)	
	+	–	?
Beispiel-formen	I am going you are going he is going	I am not going you aren't going he isn't going	am I going are you going is he going

Anwendung:
Present Tense Continuous
- bezeichnet vor allem Handlungen, die im Moment des Sprechens geschehen;
  z. B.: At the moment he is washing his car.
  Signalwörter
  just now, at the moment, Look!, Listen!

Beachte:

Dauerzustände stehen im Present Tense Simple;
z. B.: Our house stands in East Lane.

Bei Verben, die im Infinitiv einen kurzen betonten Vokal – a, e, i, o, u – haben, wird der darauffolgende Konsonant beim Anhängen von -ing verdoppelt;
z. B.: to put – putting
to sit – sitting

Bei Verben, die im Infinitiv mit stummem -e enden, fällt das -e beim Anhängen von -ing weg;
z. B.: to come – coming
to give – giving

A-Übungen (Exercises)

I. Put the verbs in brackets () into the correct Present Tense Continuous form. (Setze die Verben in Klammern in die richtige Form der Präsens Verlaufsform!)

1. The workers (to pull down) the house now.
2. Mr. Paul (to repair) his car at the moment.
3. Look! The students (to play) football.
4. I (to write) a letter just now.
5. She (to wear) jeans today.
6. Look! He (to run) through the park again.
7. Listen! They (to play) our favourite song.
8. Mother (to prepare) lunch now.
9. Listen! Mrs. Carter (to shout) at Billy.
10. The boss (to telephone) just now.

II. Translate the following sentences. (Übersetze die folgenden Sätze!)

1. Susanne besucht im Moment ihre Großmutter.
2. John ist nicht zuhause. Er spielt gerade Tennis.
3. Mary macht gerade ihre Hausaufgaben.
4. Die Millers sitzen im Moment im Garten und spielen Karten.
5. Gib mir meinen Schirm! Es regnet.
6. Hör mal! Stephen spielt Klavier.
7. Ich kann nicht kommen. Ich helfe gerade meiner Mutter.
8. Komm, wir (Let's) gehen in den Garten. Die Sonne scheint.
9. Vater schaut gerade fern und Mutter liest ein Buch.
10. Schau! Der Arzt kommt.

III. Today everything is different! Mary is late today. Write down what Mary does every day and what she is doing today. Use the following expressions. (Schreibe auf, was Mary jeden Tag macht und was sie heute tut. Benutze die folgenden Ausdrücke.)

Beispiel:
Every day Mary gets up at 6.30 a. m., but today she is still sleeping.

	every day	today
1. 7 o'clock	(to have breakfast)	(to lie in bed)
2. 8 o'clock	(to go to the bus stop)	(to have breakfast)
3. 9 o'clock	(to start working)	(to sit in the bus)
4. 10 o'clock	(to make phone calls)	(to arrive at the office)
5. 12 o'clock	(to have break)	(to work)

B-Übungen (Exercises)

I. Fill in the correct Present Tense forms, use either Simple or Continuous. (Setze die richtigen Präsensformen ein, benutze entweder das einfache Präsens oder die Verlaufsform!)

1. Every morning Betty (to get) up at 7 o'clock, but today she (to be) late.
2. Now it's 8 o'clock and Betty still (to sleep).
3. Look! Mr. Cooper (to work) in the garden. He usually (to have) a rest at this time.
4. Mary seldom (to go) to a disco, but this evening she (to dance) and (to have fun) at 'The Black Prince'.
5. Mr. Smith (to hate) housework, but because his wife (to have to stay) in bed he (to clean) the kitchen now.
6. Peter, what (to do) you now?
7. Mr. Brown (to play) tennis every weekend, but now he (to cut) his lawn instead of playing tennis.
8. Some small trees (to stand) in our front garden.
9. Listen! Mary (to play) the guitar. She (not/to play) well.
10. Where's your brother? He (to have) a shower.

II. Translate the following sentences. (Übersetze die folgenden Sätze!)

1. Schau, die Jungen spielen Handball, obwohl sie normalerweise Sport nicht mögen.
2. Während Mr. Miller ein Buch liest, schaut seine Frau fern.
3. Frankfurt liegt am Main.
4. Jeden Samstag erledigt Frau Müller ihre Einkäufe.
5. Ich mache jeden Tag zwischen 14 und 17 Uhr meine Hausaufgaben, aber heute höre ich Platten.

6. Mr. Miller raucht selten, aber heute raucht er eine Zigarre.
7. Was machst du gerade? Ich wasche meine Haare.
8. Unsere Nachbarin spielt täglich Klavier. Hörst du? Sie übt gerade.
9. Stephen fährt gewöhnlich mit dem Bus zur Schule, aber heute nimmt er die U-Bahn.
10. Ich gehe nicht sehr oft ins Kino, aber mein Bruder geht beinahe jede Woche.

Past Tense Simple – Imperfekt (Präteritum)

Bei regelmäßigen Verben

	+	–	?
Bildungsweise	Infinitiv + -ed	didn't + Infinitiv	did + Infinitiv
Beispielformen	I worked	I didn't work	did I work

Beachte:
Endet das Verb im Infinitiv auf Konsonant + y, so wird im Imperfekt aus dem y ein i;
z. B.: to carry – he carried

Bei unregelmäßigen Verben

	+	–	?
Bildungsweise	2. Verbform	didn't + Infinitiv	did + Infinitiv
Beispielformen	I went	I didn't go	did I go

Anwendung:
Past Tense Simple bezeichnet
- einmalige
- aufeinanderfolgende
- wiederholte

} Handlungen, die in der Vergangenheit angefangen haben und abgeschlossen sind.

Signalwörter
last . . ., . . . ago,
in 1950, yesterday;
z. B.: I saw him last week.

Beachte:

Im Deutschen steht oft Perfekt, wenn im entsprechenden englischen Satz Imperfekt steht. Laß Dich also nicht von der deutschen Übersetzung in die Irre führen!

Beispiel:

Gestern habe ich Peter gesehen. –
Yesterday I saw Peter.

A-Übungen (Exercises)

I. Put the verbs in brackets () into the Past Tense. Learn the irregular forms first! (Setze die Verben in Klammern ins Imperfekt! Lerne zuerst die unregelmäßigen Verben!)

1. Yesterday I (to write) a letter to Aunt Mary.
2. I (to meet) my friend Tom two days ago.
3. The Millers (to build) a house last year.
4. My father (to buy) a new car two months ago.
5. He (to get) the car from a car dealer.
6. He (not/to come) to my party last week.
7. ... my brother (to give) you the book?
8. In 1960 my parents (to marry).
9. Last week our class (to have) a party.
10. Three days ago our new neighbours (to move) in.
11. ... you (to see) the new Fellini film?
12. Yesterday I (not/to do) my homework.
13. I (to be) very busy yesterday.
14. We (to spend) our last holiday in Italy.
15. The hotel rooms there (to be) very nice.
16. The tourists (to visit) Big Ben last week.
17. When I was young, I (to learn) skiing.
18. Half an hour ago grandmother (to call).
19. The students (not/to be) quick yesterday.
20. Columbus (to discover) America.

II. Rewrite the following story in the Past Tense. You must change 21 verbs. (Schreibe die folgende Geschichte im Imperfekt! Du mußt 21 Verben verändern.)

John gets up at 7.15. He goes into the bathroom, washes, dresses, and then goes downstairs. He has breakfast at 7.30 and leaves the house half an hour later. He walks to the nearest bus stop and takes the 8.20 bus to school. He sits in class till 12.30. Then the school bell rings and the children rush to the dining hall and have lunch. They don't like the food very much, but nevertheless they eat their meals

because they are hungry. After lunch they have four more lessons. Their first subject in the afternoon is Sports. At 5 o'clock they leave school, get on a bus again and arrive at home at about 5.45.
So, yesterday...

B-Übungen (Exercises)

Translate the following sentences.
(Übersetze die folgenden Sätze!)

1. Gestern war das Wetter schön.
2. Letzten Monat hatten wir keine Zeit.
3. Wir haben unser Haus vor zwei Jahren gekauft.
4. Die Familie Berg ist gestern ausgezogen.
5. Wir haben vorigen Monat fünf Klassenarbeiten geschrieben.
6. Im letzten Zeugnis hatte ich keine schlechte Note.
7. Letzten Monat bekam ich keinen Brief von ihm.
8. Ich habe mir gestern den neuen Film im Kino angesehen.
9. Mein Bruder hat gestern den ganzen Tag gearbeitet.
10. Die Polizei fing den Dieb vor drei Wochen.
11. Ich habe vor zwei Tagen meine Brieftasche verloren.
12. Er vergaß gestern, das Buch abzuholen.
13. Mein Freund kam gestern abend nicht pünktlich.
14. Hast du das Fußballspiel gestern gesehen?
15. Wann seid ihr gestern ins Bett gegangen?

Past Tense Continuous – Imperfekt Verlaufsform

Bildungsweise:
Imperfekt von 'to be' (was/were) + Infinitiv + -ing
Imperfekt von 'to be':

I was (wasn't)	we were (weren't)
you were (weren't)	you were (weren't)
he, she, it was (wasn't)	they were (weren't)

	+	–	?
Beispiel-formen	I was going you were going	I wasn't going you weren't going	was I going were you going

Anwendung:
Past Tense Continuous bezeichnet
- den Ablauf einer Tätigkeit oder eines Vorgangs in einem bestimmten Zeitraum der Vergangenheit oder zu einem bestimmten Zeitpunkt der Vergangenheit; z. B.: Yesterday at 9 o'clock I was watching TV.

- häufig eine Handlung, die gerade stattfand, als ein neues Ereignis eintrat. Das neue Ereignis steht dagegen im Past Tense Simple;
  We were watching TV when the telephone rang.

  neues Ereignis

Beachte:
Verben mit statischer Bedeutung (siehe S. 13) haben keine Verlaufsform!

Fanden mehrere Vorgänge gleichzeitig in der Vergangenheit statt, so benutzt man bei allen Vorgängen Past Tense Continuous;
z. B.: I was watching TV while my mother was knitting.

Fanden mehrere Vorgänge nacheinander in der Vergangenheit statt, benutzt man dagegen Past Tense Simple;
z. B.: First I watched TV, then I read a book.

A-Übungen (Exercises)

I. When Mr. Miller, the boss, came into the office he saw that his employees were not working. Describe what they were doing.
(Als Herr Miller, der Chef, ins Büro kam, sah er, daß seine Angestellten nicht arbeiteten. Beschreibe, was sie taten!)

Beispiel:
Benny – to play cards.
Benny was playing cards.

1. Mrs. Peggy – to do her make-up
2. Paul – to read a newspaper
3. Mary – to drink tea
4. Simon – to sleep on the table
5. Peter and Mary – to dance
6. Susan – to make a private phone call
7. his secretary – to write a love letter
8. Mr. Smith – to flirt with Anne
9. Johnny and Stephen – to tell jokes
10. Jean – to do a crossword puzzle

II. Write down what the persons were doing at the same time.
(Schreibe auf, was die Personen gleichzeitig taten!)

Beispiel:
I was reading a book, while my brother (to watch) TV.
I was reading a book, while my brother was watching TV.

1. My mother was preparing dinner, while I (to do) my homework.
2. Peter was repairing his bike, while I (to cut) the lawn.
3. Susan (to play) in the garden, while the other children were swimming in the pool.
4. While my sister (to sleep), I (to listen) to new records with earphones.
5. Mr. Green (to work) in his garden, while his wife (to lie) in the sun.
6. Some visitors were clapping, others (to get) up from their chairs.
7. The children (to play), Mr. Miller (to write) a few letters, and Mrs. Miller (to knit).
8. While everybody (to sleep) the burglar (to try) to get into the house.
9. The sun (to shine), the Millers (to boat) on the lake and the neighbours (to rest) on the beach.
10. Mr. Cooper (to telephone), while his secretary (to make) tea for everybody.

B-Übungen (Exercises)

Decide whether to use Past Tense Simple or Past Tense Continuous.
(Entscheide, ob Du das einfache Imperfekt oder die Verlaufsform benutzen mußt!)

1. Susan (to have) a bath while her brother (to telephone).
2. Mr. Miller (to lie) on the beach, when he suddenly (to hear) a noise.
3. When my mother (to come) in, I (to smoke).
4. When the boss (to enter) the office, his employees (not/to work).
5. While the children (to play) in their room, mother (to read) the newspaper.
6. First he (to open) the bottle, then he (to sit) down and (to drink) a glass of Coke.
7. While I (to watch) TV, I (to think) 'What a terrible film!'
8. While the teacher (to explain) the new text, all the students (to write) in their exercise books, but they (not/to understand) a word.
9. The old lady (to sleep) when suddenly a window (to break).
10. The children (to do) their homework, suddenly the bell (to ring).

Present Perfect Simple – Perfekt

Bei regelmäßigen Verben

	+	–	?
Bildungsweise	have (in der 3. Person Singular 'has') +1. Verbform + -ed	haven't (in der 3. Person Singular 'hasn't') +1. Verbform + -ed	have (in der 3. Person Singular 'has') +1. Verbform + -ed
Beispielformen	I have watched he has watched	I haven't watched he hasn't watched	have I watched has he watched

Bei unregelmäßigen Verben

	+	–	?
Bildungsweise	have (in der 3. Person Singular 'has') + 3. Verbform	haven't (in der 3. Person Singular 'hasn't') + 3. Verbform	have (in der 3. Person Singular 'has') + 3. Verbform
Beispielformen	I have gone he has gone	I haven't gone he hasn't gone	have I gone has he gone

Beachte:
Im Deutschen wird das Perfekt bei einigen Verben mit einer Form von „sein", bei einigen Verben mit einer Form von „haben" gebildet;
z. B.: Er ist gegangen; ich habe gesehen.
Im Englischen wird das Present Perfect jedoch immer mit einer Form von „have" gebildet!

Anwendung:

- Present Perfect bezeichnet meist einen Vorgang, der in der Vergangenheit begonnen hat und bis in die Gegenwart andauert oder dessen Auswirkungen bis in die Gegenwart reichen.
  Signalwörter
  yet, so far, up to now, never, ever, already usw.;
  z. B.: We have never seen that film.
  Since, for, recently, lately stehen ebenfalls häufig mit dem Present Perfect.
  now, just this week, month etc today
- Present Perfect kann auch rückschauend das abgeschlossene Zustandekommen eines gegenwärtigen Zustandes bezeichnen. Der Zeitpunkt der eigentlichen Handlung interessiert dabei den Sprecher nicht.
  Beispiel:
  Prices have gone up. –
  Die Preise sind gestiegen.
- Present Perfect Simple kann auch für gewohnheitsmäßige, wiederholte Handlungen stehen;
  z. B.: I've often met him.

A-Übungen (Exercises)

I. Mary has been in hospital. When she comes home, she finds that her husband has done all the housework. Write down what her husband has already done. (Mary war im Krankenhaus. Als sie nach Hause kommt, sieht sie, daß ihr Mann die ganze Hausarbeit gemacht hat. Schreibe auf, was ihr Ehemann schon alles erledigt hat!)

Beispiel:
– to water the flowers –
He has already watered the flowers.

1. – to iron her blouses –
2. – to clean the kitchen –
3. – to make the beds –
4. – to wash the dirty shirts –
5. – to do the washing up –
6. – to repair the refrigerator –
7. – to use the vacuum cleaner –
8. – to cut the lawn –
9. – to clear up the children's room –
10. – to cook a meal –

But then she finds out that he hasn't done his own work.
(Aber dann findet sie heraus, daß er seine eigene Arbeit nicht erledigt hat.)

Beispiel:
– not/to clean his shoes –
He hasn't cleaned his shoes.

11. – not/to clear up his own room –
12. – not/to write his letters –
13. – not/to make his phone calls –
14. – not/to clean his own room –
15. – not/to repair the car –

II. Form sentences using Present Perfect Simple.
(Bilde Sätze, in denen Du das Perfekt benutzt!)

1. I (not/to see) him for years.
2. He (not/to be) here since last Monday.
3. Traffic (to come) to a standstill.
4. Since when (she/to live) here?
5. (You/ever/to be) to London?
6. (anyone/to telephone) yet?
7. She (to ask) me the same questions every day for the last two weeks.
8. My sister (to buy) a bike. Now she can cycle to school.
9. We (not/to visit) our aunt for weeks.
10. I (to work) a lot this week.
11. The taxi (just/to arrive).
12. Where (he/to go)?
13. I haven't any money at the moment because I (to lose) my handbag.
14. I (never/to speak) to our neighbour.
15. The students (to finish) their work now.

B-Übungen (Exercises)

Translate the following sentences.
(Übersetze die folgenden Sätze!)

1. Er ist schon zur Schule gegangen.
2. Die Millers leben schon seit 1980 in Deutschland.
3. Ich habe ihn seit einem Monat nicht getroffen.
4. Wir sind seit zwei Monaten nicht im Kino gewesen.
5. Bist du schon mal in New York gewesen?
6. Ich habe noch nie Pizza gegessen.
7. Gib mir das Buch zurück, wenn du es gelesen hast.
8. Herr Becker hat bereits 5 Zigaretten geraucht, seit er hier ist.
9. Hör auf zu reden! Ich habe genug von diesem Blödsinn.
10. Wie lange kennst du Jim schon?

Present Perfect Continuous – Perfekt Verlaufsform

Bildungsweise:
have (bei der 3. Person Singular 'has') + been + 1. Verbform + -ing

	+	–	?
Beispiel-formen	I have been working he has been working	I haven't been working he hasn't been working	have I been working has he been working

Anwendung:

- Beide Present Perfect-Formen (sowohl Simple als auch Continuous) betonen, daß ein Vorgang in bezug auf die Gegenwart gesehen wird.
- Present Perfect Continuous betont besonders Ablauf, Dauer und Unabgeschlossenheit eines solchen Vorgangs, Present Perfect Simple dagegen eher das Ergebnis (result) eines Vorgangs oder einer Handlung.

  Beispiel:
  He has been drinking all evening.
  He has already drunk 5 bottles of beer.

Beachte:
Im Deutschen wird oft Präsens verwendet, wenn im Englischen Present Perfect Continuous steht. Also Vorsicht beim Übersetzen!
Beispiel:
Er wohnt seit zwei Wochen hier. –
He has been living here for two weeks.

A-Übungen (Exercises)

Form sentences using the Present Perfect Continuous.
(Bilde Sätze, in denen Du die Perfekt Verlaufsform benutzt!)

1. He – to wait – for three hours.
2. They – to discuss – plans for their holidays all evening.
3. This book – to lie – under your desk the whole morning.
4. This castle – to stand – here for centuries.
5. Mr. Miller – to smoke – all evening.
6. How long – you/to learn – French?
7. The children – to stand – in this queue since 2 o'clock.
8. All the employees – to work – all day.
9. The secretary – to type – letters since lunchtime.
10. It – to snow – for three hours.

B-Übungen (Exercises)

Decide whether to use Present Perfect Simple or Present Perfect Continuous.
(Entscheide, ob Du das einfache Perfekt oder die Verlaufsform nehmen mußt!)

1. Mary (to dance) all evening. She (already/to dance) with ten boys.
2. Maud (to read) the whole weekend. She (already/to read) 200 pages.
3. I (to wait) for my girl-friend since 2 o'clock. I (already/to wait) for three hours now.
4. This man (to take) drugs for one year now. He (already/to ruin) his health.
5. Charles (to talk) to Simon for three hours now. He (not/to talk) to anybody else.
6. Simon (to read) magazines all evening. He (to read) every magazine he could find.
7. He (to write) letters for 4 hours. He (already/to write) to all of his friends.
8. Mr. and Mrs. Miller (to take) photographs all afternoon. They (to take) more than 50 photos already.
9. My mother (to make) cakes all morning. She (to make) five already.
10. The students (to do) their homework all afternoon, but they (not/to learn) their new words yet.

'Since' and 'for'

'Since' and **'for'** sind Signalwörter für Present Perfect. Beide bedeuten „seit" und machen daher Schülern oft Schwierigkeiten, da sie trotz gleicher deutscher Bedeutung nicht austauschbar sind.

a) 'since' = seit (einem bestimmten Zeitpunkt);
z. B.: since Monday = seit Montag

b) 'for' = seit (einer Zeitspanne);
z. B.: for two hours = seit zwei Stunden

Beachte:
Wenn man im Deutschen außer „seit" auch „lang" sagen kann, nimmt man 'for'; z. B.: zwei Stunden lang = for two hours

A-Übungen (Exercises)

I. Put 'since' or 'for' in front of the expressions.
(Setze 'since' oder 'for' vor die Ausdrücke!)

1. .... Easter
2. .... last summer
3. .... my birthday
4. 1965
5. .... 1st April
6. .... my childhood
7. .... 3 weeks
8. .... a few minutes
9. .... our last holiday
10. .... two days
11. .... 2 o'clock
12. .... I was young
13. .... the last 5 years
14. .... he was a child

II. Fill in 'since' or 'for'.
(Setze 'since' oder 'for' ein!)

An Interview

- 'How long have you been in London?'
- 'Oh, I've been here (1) .... 4 months now.'
- 'Have you already been to many parties (2) .... you arrived?'
- 'Actually, I haven't been to a single party (3) .... about 10 weeks.'
- 'Don't you like the people here?'
- 'Oh, I have never met such friendly and polite people (4) .... my visit to the USA.'
- 'So, you like the English. What about the language?'
- 'I've only been learning English (5) .... half a year.'
- 'What did you do before you came to England?'
- 'I've been working in Germany (6) .... the last 6 years.'
- 'What do you do in your free time?'

- 'I've been playing the piano (7) . . . . I was ten and last year I joined an orchestra and I've met many interesting people (8) . . . . then.'
- 'How long will you stay in London?'
- 'I hope (9) . . . . about 2 years. I'd like to go back to America then, because I haven't seen my friends (10) . . . . four years.

Past Tense and Present Perfect – Imperfekt und Perfekt

Die unterschiedliche Anwendungsweise von Past Tense und Present Perfect ist häufig Ursache von schweren Grammatikfehlern. Deshalb soll hier noch einmal der Unterschied zwischen Past Tense und Present Perfect hervorgehoben werden.

Past Tense	Present Perfect
a) Der Vorgang hat in der Vergangenheit angefangen und ist abgeschlossen; z. B.: I bought a bike last weekend. b) Der Vorgang hat in der Vergangenheit angefangen, ist abgeschlossen und wird als vergangenes Ereignis völlig getrennt von der Gegenwart gesehen; z. B.: My brother bought a bike two weeks ago. **Signalwörter** yesterday, . . . ago, last . . ., the other day, in 1975 usw.	a) Der Vorgang hat in der Vergangenheit angefangen und dauert noch an; z. B.: I've worked for 2 hours now. b) Der Vorgang hat in der Vergangenheit angefangen, ist gerade abgeschlossen, seine Folgen reichen jedoch bis in die Gegenwart; z. B.: My brother has just bought a bike. He can cycle to school now. **Signalwörter** so far, up to now, these 2 days, since, for, ever, never, this . . . usw.

A-Übungen (Exercises)

Put the verbs in brackets ( ) into the correct tense. Mind the signal words which tell you whether to use Past Tense or Present Perfect!
(Setze die Verben in Klammern in die richtige Zeit. Achte auf die Signalwörter, die Dir sagen, ob Du Imperfekt oder Perfekt benutzen mußt!)

1. Yesterday the pupils (to learn) 20 new words.
2. I (not/to be) in town for 2 weeks.
3. My brother (to visit) our uncle last week.
4. Two days ago our new neighbours (to move in).
5. My father (to work) in his firm since 1972.
6. I (to look for) my book all day, but I (not/to find) it yet.

7. I (not/to see) my pen-friend for a long time.
8. The other day my father (to take) me to the airport.
9. In 1980 we (to spend) our holidays in Greece.
10. The plane (to leave) half an hour ago.
11. (You/ever/to be) to Africa?
12. Yesterday our teacher (to be) 10 minutes late.
13. This man (to watch) me for half an hour now.
14. The Millers (just/to arrive).
15. Last Christmas we (to go skiing).
16. He (not/to finish) reading this book yet.
17. How many sentences (you/to write) since 2 o'clock?
18. She (not/to wear) this dress for 3 months.
19. Last lesson I (to understand) everything.
20. The author (to write) this play two years ago.

B-Übungen (Exercises)

Past Tense or Present Perfect? Translate the following sentences.
(Imperfekt oder Perfekt? Übersetze die folgenden Sätze!)

1. Ich bin gestern in Hamburg gewesen.
2. Ich war seit zwei Jahren nicht mehr in Frankfurt.
3. Er ist noch nie in Mainz gewesen.
4. Hast du schon einmal Pizza gegessen?
5. Letzte Woche habe ich eine neue Schallplatte gekauft.
6. Mein Großvater liegt schon 3 Wochen im Krankenhaus.
7. Meine Mutter geht schon seit zwei Jahren zu diesem Friseur.
8. Er ist vor zwei Stunden angekommen.
9. Seit 3 Jahren spiele ich Tennis.
10. Letztes Jahr hat Mr. Baker seinen Führerschein gemacht.
11. Er arbeitet schon seit 3 Monaten nicht mehr für diese Firma.
12. Ich bin am 1. August 1962 geboren und wohne seitdem in Berlin.
13. Seitdem ich in Spanien war, habe ich kein Spanisch mehr gesprochen.
14. Ich kenne ihn schon seit 5 Jahren, aber ich habe ihn noch nie rauchen sehen.
15. Vor zwei Stunden fingen sie an Monopoly zu spielen, und sie spielen seitdem ununterbrochen.
16. Als ich ihn das erste Mal sah, wußte ich nicht, wer er war.
17. Ich verbrachte jahrelang meinen Urlaub in Frankreich, aber seit zwei Jahren war ich nicht mehr da.
18. Seit ich das erste Mal ein Fußballspiel sah, gehe ich jeden Sonntag zum Stadion.
19. Seit einem Jahr hat er nichts von seinem Bruder gehört.
20. Ich war nie mehr in England, seit ich diesen Unfall hatte.

Past Perfect Simple and Continuous – Plusquamperfekt und Plusquamperfekt Verlaufsform

a) Past Perfect Simple – Plusquamperfekt

Bei regelmäßigen Verben

	+	–	?
Bildungsweise	had + 1. Verbform + -ed	hadn't + 1. Verbform + -ed	had + 1. Verbform + -ed
Beispielformen	I had worked	I hadn't worked	had I worked

Bei unregelmäßigen Verben

	+	–	?
Bildungsweise	had + 3. Verbform	hadn't + 3. Verbform	had + 3. Verbform
Beispielformen	I had gone	I hadn't gone	had I gone

Anwendung:

Past Perfect Simple steht für Handlungen,

- die zu einem bestimmten Zeitpunkt der Vergangenheit bereits abgeschlossen waren;
  z. B.: After they had eaten their sandwiches, they climbed up the hill.
- die vor einem bestimmten Zeitpunkt der Vergangenheit angefangen haben, aber bis zu ihm oder über ihn hinaus andauern;
  z. B.: He had already worked for this company for 2 years before he got more money.

b) Past Perfect Continuous – Plusquamperfekt Verlaufsform

	+	–	?
Bildungsweise	had + been + 1. Verbform + -ing	hadn't + been + 1. Verbform + -ing	had + been + 1. Verbform + -ing
Beispielformen	I had been working	I hadn't been working	had I been working

Anwendung:

Past Perfect Continuous wird benutzt, wenn Ablauf und Dauer eines Vorgangs betont werden sollen, der bis zu einem bestimmten Zeitpunkt der Vergangenheit andauerte oder über diesen hinausging;

z. B.: He had been working for 2 hours when she arrived.

Beachte:
Beide Past Perfect Formen treten nur im Zusammenhang mit Past Tense auf!

A-Übungen (Exercises)

I. A group of boy scouts went on a mountain climbing tour. Before they started they had already done a lot of things, e. g.: Before they started they had bought a long rope. Write down what they had done before they started.
(Eine Gruppe Pfadfinder unternahm eine Bergtour. Bevor sie aufbrachen, hatten sie schon eine Menge erledigt, z. B.: Bevor sie aufbrachen, hatten sie ein langes Seil gekauft. Schreibe auf, was sie schon getan hatten, bevor sie auf Klettertour gingen!)

1. to check their shoes
2. to collect maps
3. to prepare picnic baskets
4. to repair their rucksacks
5. to listen to the weather forecast
6. to tell their parents about their plans
7. to pack their rucksacks
8. to tell their parents their route
9. to buy films
10. to borrow grandfather's binoculars
11. to have several meetings
12. to ask their fathers for first aid material
13. to discuss their plans
14. to put their torches in their rucksacks
15. to attend a mountain climbing course

After they had started they found out that they had forgotten a few important things;
(Nachdem sie aufgebrochen waren, fanden sie heraus, daß sie einige wichtige Dinge vergessen hatten.)
e. g.: They had not packed any matches. Go on!

16. not/to check their tents
17. not/to buy enough tins
18. not/to plan their daily routes
19. not/to read enough books about climbing
20. not/to ask their teacher about the different stones

II. Put the verbs in brackets () into the correct Past Perfect form.
(Setze die Verben in Klammern in die richtige Plusquamperfektform!)

1. Before they went to the swimming pool, they (to wait for) Susan for half an hour.
2. After the children (to be) to England, they wanted to know more about the English.
3. They bought the record after they (to see) the film.
4. After the police (to catch) the thief, they found the jewels.
5. When Susan telephoned, I (to type) for 2 hours.
6. Before Mr. Miller got his driving licence, he (to learn) very hard.
7. After he (to win) the prize, he danced.
8. I (to know) him for years before we were introduced to one another.
9. Before the fire brigade arrived, they (already/to try) to rescue the person.
10. After Mr. Smith (to discover) the burglar, he phoned the police.

B-Übungen (Exercises)

I. Past Tense or Past Perfect?
(Imperfekt oder Plusquamperfekt?)

1. He (just/to have) a cup of tea when the door bell rang.
2. They (to go) to a pub after they (to finish) work.
3. After he (to finish) dinner, he (to drink) a cup of coffee.
4. He (to take) the money after he (to do) the work.
5. My aunt (not/to see) me for one year when I (to meet) her last week.
6. I (to ask) him what languages he (to learn).
7. After he (to repair) the bike, he (to go) on a bicycle tour.
8. After she (to leave), I (to remember) her name.
9. Before we (to drive) very far, we found that we (to lose) our way.
10. After Mr. Miller (to go) to work, his wife (to start) to clean the house.

II. Translate the following sentences, using either Past Tense or Past Perfect.
(Übersetze die folgenden Sätze, indem Du entweder das Imperfekt oder das Plusquamperfekt benutzt!)

1. Ich hatte das Buch schon gelesen, bevor ich den Film sah.
2. Nachdem ich eingekauft hatte, ging ich nach Hause.
3. Hast du den Film gesehen, nachdem er gegangen war?
4. Sie feierten, nachdem sie das Spiel gewonnen hatten.
5. Nachdem sie den Aufsatz geschrieben hatten, konnten sie nach Hause gehen.

Future and Future Continuous – Futur I und Futur I Verlaufsform

a) Will-Future – Futur I

	+	–	?
Bildungsweise	will (bei 1. Person Singular und Plural auch shall) + 1. Verbform	will not (= won't) (bei 1. Person Singular und Plural auch shall not oder shan't) + 1. Verbform	will (bei 1. Person Singular und Plural auch shall) + 1. Verbform
Beispielformen	I will (shall) go I'll go he will go he'll go	I will (shall) not go I won't (shan't) go he will not go he won't go	will (shall) I go will he go

Anwendung:

Die englische Sprache ist in der Verwendung des Futurs konsequenter als die deutsche, so daß häufig Futur stehen muß, wenn im Deutschen Präsens gebraucht werden kann.

- Das Will-Future dient zur Vorhersage von zukünftigen Handlungen oder Vorgängen;
  z. B.: Tomorrow the sun will shine.
- Das Will-Future kann einen Entschluß ausdrücken, der spontan im Moment des Sprechens gefaßt wird;
  z. B.: Just a moment, I'll drive you.
- Das Will-Future steht im Hauptsatz einer Conditional Clause Type I (Bedingungssatz, siehe Seite 48);
  z. B.: If the sun shines, I'll go swimming. (Im Nebensatz steht dann Präsens.)

b) Going to-Future

Bildungsweise: Präsens von 'to be' (am/are/is) + going to + 1. Verbform		
	+/–	?
Beispielformen	I am (not) going to come you are (not) going to come he/she/it is (not) going to come we are (not) going to come you are (not) going to come they are (not) going to come	am I going to come are you going to come is he/she/it going to come are we going to come are you going to come are they going to come

Anwendung:

- Das Going to-Future drückt eine Absicht aus, die zum Zeitpunkt des Sprechens bereits besteht (also keinen spontanen Entschluß wie beim Will-Future); z. B.: I'm going to see the doctor tomorrow.
- Das Going to-Future drückt eine logische Schlußfolgerung aus; z. B.: Look at the clouds! It's going to rain.

c) Future Continuous – Futur I Verlaufsform

Bildungsweise: will/shall + be + 1. Verbform + -ing			
	+	–	?
Beispiel- formen	I will/shall be going = I'll be going he will be going = he'll be going	I will/shall not be going = I won't/shan't be going he will/shall not be going = he won't be going	will/shall I be going will he be going

Anwendung:

- Future Continuous kann ausdrücken, daß ein Vorgang zu einem bestimmten Zeitpunkt der Zukunft gerade ablaufen wird; z. B.: When you get this letter, I'll be lying in the sun.
- Future Continuous kann auch ausdrücken, daß ein zukünftiger Vorgang für ganz sicher oder selbstverständlich gehalten wird; z. B.: I'll be seeing him tomorrow.

d) Present Tense Simple in futurischer Bedeutung

Present Tense Simple (Präsens) kann in futurischer Bedeutung gebraucht werden. Es bezeichnet dann Vorgänge oder Zustände, die von außenstehenden Personen oder Institutionen festgelegt sind;
z. B.: Holidays begin on Monday next week.

e) Present Tense Continuous in futurischer Bedeutung

Present Tense Continuous (Präsens Verlaufsform) kann bei Tätigkeits- und Vorgangsverben (z. B. to come, to go, to leave usw.) in futurischer Bedeutung gebraucht werden, um eine getroffene Vereinbarung oder einen festgelegten Plan auszudrücken (Beachte: Sind noch keine Vorbereitungen oder Vereinbarungen getroffen, benutzt man das 'Going to-Future'!);
z. B.: The Bakers are moving next week.

Übersicht über die Verwendung der einzelnen Futurformen

Will-Future	spontaner Entschluß/Vorhersage oder Vermutung
Going to-Future	Absicht/logische Schlußfolgerung
Future Continuous	Ablauf eines zukünftigen Vorgangs zu einem bestimmten Zeitpunkt/selbstverständliches Ereignis
Present Tense Simple	Programm oder Terminplan
Present Tense Continuous	bereits getroffene Vereinbarung oder bereits festgelegter Plan

A-Übungen (Exercises)

I. Will-Future
This year we've had a lot of snow, which caused a lot of problems. Write down what will happen if it's the same next year.
(Dieses Jahr haben wir viel Schnee gehabt, der viele Probleme verursachte. Schreibe auf, was passieren wird, wenn es nächstes Jahr genauso ist!)

Beispiel:
a lot of people – to be late for work
A lot of people will be late for work.

1. many people – to get stuck in a traffic jam
2. my father – not/to get out of his garage
3. school buses – not/to run on time
4. many students – to be late
5. street workers – to have to work hard
6. there – to be – many accidents
7. many children – to be ill
8. some cars – not/to start
9. my mother – to clear away snow every morning
10. children – to go skiing
11. house owners – to spend a lot of money for heating
12. shop owners – to sell many pullovers
13. old people – not/to be able to go outside
14. garages – to have a lot of work
15. bosses – to be angry because many workers – to be late

II. Going to-Future
Write down what the students intend to do after school.
(Schreibe auf, was die Schüler nach der Schule machen wollen!)

Beispiel:
Paul – to go home at once
Paul is going to go home at once.

1. Mary – to take the bus at 1.30
2. Simon – to have 2 more sport lessons
3. Susan – to stay in school for 1 more lesson
4. Peter and Jane – to visit their aunt
5. we – to go to McDonald's
6. I – to talk to my teacher
7. they – to walk to the station
8. the four girls – to have a look around the shops
9. the two boys – to play football
10. Marc – not/to eat anything
11. Janet – to go to her girlfriend
12. some of the boys – to take the next bus
13. a few girls – to clear up the classroom
14. Jean – to explain the new words to us
15. you – to cycle home

III. Future Continuous
The Millers will be in Spain tomorrow. They are talking about what they will be doing tomorrow afternoon. Make up sentences using Future Continuous.
(Die Millers werden morgen in Spanien sein. Sie sprechen über das, was sie morgen nachmittag tun werden. Bilde Sätze, indem Du Futur I Verlaufsform benutzt!)

Beispiel:
Simon – to lie on the beach
Simon will be lying on the beach.

1. Mr. Miller – to swim in the sea
2. Mrs. Miller – to sunbathe
3. Mary – to read a book
4. Grandfather – to sit in the sun
5. Grandmother – to have coffee in the hotel bar
6. Paul – to play badminton on the beach
7. our neighbours – to write postcards
8. Aunt Mabel – to visit the hotel-hairdresser
9. Uncle John – to talk to the other guests
10. Maud – to flirt with the waiter
11. we – not/to swim in the sea
12. we – to look at souvenirs
13. I – to rest in the hotel room

14. our dog – to run along the beach
15. you – to work in your office

B-Übungen (Exercises)

Put the verbs in brackets () into the correct Future form. Use either Will-Future or Going to-Future or Future Continuous or Present Simple or Present Continuous. (Setze die Verben in Klammern in die richtige Futurform! Benutze entweder das Will-Futur oder das Going to-Futur, die Futur-I-Verlaufsform, das Präsens oder die Präsens Verlaufsform!)

1. Just a moment! I (to help) you.
2. We (to repair) the bike tomorrow.
3. Many people (to come) when the band plays.
4. Easter Sunday (to be) on March 27th this year.
5. This time next week I (to sit) in the plane.
6. We (to have) turkey for our Christmas dinner this year.
7. I (to look) at the shops on my way home.
8. Look at the sky! It (to snow).
9. The shops (to close) in 10 minutes.
10. If it rains, the students (not/to go) swimming.
11. The test (to be) on Tuesday next week.
12. In 1990 there (to be) more cars.
13. My father (to go) for a walk if the weather is fine.
14. My grandfather (to keep) an eye on our house when we're away.
15. Alan looks pale. He (to be) ill.

Future Perfect Simple and Continuous – Futur II und Futur II Verlaufsform

a) Future Perfect Simple – Futur II

Bei regelmäßigen Verben

	+	–	?
Bildungsweise	will (bei 1. Person Singular und Plural auch shall) + have + 1. Verbform + -ed	will not (= won't) (bei 1. Person Singular und Plural auch shall not oder shan't) + 1. Verbform + -ed	will (bei 1. Person Singular und Plural auch shall) + have + 1. Verbform + -ed
Beispielformen	I will/shall have worked I'll have worked	I will/shall not have worked I won't/shan't have worked	will/shall I have worked

Bei unregelmäßigen Verben

	+	–	?
Bildungsweise	will (bei 1. Person Singular und Plural auch shall) + have + 3. Verbform	will not (= won't) (bei 1. Person Singular und Plural auch shall not oder shan't) + have + 3. Verbform	will (bei 1. Person Singular und Plural auch shall) + have + 3. Verbform
Beispielformen	I will/shall have gone I'll have gone	I will/shall not have gone I won't/shan't have gone	will/shall I have gone

b) Future Perfect Continuous – Futur II Verlaufsform

Bildungsweise: will/shall + have + been + 1. Verbform + -ing			
	+	–	?
Beispielformen	he will have been working	he will not have been working	will he have been working

Anwendung:

Future Perfect Simple und Continuous drücken Vorzeitigkeit gegenüber einem bestimmten Zeitpunkt der Zukunft aus. Der Gebrauch der Verlaufsform betont die ununterbrochene Dauer.

Beispiel:

By 2 o'clock tomorrow we will/shall have collected enough books for the jumble sale.

By tomorrow evening Jim will have been working for 5 hours.

A-Übungen (Exercises)

Ia. The youth club members will be glad when they have finished their preparations for the party on the next evening. Write down what they will have done before the party starts.

(Die Mitglieder des Jugendclubs werden froh sein, wenn sie die Vorbereitungen für die Party am nächsten Abend beendet haben. Schreibe auf, was sie vor Beginn der Party alles getan haben werden!)

Beispiel:

By seven o'clock tomorrow – to lay the table

They will have laid the table.

1. – to decorate the rooms
2. – to wash all the glasses
3. – to clean the rooms
4. – to make lemonade
5. – to build up a stage
6. – to prepare a speech
7. – to invite everybody
8. – to paint posters
9. – to check all the records
10. – to practise their dances long enough

Ib. All this takes a long time. So, by 7 o'clock tomorrow they will have been decorating the rooms for quite a long time. Go on! Use sentences 2–10 in the same way.
(All das braucht seine Zeit. So werden sie morgen um 7 Uhr schon eine ganze Weile dabei sein, die Räume zu schmücken. Fahre fort! Benutze die Sätze 2–10 in ähnlicher Weise!)

Conditional I Simple and Continuous – Konditional I und Konditional I Verlaufsform

a) Conditional I Simple – Konditional I

Bildungsweise: would (bei 1. Person Singular und Plural auch should) + 1. Verbform		
	+	–
Beispiel-formen	I would/should come he would go	I would/should not come he would not go

Anwendung:
Conditional I Simple wird verwendet
- in den Hauptsätzen von Bedingungssätzen des Typs II (siehe Seite 50). In den entsprechenden Nebensätzen steht Past Tense (Imperfekt),
  z. B.: I would buy a Rolls Royce if I had the money.
- in der indirekten Rede (Reported Speech, siehe Seite 54), wenn das einleitende Verb in einer Zeit der Vergangenheitsgruppe steht und in der direkten Rede (Direct Speech) Future (Futur I) steht.
  Beispiel:
  He said, 'I will go to England.' (Direkte Rede)
  He said he would go to England. (Indirekte Rede)
- in einfachen Hauptsätzen. Es entspricht im Deutschen einer Umschreibung mit „würde".

Beispiel:
I would like to come. – Ich würde gerne kommen.
Would you pass me the sugar, please? – Würdest du mir bitte den Zucker reichen?

A-Übungen (Exercises)

I. Put the verbs in brackets () into Conditional I.
(Setze die Verben in Klammern in den Konditional I!)

1. I (to be glad) to help you.
2. If they were rich, they (to build) a swimming pool.
3. He (to come) if I called him.
4. He (to help) you if you asked him.
5. Peter (to like) to have an ice-cream.
6. I (not/to go) if I were you.
7. He said that he (to watch) the film.
8. They answered they (to read) the letter carefully.
9. He (to be able to) answer your questions.
10. If she had her A-level, she (to go) to university.

II. Translate the following sentences.
(Übersetze die folgenden Sätze!)

1. Würdest du das Fenster bitte öffnen!
2. Ich würde gerne Tee trinken.
3. Mary würde gerne tanzen.
4. Würdest du bitte das Radio leiser stellen?
5. Sie würden gerne nach England fahren.

b) Conditional I Continuous – Konditional I Verlaufsform

Bildungsweise: would (bei 1. Person Singular und Plural auch 'should') + be + 1. Verbform + -ing		
	+	–
Beispiel-formen	I would/should be working I'd be working	I would/should not be working I wouldn't/shouldn't be working

Anwendung:
Zwischen Conditional I Simple und Continuous bestehen die gleichen Unterschiede wie bei den anderen Zeiten (siehe Seite 37).

Conditional II Simple and Continuous – Konditional II und Konditional II Verlaufsform

a) Conditional II Simple – Konditional II

Bei regelmäßigen Verben

Bildungsweise: would (bei 1. Person Singular und Plural auch 'should') + have + 1. Verbform + -ed		
	+	–
Beispiel-formen	I would/should have worked I'd have worked	I would/should not have worked I wouldn't/shouldn't have worked

Bei unregelmäßigen Verben

Bildungsweise: would (bei 1. Person Singular und Plural auch 'should') + have + 3. Verbform		
	+	–
Beispiel-formen	I would/should have gone I'd have gone	I would/should not have gone I wouldn't/shouldn't have gone

Anwendung:

Conditional II Simple steht

- in den Hauptsätzen von Bedingungssätzen des Typs III (siehe Seite 52). In den entsprechenden Nebensätzen steht Past Perfect (Plusquamperfekt); z. B.: I would/should have gone to the theatre if I had been to London.
- in der indirekten Rede (Reported Speech, siehe Seite 54), wenn das einleitende Verb in einer Zeit der Vergangenheitsgruppe steht und in der direkten Rede Future Perfect oder Conditional I steht.

  Beispiel:

  He said, 'I will have seen Big Ben by this time next week.' (Direkte Rede)
  He said he would have seen Big Ben by that time the following week. (Indirekte Rede)
- in einfachen Hauptsätzen in der Bedeutung des deutschen Konjunktivs des Imperfekts/Präteritums.

  Beispiel:

  I would/should have done that anyway.
  Ich hätte das in jedem Fall getan.

A-Übungen (Exercises)

Put the verbs in brackets () into Conditional II.
(Setze die Verben in Klammern in den Konditional II!)

1. I (to work) harder if I had known that.
2. If he had learned more, he (to pass) the exam.
3. He said he (to see) the film by 2 o'clock the next day.
4. I (to try) this special dish.
5. Mary (to finish) her letter if you hadn't disturbed her.
6. He (to ask) that anyway.
7. You (to catch) the train if you had hurried.
8. If they had gone, they (to meet) him.
9. I (not/to be) so late.
10. He (not/to do) that.

b) Conditional II Continuous – Konditional II Verlaufsform

Bildungsweise:
would (bei 1. Person Singular und Plural auch 'should') + have + been + 1. Verbform + -ing

	+	–
Beispielformen	I would/should have been working	I would/should not have been working

Anwendung:
Zwischen Conditional II Simple und Continuous bestehen die gleichen Unterschiede wie bei den anderen Zeiten (siehe Seite 37).

Gemischte Übungen zum Gebrauch der Zeiten (Aktiv)

B-Übungen (Exercises)

I. Put the verbs in brackets () into the correct tense.
(Setze die Verben in Klammern in die richtige Zeit!)

1. Paul (to spend) his holidays in Spain last year, but he said he (never/to go) there again.
2. While Peter (to talk) to his aunt last Monday, the man whom he (to meet) the previous day (to come) in.

3. Mary (never/to see) such a beautiful garden since she (to be) in England in 1983.
4. The architect complained: 'Next month you (to work) on this bridge for 10 years and it (still/not/to be) finished.'
5. After they (to see) the house, they (to decide) not to buy it. Instead they (to rent) a beautiful flat two weeks ago.
6. Susan (to have) a party. She (already/to invite) all her friends.
7. I (to drink) a glass of wine every day for the last 15 years and I (still/to do) so. I (not/to stop) doing so in the future.
8. Mrs. Sanders (not/to see) St. Paul's Cathedral yet. I (to take) her there tomorrow afternoon.
9. Before Mr. MacGregor (to come) to the city last spring, he (never/to think) of eating out in a restaurant.
10. Although John (not/to smoke) at all, Mary usually (to smoke) one cigarette after the other.
11. Mrs. Peel (to go) to Australia last November, but she (not/to write) a single letter yet.
12. Elizabeth is usually late for dinner, but yesterday she (to be) later than she (ever/to be) before.
13. Bob told me he (never/to marry) that lazy girl if she (not/to learn) to do the housework properly within the next few months.
14. Peter (just/to promise) me that he (never/to do) this again.
15. I (now/to listen) to you for over half an hour. Why (not/to tell) me last week that you (never/to hear) of Shakespeare before.

II. Translate the following sentences.
(Übersetze die folgenden Sätze!)

1. Peter war noch nie im Kino, aber er sieht jeden Abend fern.
2. Er hatte noch nie ein Bild der englischen Königin gesehen, bevor er nach England kam.
3. Ich las gerade die Zeitung, als Mary plötzlich zur Tür herein kam.
4. Nachdem Paul sich das letzte Mal verfahren hatte, sagte er, er würde nie mehr mit dem Auto nach London fahren.
5. Obwohl ich gewöhnlich ein Glas Wein zum Abendessen trinke, trinke ich heute Bier.
6. Nachdem James den Tee serviert hatte, ging er zurück in die Küche.
7. Morgen nachmittag wird der Bäcker die Sandwiches für unsere Party gemacht haben. Wir werden sie gegen 17 Uhr abholen.
8. Seit ich aus dem Urlaub zurückgekommen bin, hat die Sonne überhaupt nicht geschienen.
9. Früher ging Paul gelegentlich ins Kino, aber seit er begann, als Kellner zu arbeiten, hat er keine Zeit mehr.
10. Während Paul Schallplatten hörte, sahen seine Eltern fern.

11. Bill hatte 2 Jahre lang in Spanien gearbeitet, bevor er nach Deutschland kam.
12. Obwohl Oliver noch nie in England war, spricht er fließend Englisch.
13. Paul wollte nicht mehr zur Schule gehen, weil er kein Wort von dem verstand, was der Lehrer sagte.
14. Susan lebte von 1975 bis 1980 in England, zog dann nach Australien und wohnt seit 1984 in den USA.
15. Als ich hereinkam, spielten Paul und Susan gerade Karten.
16. Ich würde gerne nach England fahren, aber ich habe seit 2 Jahren keinen Urlaub mehr gehabt.
17. Der Zug fährt um 17.45 Uhr. Ich hoffe, wir werden rechtzeitig am Bahnhof sein.
18. Wann hast du dein neues Auto gekauft? Ich habe es noch nicht gesehen.

Passive Voice – Passiv

Die bisher behandelten Zeiten waren Aktivzeiten. Das Subjekt des Satzes tat etwas selbst. Im Passiv wird mit dem Subjekt etwas getan, und zwar von einem Handlungsträger.

Beispiel:
Aktiv: Ich öffne das Fenster.
Passiv: Das Fenster wird von mir geöffnet.

Bildungsweise:	
Simple:	Form von 'to be' + 3. Verbform (bei regelmäßigen Verben 1. Verbform + -ed); z. B.: He is washed.
Continuous:	Form von 'to be' + being + 3. Verbform (bei regelmäßigen Verben 1. Verbform + -ed); z. B.: He is being washed.

Beachte:
Im Deutschen wird das Passiv mit einer Form von ‚werden' gebildet.
Beispiel:
Ich werde gewaschen.
I am washed.

Tabellarische Übersicht über die Zeiten im Passiv

Infinitive Passive		to be washed
Present Tense (Präsens)	S* C**	am/are/is washed am/are/is being washed
Past Tense (Imperfekt/Präteritum)	S* C**	was/were washed was/were being washed
Present Perfect (Perfekt)	S* C**	have/has been washed wird nicht verwendet
Past Perfect (Plusquamperfekt)	S* C**	had been washed wird nicht verwendet
Future (Futur I)	S* C**	will be washed wird nicht verwendet
Future Perfect (Futur II)	S* C**	will have been washed wird nicht verwendet
Conditional I (Konditional I)	S* C**	would/should be washed wird nicht verwendet
Conditional II (Konditional II)	S* C**	would/should have been washed wird nicht verwendet

*S = Simple
**C = Continuous

Umwandlung eines Aktivsatzes in einen Passivsatz

Beispiel:

Aktiv: Mr. Miller took Peter to hospital.
(Subjekt) (Prädikat) (Objekt) (Ortsbestimmung)

Passiv: Peter was taken to hospital by Mr. Miller.
(Subjekt) (Prädikat) (Ortsbestimmung) (Objekt)

Beachte:
Bei der Umwandlung eines Aktivsatzes in einen Passivsatz werden Subjekt und Objekt vertauscht. Die Zeit wird beibehalten.

Beispiel mit einem Personalpronomen (personal pronoun) als Objekt:

Aktiv: Mr. Miller took him to hospital.

Passiv: He was taken to hospital by Mr. Miller.

Beachte:

Bei der Umwandlung eines Aktivsatzes mit Pronomen als Objekt in einen Passivsatz ändert sich der Kasus des Pronomens:

Aus	'me'	wird	'I'
Aus	'him'	wird	'he'
Aus	'her'	wird	'she'
Aus	'us'	wird	'we'
Aus	'them'	wird	'they'

Im Deutschen ist das anders:
Mother told us to go home.
We were told to... (Uns wurde gesagt...)

Beispiel mit zwei Objekten im Aktivsatz:

Aktiv:	Mr. Miller (Subjekt)	offered (Prädikat)	me (Objekt 1)	a cup of tea. (Objekt 2)
Passiv: 1)	I (S)	was offered (P)	a cup of tea (O)	by Mr. Miller. (O)
2)	A cup of tea (S)	was offered (P)	to me (O)	by Mr. Miller. (O)

Beachte:

Hat der Aktivsatz zwei Objekte, so gibt es zwei mögliche Passivsätze. Jedes der beiden Objekte des Aktivsatzes kann Subjekt eines Passivsatzes werden.

Das präpositionale Objekt mit 'by' (by-agent)

Am Ende eines Passivsatzes kann der Handlungsträger (derjenige, von dem etwas gemacht wird) genannt werden;
z. B.: von Mr. Miller = by Mr. Miller
Er wird jedoch nur genannt, wenn er für die Aussage von Wichtigkeit ist. Ein unpersönlicher Handlungsträger kann weggelassen werden.

Beispiel:
Aktiv: Someone opened the box.
Passiv: The box was opened (by someone).

A-Übungen (Exercises)

I. Put the following sentences into the Passive Voice.
(Setze die folgenden Sätze ins Passiv!)

1. We will invite our neighbours.
2. We paid the bill last week.
3. Mother is cooking the vegetables.
4. The teacher explained the sentence.
5. My father had given away the book.
6. The policeman has always helped the old lady.
7. The lady looks after the children.
8. Father repaired my bike last weekend.
9. The company built the house.
10. Mr. Baker will open a new restaurant next week.
11. He hasn't translated the sentences yet.
12. The workers have already cleaned the street.
13. The secretary posted the letter yesterday.
14. My mother sends me to the baker.
15. Mrs. Cooper types ten letters every morning.

II. Put into the Passive Voice. Mind the pronouns!
(Setze ins Passiv! Achte auf die Pronomen!)

1. Mr. Miller asked her to open the window.
2. Father took me to school.
3. Mary invited him.
4. I will look after him.
5. She always admired her.
6. Our class won it last year.
7. Mary introduces us to Mr. Baker.
8. Mr. Cooper had opened it carefully.
9. We saw her in Frankfurt yesterday.
10. Thieves have stolen them.

B-Übungen (Exercises)

I. Put into the Passive Voice. Sometimes you can form two Passive sentences.
(Setze ins Passiv! Manchmal kannst du zwei Passivsätze bilden!)

1. Mr. Cooper showed the visitors the rooms. (2)
2. Somebody built this house last year.
3. People mustn't feed the animals.
4. You can't open this box.
5. The wind blew his hat down the street.
6. People all over the world speak English.
7. The teacher will describe the famous buildings to us.
8. She passed me the butter.
9. They have promised us a present. (2)

10. She had written him a letter. (2)
11. The waiter brought us a huge bottle. (2)
12. He threw me the ball.
13. People used this building as a prison.
14. No one has ever beaten me at chess.
15. You must write the answers down.

II. Translate the following Passive Voice sentences.
(Übersetze die folgenden Passivsätze!)

1. Die Gemälde sind gestern gestohlen worden.
2. Uns wurde ein Brief geschickt.
3. Ihm wurde eine Tasse Tee angeboten.
4. Nächstes Jahr wird das Haus gestrichen.
5. Wir sind zur Party eingeladen worden.

Conditional Clauses (If-Clauses) – Bedingungssätze

If-Sätze sind Nebensätze, die eine Bedingung („wenn. . ." in der Bedeutung von „falls. . .") ausdrücken. Sie sind mit Hauptsätzen kombiniert.

Beispiel:
Wenn (unter der Bedingung, daß) das Wetter schön ist, gehe ich schwimmen.

Die If-Sätze bereiten oft Schwierigkeiten, da im Englischen genau festgelegt ist, welche Zeit (tense) im If-Satz (if-clause) und welche im Hauptsatz (main-clause) stehen muß.
Es gibt drei verschiedene If-Satz-Typen (types), die verschiedene Arten von Bedingungen ausdrücken.

Type I: Probable Condition – wahrscheinliche Bedingung

Beispiel:	If the sun shines,	he will go swimming.
	(Wenn die Sonne scheint,	geht er schwimmen.)
Zeit (tense):	Präsens (Present Tense)	Futur I (Future)
Bildungsweise:	1. Verbform; in der 3. Person Singular + -s	will + 1. Verbform
Art der Bedingung:	Die Bedingung (wenn die Sonne scheint) ist erfüllbar. Es ist wahrscheinlich (probable), daß die Sonne scheint.	

Kurzregel (Typ I):
Steht im If-Satz Präsens (Present Tense), so steht im Hauptsatz Futur I (Future).

A-Übungen (Exercises)

I. Put the verbs in brackets () into the correct tense.
(Setze die Verben in Klammern in die richtige Zeit!)

1. If the weather is fine, we (to have) a picnic.
2. If it rains, I (to take) an umbrella.
3. If I (to find) a bike, I will go on a bicycle tour.
4. If she (to come), we will go to the cinema.
5. The students will see Big Ben if they (to visit) London.

6. I (to write) a letter if I (to have) time.
7. If I (to get) my money back, I (to buy) some new books.
8. If my brother (to get) a camera for his birthday, he (to take) a lot of photos.
9. If I (to meet) him, I (to tell) him.
10. I (to go) to a new school if we (to move).

II. Translate the following sentences!
(Übersetze die folgenden Sätze!)

1. Wenn ich mein Taschengeld bekomme (to get!), kaufe ich die Schallplatte.
2. Wir fahren nach London, wenn wir ein Hotel finden.
3. Wenn es regnet, werden wir Monopoly spielen.
4. Wenn ich dein Buch finde, gebe ich es dir.
5. Wir werden umziehen, wenn wir eine größere Wohnung finden.

B-Übungen (Exercises)

I. Put the verbs in brackets () into the correct forms.
(Setze die Verben in Klammern in die richtige Form!)

1. If my boy-friend (can afford) it, he (to buy) me a ring.
2. If you (to learn) the new words, you (to be able) to get a good mark.
3. If you (to send) us the photos, we (to be glad) to send you the money.
4. I (not/to be able to buy) the book I need if my father (not/to lend) me some money.
5. Our performance (not/to be) a great success if we (not/to work) hard.

II. Your theatre group at school is planning a performance. You need a few more things. You have to persuade your headmaster. Give arguments.
(Eure Theatergruppe in der Schule plant eine Aufführung. Ihr braucht einige zusätzliche Dinge. Du sollst den Rektor überzeugen. Nenne einige Argumente.)

Beispiel:
to get the hall – to practise every afternoon
If we get the hall, we will practise every afternoon.

1. to get some extra money – to be able to buy new costumes
2. to have a free day on Saturday – to work extremely hard on Monday
3. the performance/to be a success – the school/to become famous
4. to put advertisements in the newspaper– a lot of people/to come

Beachte:
'Can' und 'must' können Zukünftiges ausdrücken. Ihr findet daher in diesen Fällen manchmal Präsens statt Futur im Hauptsatz;
z. B.: If the sun shines, you can go swimming.

Type II: Improbable Condition – unwahrscheinliche Bedingung

Beispiel:	If I ate too much,	I would feel sick.
	(Wenn ich zuviel äße,	fühlte ich mich krank.)
Zeit (tense):	Imperfekt/Präteritum (Past Tense)	Konditional I (Conditional I)
Bildungsweise:	regelmäßige Verben: 1. Verbform + -ed unregelmäßige Verben: 2. Verbform	would + 1. Verbform
Art der Bedingung:	1. Die Bedingung (wenn ich zuviel äße, was ich aber wohl nicht tun werde) ist unwahrscheinlich (improbable). 2. Die Bedingung ist nicht erfüllbar. Beispiel: If he were still alive, he'd be angry. Wenn er noch lebte (was er aber nicht tut), wäre er wütend.	

Kurzregel (Typ II):
Steht im If-Satz Imperfekt/Präteritum (Past Tense), so steht im Hauptsatz Konditional I (Conditional I).

Beachte:
Im If-Satz steht statt 'was' 'were'!
Beispiel: If I were you, I'd go home.

A-Übungen (Exercises)

I. Put the verbs in brackets () into the correct tense.
(Setze die Verben in Klammern in die richtige Zeit!)

1. If I (to have) a lot of money, I'd buy a Rolls Royce.
2. If he (to be) my friend, I would invite him.
3. The Millers would go on holiday if they (to have) time.
4. If Peter learned more, he (to be) better at school.
5. If I (to find) £100, I (to go) to the lost property office.
6. We (to call) the police if we (to see) a burglar.
7. If the students (to have) no school, they (to be) happy.
8. My father (to build) a swimming pool if he (to have) the time.
9. If I (to phone), he (to come) at once.
10. If Mary (to come) home late, her mother (to be) very angry.

II. Make sentences.
(Bilde Sätze!)

Beispiel:
to see a camel in the garden – to call the zoo
If I saw a camel in the garden, I'd call the zoo.

1. to get 1000 DM – to buy a motorbike
2. to be you – not to be so lazy
3. to find a wallet – to take it to the police
4. to see an accident – to call the ambulance
5. to be in your situation – to tell my parents

B-Übungen (Exercises)

I. Put the verbs in brackets () into the correct tense.
(Setze die Verben in Klammern in die richtige Zeit!)

1. If I (to have) a broken leg, I (not to be able) to work so much.
2. Your parents (not to have) to tell you to come home so early if you (to be) more reliable.
3. The grocer (to give up) his shop if the company (to build) a new supermarket.
4. If you (to attack) us, we (to be able) to defend ourselves.
5. If he (to be) still alive, he (to tell) you what to do.

II. Translate the following sentences.
(Übersetze die folgenden Sätze!)

1. Wenn die Stadt kein Geld hätte, die Altersheime zu unterhalten, wären viele alte Leute hilflos.
2. Wenn ich ein Auto hätte, dürfte mein Bruder damit fahren.
3. Ich würde Mathematik studieren, wenn ich nicht so viele Fehler machte.
4. Wir könnten viel öfter ausgehen, wenn wir mehr Zeit hätten.

Type III: Impossible Condition – unmögliche Bedingung

Beispiel:	If I had been to London, I would have visited the 'Museum of London'. (Wenn ich in London gewesen wäre, hätte ich das ‚Museum of London' besucht.	
Zeit (tense):	Plusquamperfekt (Past Perfect)	Konditional II (Conditional II)
Bildungsweise:	regelmäßige Verben: had + 1. Verbform + -ed	would + have + 1. Verbform + -ed
	unregelmäßige Verben: had + 3. Verbform	would + have + 3. Verbform
Art der Bedingung:	Die Bedingung (wenn ich in London gewesen wäre, was ich aber nicht war) ist unmöglich (impossible), da sie in der Vergangenheit nicht gegeben war.	

Kurzregel (Typ III):
Steht im If-Satz Plusquamperfekt (Past Perfekt), so steht im Hauptsatz Konditional II (Conditional II).

A-Übungen (Exercises)

I. If you had been to London, what would you have done?
(Wenn Du in London gewesen wärst, was hättest Du unternommen?)

Beispiel:
to go to the theatre
If I had been to London, I would have gone to the theatre.

1. to see Madame Tussaud's
2. to watch the Changing of the Guards
3. to spend hours in a museum
4. to see the Tower
5. to go shopping

II. Put the verbs in brackets () into the correct tense.
(Setze die Verben in Klammern in die richtige Zeit!)

1. If you had read the book, you (to know) it.
2. If Paul (not to forget) his book, he wouldn't have been so late.
3. I wouldn't have bought the books if I (to know) the price.
4. If I (to be) in England for such a long time, I (to learn) English.
5. If the police (to come) earlier, he (not to escape).
6. The house (not to burn down) if the firemen (to arrive) at once.

7. If you (to meet) him, you (to like) him.
8. If my mother (not to be) ill, I (to come) to your party.
9. If I (to have) the money, I (to buy) the car.
10. Maud (to sell) the picture at once if she (to have) a customer.

B-Übungen (Exercises)

Think of the situation you were in and draw conclusions.
(Denk an die Situation, in der Du warst, und ziehe Schlußfolgerungen!)

Beispiel:
You wanted to go swimming, but it was raining.
If it hadn't been raining, I would have gone swimming.

1. You were often tired at school, because you had stayed up late in the evening.
2. You had to go to the dentist, because you had eaten too many sweets.
3. You saw a nice dress in the shop, but you hadn't got enough money.
4. You wanted to go to a disco, but your father didn't allow it.
5. You wanted to leave school and start working, but your parents told you to do your exam first.

Gemischte Übungen zum Gebrauch der Bedingungssätze

B-Übungen (Exercises)

Put the verbs in brackets () into the correct tense.
(Setze die Verben in Klammern in die richtige Zeit!)

1. If I (to be) you, I would help him.
2. The dog would not have bitten him if he (not to run) away.
3. If he goes on eating like that, he (to get) pretty fat.
4. I (never to come) here if I had known that Peter was here.
5. If you don't leave my house at once, I (to call) the police.
6. John would come immediately if he (to know) that I had got a cheese cake for him.
7. If London (to be) in Italy, it would be much warmer there.
8. I (to open) the door if I had heard the bell.
9. He (never to learn) English if he doesn't learn his words.
10. Aunt Mary (never can come) if you had not picked her up at the airport.

Reported Speech – indirekte Rede

Der Gebrauch der Zeiten in der indirekten Rede unterliegt im Englischen ganz bestimmten Regeln. Zwei Faktoren bestimmen, welche Zeit in der indirekten Rede stehen muß:

1. die Zeit des einleitenden Verbs (he says, asked usw.),
2. die Zeit, die in der direkten Rede stand.

Bei Punkt 1 gibt es zwei Möglichkeiten:

a) Das einleitende Verb steht in einer Zeit der Gegenwartsgruppe (Present Tense, Present Perfect, Future oder Future Perfect).

Beispiel:

He says	I'll say
He has said	You'll have said

b) Das einleitende Verb steht in einer Zeit der Vergangenheitsgruppe (Past Tense, Past Perfect, Conditional I oder II).

Beispiel:

He said	I would say
He had said	I would have said

Regel zu a) Steht das einleitende Verb in einer Zeit der Gegenwartsgruppe, so bleibt die Zeit der direkten Rede in der indirekten erhalten.

Beispiel:
He says, 'I'll come.' (Direkte Rede)
He says that he'll come. (Indirekte Rede)
I say, 'Peter is my friend.' (Direkte Rede)
I say that Peter is my friend. (Indirekte Rede)

Regel zu b) Steht das einleitende Verb in einer Zeit der Vergangenheitsgruppe, so wird die Zeit der direkten Rede folgendermaßen verändert:

Aus ... wird in der indirekten Rede	
Present Tense	Past Tense (Beispiel 1)
Past Tense	Past Perfect (Beispiel 2)
Present Perfect	Past Perfect (Beispiel 3)
Past Perfect	Past Perfect (Beispiel 4)
Future	Conditional I (Beispiel 5)
Future Perfect	Conditional II (Beispiel 6)
Conditional I	Conditional II (Beispiel 7)
Conditional II	Conditional II (Beispiel 8)

Beispiele:

zu (1): He said, 'I sometimes go to London.' (Direkte Rede)
He said that he sometimes went to London. (Indirekte Rede)

zu (2): He said, 'I went to London.' (Direkte Rede)
He said that he had gone to London. (Indirekte Rede)

zu (3): He said, 'I have gone . . .' (Direkte Rede)
He said that he had gone . . . (Indirekte Rede)

zu (4): He said, 'I had gone . . .' (Direkte Rede)
He said that he had gone (Indirekte Rede)

zu (5): He said, 'I'll go . . .' (Direkte Rede)
He said that he would go . . . (Indirekte Rede)

zu (6): He said, 'I will have gone . . .' (Direkte Rede)
He said that he would have gone . . . (Indirekte Rede)

zu (7): He said, 'I'd go . . .' (Direkte Rede)
He said that he would have gone . . . (Indirekte Rede)

zu (8): He said, 'I would have gone . . .' (Direkte Rede)
He said that he would have gone . . . (Indirekte Rede)

Bei der Umformung muß darauf geachtet werden, daß eine Verlaufsform auch nach der Umformung Verlaufsform ist.

Beispiel:

He said, 'I'm reading a book.' (Direkte Rede)
He said that he was reading a book. (Indirekte Rede)

Änderungen von Zeitangaben

Steht das einleitende Verb in einer Zeit der Vergangenheitsgruppe, so werden Zeitangaben der direkten Rede folgendermaßen verändert:

Aus	wird in der indirekten Rede
this (morning)	that (morning)
today/this day	that day
next (week)	the following (week)
yesterday	the day before
tomorrow	the next day
at this moment	at that moment
these (days)	those (days)
now	then
two months ago	two months before
last	before

Beispiel:

'I shall go to the market this morning,' she said. (Direkte Rede)
She said she would go to the market that morning. (Indirekte Rede)

Die Anknüpfung von indirekten Sätzen

a) Aussagesatz

Formt man direkte Aussagesätze (statements) in indirekte um, so steht nach dem einleitenden Verb ein 'that'. Dieses kann jedoch wahlweise wegfallen.

Beispiel:
He said, 'I'll come.'
He said that he would come.
oder
He said he would come.

b) Fragesatz

a) Formt man direkte Fragesätze (questions) mit Fragewort (z. B. when, how, . . .) in indirekte um, so steht nach dem einleitenden Verb ebenfalls das Fragewort.

Beispiel:
He asked, 'When are you coming?'
He asked when I was coming.

b) Fragesätze ohne Fragewort werden in der indirekten Rede mit 'if' oder 'whether' (ob) eingeleitet.

Beispiel:
He asked, 'Are you coming?'
He asked if (whether) I was coming.

Beachte die veränderte Satzstellung bei indirekten Fragen und den Wegfall der Umschreibung mit 'do'. In verneinten indirekten Fragesätzen bleibt die Umschreibung mit 'do' jedoch erhalten;
z. B.: He asked if I didn't like him.

c) Befehlssatz

Indirekte Befehle (commands) fallen nicht unter die Regeln der Zeitenfolge in der indirekten Rede. Sie werden immer, egal welche Zeit das einführende Verb hat, mit dem Infinitiv gebildet.

Beispiel:
He says to her, 'Go home!'
He tells her to go home.
He said to her, 'Go home!'
He told her to go home.

Verneinter Befehl:

Beispiel:
He said to her, 'Don't go home!'
He told her not to go home.

Beachte:
Beim verneinten Befehl fällt die Umschreibung mit 'do' weg.

A-Übungen (Exercises)

I. Put into Reported Speech.
(Setze in die indirekte Rede!)

a) Statements (Aussagesätze)
1. Mrs. Miller says, 'I will be at home tomorrow.'
2. Susan remarks, 'Peter is watching TV.'
3. 'I have breakfast at 7 o'clock every day,' Mary says.
4. Mr. Baker says, 'I was ill yesterday.'
5. The secretary tells the boss, 'You must sign these letters.'

b) Questions (Fragesätze)
1. Mr. Cooper asks, 'Will you be at home tomorrow?'
2. The boss wants to know, 'When did you come?'
3. The secretary asks, 'Has Mr. Miller arrived?'
4. 'Who is that lady?' he asks his friend.
5. 'Where did you park your car?' Paul wants to know.

c) Commands (Befehlssätze)
1. The bus conductor tells us, 'Mind the steps!'
2. 'Write these sentences!' the teacher tells us.
3. 'Don't eat chocolate in the living-room!' Mother tells Billy.
4. Father tells Susan, 'Don't play with the knife!'
5. The boss tells his secretary, 'Answer these letters at once, please!'

II. Put into Reported Speech.
(Setze in die indirekte Rede!)

a) Statements (Aussagesätze)
1. 'Last year the Millers had a serious accident,' our neighbour told us.
2. 'We'll have to learn a lot tomorrow,' the students complained.
3. Mr. Smith complained, 'My son never does his work properly.'
4. Susan had said, 'After I had read the book, I bought it.'
5. The boys remarked, 'The article was published in our school magazine.'

b) Questions (Fragesätze)

1. 'Are you leaving next Sunday?' she asked.
2. 'What do you do with all that money?' he wanted to know.
3. 'Why don't you buy a dictionary?' his mother asked.
4. Mary asked, 'Who gave you this present?'
5. The teacher asked, 'When are you going to do your homework properly?'

c) Commands (Befehlssätze)

1. 'Don't throw away this paper!' the clerk told me.
2. 'Please be in time!' my mother asked me.
3. Susan told her brother, 'Don't use my record-player!'
4. The warden told the students, 'Don't go out after 10 o'clock!'
5. 'Don't feed the animals!' the man told us.

B-Übungen (Exercises)

Put into Reported Speech.
(Setze in die indirekte Rede!)

1. 'Are you going to come with me to the football stadium next Saturday?' he asked.
2. Mr. Cooper told us, 'Don't write your homework in pencil, but in ink!'
3. 'What would you have done if you had not met John?' she wanted to know.
4. 'Why did John not go to England last spring?' Peter asked.
5. Our landlady told us, 'These rooms haven't been used for three months.'
6. Mary asked, 'Didn't you tell me that you'd washed up all the dishes?'
7. 'Why didn't you use your book instead of using mine?' my brother asks.
8. The teacher asked, 'Why has he never told us that he had had problems before he came here?'
9. Ann complained, 'My boy-friend has never bought any flowers for me.'
10. The lady answers, 'I'm never going to sell my parrot!'
11. The teacher told the students, 'If you don't learn your new words, you'll never pass the exam.'
12. The inspector asked the burglar, 'Why did you not steal the TV when you found out that nobody was at home?'
13. The burglar replied, 'If I had stolen the TV, I would not have been able to run away quickly.'
14. The inspector exclaimed, 'I'll never understand those burglars!'
15. 'Do you think it'll rain tomorrow?' my brother wanted to know.
16. 'Who has already finished?' the teacher asked.
17. The lady said, 'Our most expensive bowl was broken when she was tidying up the room.'
18. 'I hope she will succeed,' the old man replied.
19. 'Did the man speak Italian?' she asked.
20. He admitted, 'It must be done immediately.'

Auxiliary Verbs – Hilfsverben

Im Englischen unterscheidet man zwei Arten von Hilfsverben:

1. die vollständigen Hilfsverben (to have, to be, to do)
2. die unvollständigen Hilfsverben, die nur eine oder zwei Formen bilden können (can, may, shall, will, must, ought to, used to, need).

The Primary Auxiliaries – die vollständigen Hilfsverben

To have, to be, to do können sowohl als Hilfsverb wie auch als Vollverb gebraucht werden:

a) to have = haben

Stammformen: to have/has - had - had

Beispiel:
als Hilfsverb: He has written these sentences.
als Vollverb: He has a good job.

b) to be = sein

Stammformen: to be/am/are/is - was/were - been

Beispiel:
als Hilfsverb: He is writing these sentences.
als Vollverb: He is a doctor.

c) to do = tun

Stammformen: to do/does - did - done

Beispiel:
als Hilfsverb: He didn't write these sentences.
als Vollverb: He did a good job.

The Modal Auxiliaries – die unvollständigen Hilfsverben

Die unvollständigen Hilfsverben werden anders als im Deutschen nur als Hilfsverben gebraucht.

Beispiel:
Er muß zur Schule. –
He must go to school.
Lediglich 'need' (benötigen) kann als Vollverb gebraucht werden;
z. B.: I need money.

Die unvollständigen Hilfsverben bilden entweder nur eine Präsensform oder eine Präsens- und Imperfektform. Fehlende Formen und Infinitiv werden durch bedeutungsverwandte Verben oder Ausdrücke umschrieben.

a) can = können

Formen: + can/could
— cannot (can't) could not (couldn't)
Ersatzverb: to be able to
Formen: to be (am/are/is) able to – was/were able to – been able to

Mit 'can' kann man also nur Präsens (Present Tense) oder Imperfekt (Past Tense) bilden. Für alle anderen Zeiten (auch Futur!) braucht man eine Form von 'to be able to'.

Beispiel:
He will be able to come. – Er wird kommen können.

b) may = dürfen

Formen: + may/might
— may not/might not (mightn't)
Ersatzverb: to be allowed to
Formen: to be (am/are/is) allowed to – was/were allowed to – been allowed to

Mit 'may' kann man nur Präsens (Present Tense) bilden. Die Imperfektform 'might' drückt lediglich Unsicherheit, nicht aber Vergangenheit aus.

Beispiel:
He might come. –
Es könnte vielleicht sein, daß er kommt.

Das Ersatzverb 'to be allowed to' wird also für alle Zeiten außer Präsens benötigt.

Beispiel:
He was allowed to come. –
Er durfte kommen.

c) shall/will = werden

Formen: + shall/should
+ will/would
− shall not (shan't)/should not (shouldn't)
− will not (won't)/would not (wouldn't)

'shall'/'will' sind Bestandteile der Futurformen, 'should'/'would' der Konditionalformen. 'Would' kann auch Entschlossenheit oder Gewohnheit ausdrücken.

Beispiel:
My sister would always go to the youth club. –
Meine Schwester ging gewöhnlich zum Jugendclub.

d) must = müssen

Formen: + must / –
− need not (needn't) / –

Beachte:
Die Verneinung von 'must' ist 'need not'!
'Must not' heißt „nicht dürfen"!

Ersatzverb: to have to
Formen: to have/has to – had to – had to

Mit 'must' kann man dementsprechend nur Präsens (Present Tense) bilden. Für alle anderen Zeiten benötigt man Formen des Ersatzverbs 'to have to'.

Beispiel:
He had to come. –
Er mußte kommen.

e) ought to/should = sollten

Formen: + ought to / –
+ should / –
− ought not to (oughtn't to) / –
− should not (shouldn't) / –

'Ought to'/'should' werden benutzt, um auszudrücken, daß etwas ratsam ist oder eine moralische Verpflichtung darstellt.

Beispiel:
You ought to (should) do your homework properly! –
Du solltest deine Hausaufgaben ordentlich machen!

f) used to = pflegten (Gewohnheit)

Formen: + used to / –
— used not to / –

'Used to' bezieht sich stets auf die Vergangenheit. Es bezeichnet gewohnheitsmäßige oder wiederholte Tätigkeiten in der Vergangenheit.

Beispiel:
He used to go swimming every day. –
Er pflegte jeden Tag schwimmen zu gehen.

g) need = brauchen

('Need' als Vollverb hat die Bedeutung „benötigen".)
Formen: + need / –
— need not (needn't) / –

Als unvollständiges Hilfsverb wird 'need' in Frage- und verneinten Präsenssätzen gebraucht. Es dient als Verneinung von 'must' und hat deshalb auch das gleiche Ersatzverb '(not) to have to'.

Beispiel:
He need not come. –
Er muß nicht kommen.
He didn't have to come. –
Er mußte nicht kommen.

A-Übungen (Exercises)

I. Form sentences using Past Tense.
(Bilde Sätze, in denen Du Imperfekt benutzt!)

1. Mr. Miller – must – to wait – till 2 o'clock
2. Susan – can – to translate – all the sentences
3. My parents – must – to sell their car
4. Peter – may – to go – to the disco

5. The children – may not – to play football
6. The students – must – to write – 2 pages
7. I – must – to be – home – at 10 o'clock.
8. Mr. Baker – must – to pay £200
9. The girls – may not – to open – this parcel
10. You – may not – to open – this parcel

II. Form sentences using Future.
(Bilde Sätze, in denen Du das Futur I benutzt!)

1. He – can – to go – to the youth club tomorrow
2. Next year – I – can – to speak English fluently
3. She – may not – to come – to your party
4. Tomorrow – the old lady – can – to walk again
5. You – must – to write – the letters tomorrow
6. The secretary – cannot – to answer all phone calls tomorrow
7. Next year the boys – may – to work – in their holidays
8. You – may not – to go on a mountain climbing tour
9. When – she – can – to speak English correctly?
10. Why – you – must – to work – next Saturday?

B-Übungen (Exercises)

I. Put the verbs in brackets () into the correct tense.
(Setze die Verben in Klammern in die richtige Zeit!)

1. He (not/can/to spend) his holidays in this hotel since his wife died.
2. Two weeks ago he (not/may/to join) this club.
3. Next year the Millers (can/to afford) to buy a new car.
4. When she was young, she (can/to play) tennis quite well.
5. When he heard the news, he (not/can/to believe) it at first.
6. Mr. Miller (must/to work) overtime last weekend, because his secretary (not/can/to come) to the office.
7. Two years ago she was too young (may/to go) to a youth hostel on her own.
8. If he were my son, he (not/may/to stay out) so long.
9. If you try hard, you (can/to pass) the examination.
10. His boss told him that he (must/to be) in the office at 7 o'clock the following day.
11 For five weeks I (not/can/to speak) to him on the phone.
12. After he (can/to repair) the car, he told his brother at once.
13. In a few years we (must/to look for) a bigger flat.
14. The family (must/to move) because the owner wanted the house for himself.
15. A violinist (must/to practise) every day if he wants to get good jobs.

II. Translate the following sentences.
(Übersetze die folgenden Sätze!)

1. Du solltest jeden Abend einige Seiten in deinem Buch lesen.
2. Sie mußten früh nach Hause gehen, da ihr Sohn krank war.
3. Seit wann kannst du so gut Gitarre spielen?
4. Du weißt, daß du das nicht tun darfst!
5. Sie werden nicht vor 6 Uhr gehen dürfen.
6. Würdest du bitte das Fenster öffnen!
7. Du darfst es ihr nicht erzählen!
8. Du solltest dir endlich das Rauchen abgewöhnen.
9. Du brauchst mir nicht zu helfen, wenn du nicht dazu in der Lage bist.
10. Könntest du bitte Mary fragen, ob ich mit ihr fahren darf?
11. Würdest du mir mitteilen, wann er kommen kann?
12. Wann wird Herr Schmidt endlich richtig Französisch sprechen können?
13. Warum mußtest du gestern so lange fernsehen?
14. Du brauchst mir keine Antwort zu geben, wenn du nicht willst.
15. Wenn sie heute eine Stunde länger bleiben können, brauchen sie morgen nicht zu kommen.

Die Umschreibung mit 'do'

Zur Bildung einer englischen Frage oder eines verneinten Satzes sind im allgemeinen zwei Verben notwendig:
1. ein Hilfsverb,
2. ein Vollverb.

Beispiel:
Can you come tonight?
(HV) (VV)
He cannot come tonight.
(HV) (VV)

Enthält der Satz kein Hilfsverb, so wird eine Form von 'do' zur Bildung von Fragen und verneinten Sätzen verwendet.

Beispiel:
Do you come to England every year?
(HV) (VV)
He doesn't come to England every year.
(HV) (VV)

Da alle Zeiten außer Präsens (Present Tense Simple) und Imperfekt (Past Tense Simple) durch Hilfsverben gebildet werden, ist eine Umschreibung mit 'do' nur für diese beiden Zeiten nötig.

Beachte:
'to do' kann auch Vollverb sein;
z. B.: He does his homework every day.
In Fragen und verneinten Sätzen ist dann zusätzlich eine Form von 'do' für die Umschreibung erforderlich.

Beispiel:
He doesn't do his homework.
Did he do his homework?

Bei der Umschreibung mit 'do' trägt das Hilfsverb 'do' die Zeit und die Person. Das nachfolgende Vollverb steht im Infinitiv.

Beispiel:
He doesn't eat. (3. Person Singular)
Did he eat? (Imperfekt)

Ausnahmen von der Umschreibung mit 'do'

a) Eine Frage wird nicht mit 'do' umschrieben, wenn das Fragewort nach dem Subjekt des Antwortsatzes fragt. Dies ist immer der Fall bei Fragen mit 'who' = wer.

Beispiel:
Who called me? –
Peter called you. (Peter = Subjekt)

Auch Fragen mit 'which' können nach dem Subjekt fragen und werden dann nicht mit 'do' umschrieben.

Beispiel:
Which car stands in the garage? –
The red car stands in the garage. (The red car = Subjekt)

b) In Fragen und verneinten Sätzen mit einer Form von 'to be' gibt es keine Umschreibung mit 'do'.

Beispiel:
Is he at home? –
He isn't at home.

c) In verneinten Sätzen wird 'do' nicht angewendet, wenn 'not' nicht das Verb, sondern ein anderes Wort verneint.
z. B.: Not everybody wanted to come.

A-Übungen (Exercises)

I. Form negative sentences.
(Bilde verneinte Sätze!)

1. He likes ice-cream.
2. Mr. Miller can eat five hamburgers.
3. Mrs. Miller was in hospital yesterday.
4. Mary had a party yesterday.
5. Paul wrote three letters yesterday.
6. The children play football every day.
7. The children are playing football now.
8. I did my homework properly.
9. Peter plays the piano well.
10. I watched TV last Sunday.
11. They will see Big Ben.
12. Mother bought a new book last week.
13. He spends a lot of money on records.
14. Peter comes too late.
15. I clean my bike every week.

II. Form questions starting with the given interrogative pronoun.
(Bilde Fragen, die mit den vorgegebenen Fragewörtern beginnen!)

1. Last week we went on a climbing tour.
   a) what   b) when   c) who
2. Mr. Baker works in an office in Frankfurt.
   a) who   b) where
3. Susan gets up at 7 o'clock every day.
   a) what   b) when   c) who
4. Yesterday the boys sat in class from 8 to 12 o'clock.
   a) who   b) when   c) where
5. Last year Peter won a prize in London.
   a) when   b) what   c) who   d) where

B-Übungen (Exercises)

I. Form questions which can be answered by the words underlined.
(Bilde Fragen, die sich mit den unterstrichenen Satzteilen beantworten lassen!)

1. Last night I woke up at 3 o'clock.
2. My parents always spend their holidays in Italy.
3. My boss works very hard.
4. The students wrote a difficult test last week.
5. He always listens to pop music.
6. The workers went on strike last month.
7. This lady cleans the windows every day.
8. My brother sold his car last week.
9. Two weeks ago I met Mr. Paul.
10. My friend works as a mechanic.

II. Translate the following sentences.
(Übersetze die folgenden Sätze!)

1. Wann stehst du morgens auf?
2. Schaust du oft fern?
3. Ich gehe nicht ins Kino.
4. Hast du gestern deine Vokabeln gelernt?
5. Kennst du meinen Bruder?
6. Ich lese keine Comics.
7. Wie komme ich zur Hauptstraße?
8. Warum kaufst du dir kein neues Fahrrad?
9. Gehst du immer noch jeden Morgen zur Bushaltestelle?
10. Erkennst du deinen alten Freund nicht wieder?

Infinitive and Gerund – Infinitiv und Gerundium

Infinitiv und Gerundium gehören zu den infiniten (ungebeugten) Verbformen. Sie sind im Gegensatz zu den finiten (gebeugten) Verbformen nicht durch Person und Zeit bestimmt.

Infinitive – Infinitiv

	Infinitiv Aktiv	Infinitiv Passiv
Präsens Perfekt	(to) ask (to) have asked	(to) be asked (to) have been asked

Es gibt den Infinitiv mit und ohne 'to'.

Der Infinitiv ohne 'to' steht

- wie im Deutschen nach unvollständigen Hilfsverben (Ausnahme: ought to); z. B.: I can help him.
- nach den Ausdrücken: had better / would rather / would sooner usw.
  Beispiel:
  I'd rather not come. –
Ich möchte lieber nicht kommen.
- nach Verben der Wahrnehmung (to see, to hear, to feel, to watch) + Objekt, nach to make (= veranlassen) + Objekt und nach to let (= zulassen) + Objekt; z. B.: I saw him enter the pub.

Der Infinitiv mit 'to' steht

- anstelle eines indirekten Fragesatzes in Verbindung mit Fragewörtern oder mit 'whether/if' nach Verben wie to ask, to decide, to forget, to know, to learn, to remember, to show, to teach, to tell, to wonder usw.
  Beispiel:
  I'll ask her how I can do it
  I'll ask her how to do it.
- anstelle eines Relativsatzes nach Substantiven mit nachgestellter Präposition; z. B.: I had no paper to write on.

- nach Zahlwörtern und Superlativen wie the first, the last, the only thing usw.; z. B.: He was the last to come.
- nach Verben des Befehlens, Veranlassens (außer 'to make') und Zulassens (außer 'to let') wie to advise, to allow, to ask, to cause, to expect, to order, to tell (= befehlen), to want usw. + Objekt; z. B.: I told him to come in time.

Beachte:
Nach 'to want' kann nie 'that', sondern nur der Infinitiv stehen.
Beispiel:
I want to sleep.
I want him to go home.

- nach 'too' + Adjektiv; z. B.: He is too old to go to the disco.
- nach Adjektiv + 'enough'; z. B.: He is old enough to go alone.
- nach 'for' + Objekt; z. B.: It's time for him to start.
- zum Ausdruck des Zwecks; z. B.: You have to come (in order) to help me.

Beachte:
Ist bei den Infinitivkonstruktionen mit Objekt das Objekt ein Pronomen, so steht dies natürlich im Objektfall (object case).
Beispiel:
I want him to come.
I want them to work more quickly.
(Ich möchte von ihm/von ihnen, daß . . .)

Im Deutschen ist eine solche Infinitivkonstruktion nicht möglich.

Der Infinitiv Passiv steht

- nach 'to be' und 'to remain' bei passivischem Sinn; z. B.: The book was not to be found.

Ausnahmen

Infinitiv Aktiv steht trotz Passivsinn nach
- there + Form von 'to be'; z. B.: There is no time to lose.

- nach Adjektiven wie difficult, easy, hard, pleasant, nice;
  z.B.: The book is difficult to understand.
- bei 'to blame' (= tadeln) und 'to let' (= vermieten);
  z.B.: The flat is to let.

A-Übungen (Exercises)

I. Put in infinitive with or without 'to'.
(Setze den Infinitiv mit oder ohne 'to' ein!)

1. He had better (to go) now.
2. Sheila can (to go) home now.
3. Mary has (to work) every day.
4. She cannot (to come) today.
5. You must learn a lot in order (to pass) the test.
6. You ought (to see) the film.
7. I'd rather (not/to talk) about this.
8. We want (to go) to bed now.
9. It is impossible (to go) swimming in this weather.
10. You needn't (to clean) your room today.

II. Shorten the following sentences by using infinitive constructions.
(Verkürze die folgenden Sätze, indem Du Infinitivkonstruktionen benutzt!)

1. I will tell you how you can write this letter.
2. She is always the first who comes.
3. He could not find a tool he could repair the machine with.
4. Mary was the oldest girl who took part in the competition.
5. Billy was the first who reached the house.
6. He will show you where you can put your bike.
7. Mr. Miller remembers how he must type that in future.
8. Susan was the last who arrived at the youth hostel.
9. Mary said she had nothing she could give Peter.
10. She didn't know whether she should call the police.

B-Übungen (Exercises)

Translate the following sentences. Use infinitive constructions.
(Übersetze die folgenden Sätze. Benutze Infinitivkonstruktionen!)

1. Es ist schwierig für einen Indianer, eine gute Arbeit zu finden.
2. Der Chef erwartet von seinen Arbeitern, daß sie die Arbeit bis 5 Uhr erledigt haben.
3. Der Junge ist alt genug, um auf sich selbst aufzupassen.

4. Es war zu spät, um ins Kino zu gehen.
5. Erinnere mich daran, daß ich die Fenster schließe.
6. Ich möchte, daß er seine Hausaufgaben ordentlich erledigt.
7. Das Haus ist für eine so große Familie zu klein, um darin zu leben.

Gerund – Gerundium

Das Gerundium ist ein Substantiv (noun), das von einem Verb (verb) abgeleitet ist (= substantiviertes Verb). Im Deutschen bildet man das Gerundium durch Großschreibung des Infinitivs;
z. B.: Das Lesen ist mein Hobby.

Bildungsweise: Infinitive + -ing
Beispielform: reading
Rechtschreibbesonderheiten: siehe Present Tense Continuous (Seite 14 f)

Das Gerundium steht
- als Subjekt;
  z. B.: Reading is my hobby.
- nach Ausdrücken wie no use, no good, to be busy, to be near, to be like, worth, can't stand, can't help;
  z. B.: It's no good arguing.
- nach bestimmten Verben als Objekt;

nach to admit*	– zugeben
to avoid	– vermeiden
to consider	– in Betracht ziehen
to deny*	– abstreiten
to dislike	– nicht mögen
to enjoy	– Freude haben an
to mind	– etwas dagegen haben
to miss	– verpassen
to practise	– üben
to risk	– riskieren
to stop	– aufhören
to understand	– verstehen

  * Diese Verben können auch vor einem Nebensatz mit 'that' stehen.
  Beispiel:
  He admitted having stolen the money.
  He admitted that he had stolen the money.
- nach Präpositionen, wie after, in spite of, before, instead of, without, by, on usw.;
  z. B.: After playing cards they watched TV.
- nach Ausdrücken mit Präpositionen;

nach to insist on	– bestehen auf
to be good at	– gut sein in
to be interested in	– interessiert sein an
to be fond of	– begeistert sein von
to be used to	– gewöhnt sein an
to be afraid of	– sich fürchten vor
to be looking forward to	– sich freuen auf
to be for/against	– dafür/dagegen sein
to give up	– aufgeben
to go on	– weitermachen (mit)
to keep on	– fortfahren (mit)
to put off	– aufschieben
to care for	– sich kümmern um
to be keen on	– begeistert sein von
to succeed in	– Erfolg haben mit
hope of	– Hoffnung auf
no point in	– keinen Zweck
the chance of	– die Chance zu
opportunity of	– die Gelegenheit zu
reason for	– der Grund für

z. B.: They were used to travelling by train.

Gerundium oder Infinitiv?

a) Folgende Verben können entweder mit Infinitiv oder mit Gerundium stehen, ohne daß ein Bedeutungsunterschied entsteht: to begin, to start, to continue.
Beispiel:
She started to argue.
She started arguing.

b) Nach to like, to love, to prefer, to hate steht Gerundium, um eine allgemeine Vorliebe oder Abneigung auszudrücken;
z. B.: Children like playing.
Nach to like, to love, to prefer, to hate steht Infinitiv für konkrete Einzelfälle (vor allem mit 'would') oder eingeschränkte Aussagen;
z. B.: I would love to come.

c) Folgende Verben können entweder mit Gerundium oder mit Infinitiv stehen, wobei die Bedeutung jedoch jeweils eine andere ist:

to remember + Gerundium	to remember + Infinitiv
sich erinnern, etwas getan zu haben	daran denken, etwas zu tun

to regret + Gerundium
bereuen, etwas getan zu haben

to regret + Infinitiv
bedauern, etwas tun zu müssen

Beispiel:
I remember having bought the milk.
I remember to buy the milk.

A-Übungen (Exercises)

Finish the following sentences. Use the expressions in brackets + Gerund.
(Beende die folgenden Sätze. Benutze die Ausdrücke in Klammern + Gerundium!)

Beispiel:
I don't want to learn (I don't feel like . . .)
I don't feel like learning.

1. Don't take this dress. It's too old. (It's not worth . . .)
2. Don't wait for Peter. (There is no use . . .)
3. You can smoke. (I don't mind . . .)
4. Peter doesn't watch TV very often. (He isn't interested in . . .)
5. I'm very glad to see you next month. (I'm looking forward to . . .)
6. I read many books. (I'm fond of . . .)
7. I don't travel a lot. (I'm not used to . . .)
8. Jim is a very good dancer. (He's good at . . .)
9. I don't think we can win the prize. (There's no hope of . . .)
10. In England we can speak English. (We have the opportunity of . . .)
11. I wouldn't smoke any more (I would give up . . .)
12. Peter reads a lot of English magazines. (He's interested in . . .)
13. Mrs. Miller has a lot of work. She is cleaning the kitchen. (She's busy . . .)
14. He will get the job. (He will succeed in . . .)
15. Mr. Miller is not a very good speaker. (He is afraid of . . .)

B-Übungen (Exercises)

Gerund or Infinitive?
(Gerundium oder Infinitiv?)

1. Would you mind (to lend) me £5. I'd like (to buy) a present for Peter.
2. What's the advantage of (to have) a motorbike?
3. He is very fond of (to try) (to repair) this car.
4. He told her (to start) (to look for) a better job.
5. I have to ask him (to stop) (to play) the piano so late.
6. My father hates (to get up) early.
7. Would you like (to come) to my party next week?

8. Mrs. Baker asked her guests (to start) (to eat) now without (to wait) for the other guests (to come).
9. They tried (not/to be nervous).
10. The choir started (to sing) without (to practise).
11. He won't forget (to visit) the Tower of London.
12. My brother is not used to (to drive) a sports car.
13. She remembered (to meet) him in London some weeks ago.
14. My grandmother doesn't like (to go out) alone.
15. I forgot (to remind) you (to tell) your friend (not/to come) too late.

Question Tags and Short Answers – Frageanhängsel und Kurzantworten

Question Tags – Frageanhängsel

Question Tags sind durch Komma abgetrennte Frageanhängsel am Ende eines Satzes, die etwa die Bedeutung von „nicht wahr“ haben.

Beispiel:
He's a nice boy, isn't he?
Er ist ein netter Junge, nicht wahr?

Regel 1

a) Ist der Satz verneint, ist das Frageanhängsel nicht verneint;
z. B.: He can't come, can he?
b) Ist der Satz nicht verneint, ist das Frageanhängsel verneint;
z. B.: He can come, can't he?

Regel 2

a) Ist ein Hilfsverb im Satz, wird dieses im Frageanhängsel wieder aufgegriffen;
z. B.: She can speak English, can't she?
b) Ist kein Hilfsverb im Satz, wird im Frageanhängsel eine Form von 'to do' benutzt;
z. B.: She likes ice-cream, doesn't she?
Die Form von 'to do' richtet sich nach Zeit und Person des Satzes.

Ausnahmen

Befehle (Commands) haben 'will/won't' als Kurzanhängsel;
z. B.: Call me at 5 o'clock, will you?

A-Übungen (Exercises)

Add the correct question tags.
(Füge die richtigen Frageanhängsel hinzu!)

1. He is late, . . .
2. You eat very slowly, . . .
3. He didn't come, . . .

4. They arrived last week, . . .
5. I had better leave, . . .
6. She will come, . . .
7. He loves reading, . . .
8. They are playing cards, . . .
9. He couldn't go, . . .
10. The boy broke the window, . . .
11. You are much older than he, . . .
12. He has a lot of records, . . .
13. You have a car, . . .
14. She didn't know him, . . .
15. You were there, . . .
16. You won't go, . . .
17. That boy won the prize, . . .
18. You don't have to go, . . .
19. She is reading, . . .
20. She isn't at home, . . .
21. I ought to call him, . . .
22. Give me a ring, . . .
23. You bought a new car, . . .
24. You can't speak Italian, . . .
25. You often go to the disco, . . .

Short Answers – Kurzantworten

Short answers benutzt man bei Entscheidungsfragen (ja/nein), um zu vermeiden, daß man den ganzen Inhalt noch einmal wiederholen muß. 'Yes' oder 'no' alleine sind im Englischen als Antworten unzulässig.

Beispiel:
Have you got a car? Yes, I have.
No, I haven't.

Regel 1

Lautet die Antwort 'yes', ist das Verb bejaht.
Lautet die Antwort 'no', ist das Verb verneint.

Regel 2

Das Hilfsverb der Frage wird in der Kurzantwort wieder aufgegriffen.

Beispiel:
Can you speak English? Yes, I can.
No, I can't.
Does he like ice-cream? Yes, he does.
No, he doesn't.

A-Übungen (Exercises)

Answer the following questions.
(Beantworte die folgenden Fragen!)

1. Can Peter ride a motorbike? Yes, . . .
2. Do you like lemonade? No, . . .
3. Has Mary got a car? Yes, . . .
4. Have the children got a football? Yes, . . .
5. Must you learn hard? No, . . .
6. Does your mother go to work? Yes, . . .
7. Is Peter at home? No, . . .
8. Can I go swimming? Yes, . . .
9. Are you a student? No, . . .
10. Did Susan come to your party? No, . . .
11. Will Anne come with us? No, . . .
12. Have you ever met my brother? No, . . .
13. Has he ever seen the film? Yes, . . .
14. Is Paul going to join us? No, . . .
15. Had she got a job before she started to work here? Yes, . . .
16. Was Bill reading when you came? Yes, . . .
17. Were the boys at home? No, . . .
18. Couldn't you come yesterday? No, . . .
19. Weren't you able to write this report? No, . . .
20. Did you do that yourself? Yes, . . .
21. Haven't you heard of Maud? No, . . .
22. Did you go on holiday last year? Yes, . . .
23. Doesn't Susan go to school? No, . . .
24. Would you go if you were in my position? Yes, . . .
25. Can you help me? Yes, . . .

The Noun – das Substantiv

Bei den englischen Substantiven gibt es eigentlich nur zwei Bereiche (Genitiv und Plural), die Schülern Schwierigkeiten bereiten können, da es bei der Deklination kaum noch Endungen gibt. Ein Substantiv kann in vier Fällen – auch Kasus genannt – (cases) stehen:

a) Nominativ	– subject case
b) Genitiv	– genitive
c) Dativ	– object case
d) Akkusativ	– object case

Beispiel:

Singular	Plural
a) the girl	the girls
b) the girl's	the girls'
c) the girl	the girls
d) the girl	the girls

Wie diese Beispiele zeigen, gibt es lediglich im Genitiv und im Plural Endungen. Akkusativ- oder Dativobjekte sind nicht durch Endungen gekennzeichnet, sondern durch ihre Stellung im Satz:
1. Subjekt, 2. Prädikat, 3. Objekt.

The Plural – der Plural

Die regelmäßige Bildung des Plurals geschieht durch Anhängen der Pluralendung -s an das Substantiv;
z. B.: the boy – the boys
der Junge – die Jungen

Besonderheiten

a) Nach Zischlauten wird -es angehängt;
z. B.: the bus – the buses
der Bus – die Busse
b) Substantive auf -y (nach Konsonant) haben im Plural -ies;
z. B.: the country – the countries
das Land – die Länder
c) Substantive auf -o haben im Plural oft die Endung -es;
z. B.: the potato – the potatoes
die Kartoffel – die Kartoffeln
(Neue Lehnwörter haben dagegen meist einfaches -s;
z. B.: kilos, pianos, studios, tobaccos.)

d) Einige Substantive auf -f oder -fe bilden den Plural auf -ves;
z. B.: the knife – the knives
das Messer – die Messer
Die wichtigsten sind: life, wife, leaf, loaf, thief, calf, half, shelf, wolf.

e) Lehnwörter aus dem Lateinischen oder Griechischen behalten ihre ursprüngliche Pluralform oft bei;
z. B.: the crisis – the crises
die Krise – die Krisen
Dazu gehören: analysis – analyses; bacillus – bacilli; basis – bases; minimum – minima; stimulus – stimuli; thesis – theses.

f) In wenigen Fällen erfolgt unregelmäßige Pluralbildung;
z. B.: the man – the men
der Mann – die Männer
Dazu gehören: woman – women; foot – feet; goose – geese; tooth – teeth; mouse – mice; louse – lice; child – children; ox – oxen.

g) Singular und Plural haben in wenigen Fällen die gleiche Form;
z. B.: the fish – the fish
der Fisch – die Fische
Dazu gehören:
- Nationalitäten auf -ese;
  z. B.: Japanese
- technische Geräte auf -craft;
  z. B.: hovercraft
- manche Tiere (besonders Fische und Jagdtiere);
  z. B.: sheep, salmon, trout, deer, grouse
- auch: The French, The Swiss.

Pluralbildung bei zusamengesetzten Substantiven

Normalerweise tritt das Plural -s an das übergeordnete Substantiv;
z. B.: the mouse-trap – the mouse-traps
die Mausefalle – die Mausefallen
(Das -s tritt an 'trap', da das zusammengesetzte Substantiv die Bedeutung „Falle" und nicht „Maus" hat.)

Besonderheiten

a) Ist kein übergeordnetes Substantiv vorhanden, tritt das -s ans Ende;
z. B.: the breakdown – the breakdowns
die Panne – die Pannen

b) Bei Zusammensetzungen aus man/woman + Substantiv treten beide Bestandteile in den Plural, wenn eine Geschlechtszugehörigkeit gemeint ist;
z. B.: the woman teacher – the women teachers
die Lehrerin – die Lehrerinnen

A-Übungen (Exercises)

Put into the plural.
(Setze in den Plural!)

1. car
2. lady
3. house
4. fisherman
5. desk
6. lamp
7. rose
8. wish
9. hat
10. match
11. tomato
12. copy
13. garage
14. class
15. teacher
16. bridge
17. apple
18. child
19. day
20. student
21. bicycle
22. driver
23. dress
24. cup
25. dog
26. suitcase
27. record
28. policeman
29. woman
30. ticket

B-Übungen (Exercises)

Put into the plural.
(Setze in den Plural!)

1. passer-by
2. idea
3. thesis
4. commander-in-chief
5. sit-in
6. mouse
7. merry-go-round
8. woman-clerk
9. hero
10. tooth
11. woman-hater
12. chairman
13. grown-up
14. songwriter
15. aircraft
16. looker-on
17. ideal
18. man-servant
19. root
20. broadcasting-station
21. thief
22. chimney
23. horseman
24. chimney-sweeper
25. bacillus
26. city
27. life
28. mother-in-law
29. negro
30. half

Singular or Plural – Singular oder Plural

Es gibt Substantive, die nur Singular- oder Pluralform haben, deren Bedeutung sich aber nicht unbedingt mit der Form deckt. Man muß folgende Gruppen unterscheiden:

a) Substantive, die im Singular stehen und bei denen das dazugehörige Verb ebenfalls Singularform hat; es sind:
   - Materialbezeichnungen, wie z. B. coal, wood, iron, oil, salt, butter, water usw.;
     z. B.: Butter is rather expensive.
   - einige Sammelbegriffe, viele davon auf -ry, wie z. B.: machinery, jewellery, cutlery, crockery, garbage, luggage, hair, furniture usw.;
     z. B.: My hair is still wet.
   - viele abstrakte Begriffe, wie z. B. information, advice, knowledge, damage, progress, strength, confusion, work usw.;
     z. B.: His information was very useful.

   Den Gebrauch einiger dieser Substantive kann man variieren durch den Einsatz von 'a piece of' oder 'pieces of';
   z. B.: a piece of luggage,
   pieces of information.

b) Substantive, die Singularform, aber Pluralbedeutung haben und bei denen das dazugehörige Verb im Plural steht; es sind:
Sammelbegriffe (collective nouns), wie z. B. police, people, cattle, government, family, jury, company, staff, firm, class, club, band, choir, audience, group, party, couple usw., wenn die Tätigkeit oder der Zustand der einzelnen Gruppenmitglieder gemeint ist.
Beispiel:
The family are taking their seats.
aber: The Kennedy family is famous.

c) Substantive, die Pluralform, aber Singularbedeutung haben und bei denen das dazugehörige Verb im Plural steht; es sind:
- Werkzeuge und Kleidungsstücke, die aus zwei gleichartigen Teilen bestehen, wie z. B. earphones, scales, scissors, binoculars, glasses, pyjamas, shorts, trousers, jeans usw.;
  Beispiel:
  My jeans are dirty. –
  Meine Jeans ist schmutzig.
- Einzelstücke werden durch 'a pair of . . .' bezeichnet;
  z. B.: a pair of scissors – eine Schere;
- stairs, goods, clothes, belongings u. a.

d) Substantive, die Pluralform, aber Singularbedeutung haben und bei denen das dazugehörige Verb im Singular steht; es sind:
- Bezeichnungen für Fächer auf -cs, wie z. B. mathematics, physics, politics usw.;
- viele Spiele, wie z. B. darts, billiards, dominoes usw.;
- einige Krankheiten, wie z. B. mumps, measles;
- news, the United States.
  Beispiel:
  Here is the news. –
  Hier sind die Nachrichten.

A-Übungen (Exercises)

Put the verb into the correct form. Use Present Tense Simple.
(Setze das Verb in die richtige Form. Benutze einfache Gegenwart!)

1. The furniture in the room (to be) very expensive.
2. Your advice (to be) very useful.
3. His clothes (to be) old.
4. Physics (to be) an interesting subject.
5. The audience (to take) their seats.
6. Darts (to be) a popular game in England.

7. These stairs (to be) slippery.
8. The police (to come) at once.
9. The earphones (to be) on the table.
10. These goods (to be) very expensive.
11. The band (to put) away their instruments.
12. Our homework (to seem) very difficult.
13. When (to be) the news on AFN?
14. Coal (to cost) 50 p more a ton.
15. Where (to be) my glasses?
16. Ladies' clothes (to be) on the third floor.
17. The United States (to promise) help to her friends.
18. Measles (to be) an unpleasant disease.
19. People (to talk) a lot.
20. The class (to work) on their projects.

B-Übungen (Exercises)

Translate the following sentences.
(Übersetze die folgenden Sätze!)

1. Sein Fernglas war sehr teuer.
2. Mathematik ist mein Lieblingsfach.
3. Die Firma baut gerade ein neues Bürogebäude.
4. Billiard wird oft in Pubs gespielt.
5. Hier sind die 10 Uhr Nachrichten.
6. Pauls Hose ist sehr modern.
7. Die Polizei sucht den Dieb.
8. Die Möbel sind aus dem 18. Jahrhundert.
9. Diese Treppe ist sehr gefährlich.
10. Das Besteck besteht aus 24 Teilen.
11. Großer Schaden wurde verursacht.
12. Diese Informationen waren nicht sehr nützlich.
13. Wo ist die Waage?
14. Die Belegschaft ist schon gegangen.
15. Diese Schere ist ein Geschenk meiner Tante.

The Genitive – der Genitiv

Bildungsweise:

a) Der s-Genitiv

im Singular
Substantiv + ' + s;
z. B.: Mary's book

im Plural
Substantiv + s + ';
z. B.: the girls' room

Besonderheiten

- Hat ein Substantiv im Plural nicht die Endung -s, so bildet man den Genitiv wie bei einem Singularwort;
  z. B.: the children's room.
- Hat ein Substantiv bereits im Singular ein -s, so bildet man den Genitiv wie bei einem Pluralwort;
  z. B.: Davis' car.

b) Der of-Genitiv

Singular und Plural:
of + Artikel/Pronomen + Substantiv;
z. B.: the colour of the book.

Anwendung:

a) Zum Ausdruck eines Besitzverhältnisses steht bei Personen und Tieren mit Namen gewöhnlich der s-Genitiv;
   z. B.: Mary's book – Marys Buch.
b) Bei Sachbezeichnungen steht gewöhnlich der of-Genitiv;
   z. B.: the colour of roses – die Farbe von Rosen.
c) Zur Angabe eines Zeitmaßes steht der s-Genitiv;
   z. B.: an hour's walk – ein einstündiger Spaziergang.
d) Zur Bezeichnung von Örtlichkeiten bei Geschäften, Wohnungen usw. steht der s-Genitiv;
   z. B.: at the chemist's – in der Apotheke
   at the Millers' – bei den Millers

A-Übungen (Exercises)

I. Write the s-Genitive.
(Schreibe den s-Genitiv!)

1. (the girls) books
2. (Mr. Miller) car

3. (Sally) friend
4. (the boy) football
5. (Mr. Harris) house
6. (the lady) hat
7. (the men) club
8. (my brother) pencil
9. (my sister) room
10. (the Millers) garden
11. (my father) suitcase
12. (the students) work
13. (Anne) handbag
14. (the teacher) book
15. (the woman) purse
16. (the women) meeting
17. (five minutes) walk
18. (my sister) report
19. (the clerk) job
20. (the secretaries) desks

II. Decide whether to use s- or of-Genitive.
(Benutze entweder den s- oder den of-Genitiv!)

1. (Susan) record-player
2. (the house) rooms
3. (our dog) blanket
4. (the book) size
5. (my uncle) motorbike
6. (three days) work
7. (the animals) killing
8. (the director) office
9. (an hour) rest
10. (the bosses) umbrellas
11. (the house) roof
12. (the baby) bed
13. (the room) door
14. (milk) a glass
15. (the road) end
16. (the men) department
17. (John) moped
18. (my friend) bike
19. (the Browns) friends
20. (the newspaper) page

B-Übungen (Exercises)

Translate the following expressions.
(Übersetze die folgenden Ausdrücke!)

1. der Ball meines kleinen Bruders
2. die Sekretärin von Herrn Schmidt
3. der Geburtstag meiner Schwester
4. ein sechsmonatiger Kurs
5. die Seiten des Buches
4. die Tests der Schüler
7. die Zeitung von heute
8. die Spielzeuge der Kinder
9. der Preis des Autos
10. die Morgenpost
11. die Melodie des Liedes
12. die Freunde von Paul
13. die Frau meines Bruders
14. der Onkel von Fred und Peter
15. die Lebenshaltungskosten

The Article – der Artikel

Wie im Deutschen gibt es im Englischen bestimmte (definite) und unbestimmte (indefinite) Artikel. Allerdings existiert im Englischen keine Unterscheidung nach männlich, weiblich oder sächlich.

The Definite Article – der bestimmte Artikel

Wird nach dem bestimmten Artikel a, e, i, o, u gesprochen, so spricht man den Artikel the [ðiː] statt [ðə] aus, z. B. the car [ðə] – the apple [ðiː].

Anders als im Deutschen steht kein bestimmter Artikel

- bei abstrakten Begriffen, wie z. B. life, time, nature, work, history usw.
  Beispiel:
  Life is hard. –
  Das Leben ist schwer.

- bei Eigennamen, Ländern, Bergen, Seen im Singular, bei Straßen-, Brücken- und Gebäudenamen;
  Beispiel:
  Oxford Street is a shopping street in London. –
  Die Oxford Street ist eine Einkaufsstraße in London.

- bei Monatsnamen, Wochentagen, Tages- und Mahlzeiten, Jahreszeiten;
  Beispiel:
  Dinner is ready. –
  Das Abendessen ist fertig.

- bei Institutionen, wie z. B. school, church, hospital, prison, wenn die Funktion gemeint ist und nicht das Gebäude;
  Beispiel:
  I go to school every morning. –
  Ich gehe jeden Morgen zur Schule.
  aber: The school ist near the church. –
  Die Schule ist in der Nähe der Kirche.

- bei 'by' + Verkehrsmittel;
  Beispiel:
  I go by bus. –
  Ich fahre mit dem Bus.

- bei 'most' (= fast alle);
  Beispiel:
  Most people think so. –
  Die meisten Leute denken das.
- Anders als im Deutschen steht bei Musikinstrumenten ein bestimmter Artikel;
  Beispiel:
  He plays the piano. –
  Er spielt Klavier.

Stellung des bestimmten Artikels

Der bestimmte Artikel steht hinter half, double, both und all (aus einer bestimmten Anzahl);
z. B.: half the time.

The Indefinite Article – der unbestimmte Artikel

Wird nach dem unbestimmten Artikel a, e, i, o, u gesprochen, so steht 'an' statt 'a';
z. B.: an egg
an honest man [ˈɒn…]

aber: a university [ju:…]

Anders als im Deutschen steht der unbestimmte Artikel im Englischen
- bei Berufen, Volksgruppen, religiösen Gruppen oder Parteien, wenn die Person als Vertreter einer solchen Gruppe charakterisiert wird;
  Beispiel:
  She works as a teacher. –
  Sie arbeitet als Lehrerin.
- bei festen Ausdrücken, wie z. B.

to come to an end	– zum Ende kommen
to be in a hurry	– in Eile sein
it's a pity	– es ist schade
to have a temperature	– Fieber haben
to have a headache	– Kopfschmerzen haben
as a rule	– in der Regel
for a change	– zur Abwechslung
without a break	– ohne Unterbrechung;

- vor Mengen-, Maß- und Zeiteinheiten in der Bedeutung pro/je;
  Beispiel:
  The wine costs £1 a bottle. –
  Der Wein kostet ein Pfund pro Flasche.

- nach 'as';
  z. B.: as a present – als Geschenk.

Stellung des unbestimmten Artikels

Der unbestimmte Artikel steht hinter such, half, quite, rather, so + Adjektiv, too + Adjektiv;
z. B.: such a nice dress
too long a story
Er steht ausschließlich bei zählbaren Begriffen, d. h. nur bei solchen, die „viele/wenige" vor sich haben können;
z. B.: Don't buy such an expensive book.
('book' = zählbar, viele Bücher)
aber: Don't talk such nonsense.
('nonsense' = unzählbar)

A-Übungen (Exercises)

I. Put 'a' or 'an' in front of the word(s).
(Setze 'a' oder 'an' vor das Wort/die Wörter!)

1. suitcase
2. house
3. apple
4. end
5. umbrella
6. teacher
7. bike
8. answer
9. good answer
10. cow
11. window
12. animal
13. street
14. hour
15. boy
16. European country
17. student
18. car
19. girl
20. English girl

II. Put in 'a' or 'an' where necessary.
(Setze 'a' oder 'an' ein, wenn notwendig!)

1. He is . . . taxi driver.
2. It's . . . pity you can't come.
3. We watched . . . good film on TV last night.
4. I got the book as . . . present from my uncle.
5. . . . friend of mine went to Italy last year.
6. I'm in . . . great hurry.
7. I eat . . . apple . . . day.
8. It's such . . . cold night.
9. I saw . . . nice coat yesterday.
10. Don't make such . . . trouble.

III. Put in 'the' where necessary.
(Setze 'the' ein, wenn notwendig!)

1. When does . . . school begin?
2. . . . church was built in the 18th century.
3. Where did . . . life come from?
4. Last year we visited . . . Turkey.
5. I gave him . . . book from your shelf.
6. I saw . . . Buckingham Palace.
7. They took the injured man to . . . hospital.
8. . . . summer is . . . best season.
9. . . . teacher asked . . . students many questions.
10. I'd like to see . . . Mr. Miller.

B-Übungen (Exercises)

I. Put in 'a', 'an' or 'the' where necessary.
(Setze 'a', 'an' oder 'the' ein, wenn notwendig!)

1. You are not allowed to drive faster than 50 miles . . . hour.
2. He is . . . American.
3. Even though it was . . . summer, many visitors had . . . bad cold.
4. This is . . . school my brother goes to.
5. In which part of . . . England do you live?
6. In . . . summer you can sit in . . . Hyde Park.
7. I saw Mr. Baker in . . . Station Road before . . . breakfast.
8. There were quite . . . lot of people at . . . party.
9. We went swimming for . . . change.
10. You have to come to . . . office in . . . time.
11. Paul plays . . . violin very well.

12. He had . . . terrible headache yesterday.
13. Many children don't like . . . Irish Stew.
14. These apples are 80p . . . pound.
15. My colleague is known as . . . good doctor.
16. In this picture you can see . . . Westminster Bridge.
17. All . . . boys in our class came to . . . meeting.
18. . . . boy was ill. He had . . . temperature.
19. It's too hot . . . day to go for . . . walk.
20. . . . literature is often difficult to understand.

II. Put the definite or indefinite article in the right place if necessary.
(Setze den bestimmten oder unbestimmten Artikel an die richtige Stelle, wenn notwendig!)

1. There were (quite) lot of people in the hotel.
2. I didn't know that she was (such) person.
3. It's (too) cold day to go swimming.
4. (all) houses in the street were pulled down.
5. It took me (double) time to reach the valley.
6. (both) ladies were rich.
7. She is (such) friendly girl.
8. Two weeks ago my brother had (rather) bad cold.
9. The boys drank (half) bottle of Coke.
10. (half) hour later she finally arrived.

'Much' and 'Many'/ '(A) Little' and '(A) Few'

'Much', 'many', '(a) little', '(a) few' können vor einem Substantiv oder einer of-Gruppe stehen oder sich auf ein bereits genanntes Substantiv beziehen.

a) **'Much'** (viel) und **'(a) little'** (wenig) beziehen sich auf unzählbare Substantive mit Singularbedeutung.
Beispiel:
I haven't got much time.
There's little hope.

Sie können auch ohne Bezug auf ein Substantiv stehen (viel oder vieles).
Beispiel:
Much was said.
Little has been done to help them.

b) **'Many'** (viele) und **'(a) few'** (wenige) beziehen sich auf zählbare Substantive im Plural.
Beispiel:
Have you got many books?
Only a few books were interesting.

Ohne Bezug auf ein Substantiv stehen sie nur in der Bedeutung von viele/wenige/einige Leute;
z.B.: How many live in this house?

Beachte:
In bejahten Sätzen nimmt man
statt 'much' oft 'a lot (of)', 'plenty (of)', 'a great deal (of)';
statt 'many' oft 'a lot (of)', 'plenty (of)', 'a large number (of)'.

Die Steigerungen von 'much'/'little' und 'many'/'few' lauten:	
zählbar	unzählbar
many – more – most viele – mehr – die meisten a few – fewer – fewest wenige – weniger – die wenigsten	much – more – most viel – mehr – der/die/das meiste a little – less – least wenig – weniger – der/die/das wenigste

A-Übungen (Exercises)

I. Put 'much' or 'many' in front of the nouns.
(Setze 'much' oder 'many' vor die Substantive!)

1. apples
2. water
3. money
4. pencils
5. cups of tea
6. books
7. nonsense
8. students
9. coins
10. time
11. beer
12. tins
13. dogs
14. people
15. houses
16. children
17. wine
18. bottles of wine
19. fun
20. cigarettes

II. Put '(a) little' or '(a) few' in front of the nouns.
(Setze '(a) little' oder '(a) few' vor die Substantive!)

1. films
2. literature
3. newspapers
4. lemonade
5. help
6. glasses

7. records
8. flats
9. air
10. letters
11. plates
12. tea
13. stories
14. days
15. cars
16. rivers
17. minutes
18. boys
19. rubbish
20. girls

B-Übungen (Exercises)

Translate the following expressions.
(Übersetze die folgenden Ausdrücke!)

1. viele Blumen
2. weniger Geld
3. die wenigsten Kinder
4. die meisten Taschen
5. weniger Bücher
6. mehr Tee
7. die meisten Hamburger
8. weniger Felder
9. mehr Fächer
10. die meisten Freunde
11. die wenigsten Briefe
12. mehr Zimmer
13. mehr Glück
14. weniger Autos
15. viel Müll
16. wenig Zucker
17. wenig Kunst
18. viel Frieden
19. die meiste Energie
20. die wenigsten Unfälle

The Adjective – Comparison
Das Adjektiv – Steigerung

Die meisten Adjektive können gesteigert werden, d. h., man kann zu der Grundstufe (Positiv) eine Steigerunsstufe (Komparativ) und eine Höchststufe (Superlativ) bilden.

Steigerung mit -er/-est

Mit -er/-est werden gesteigert
- einsilbige Adjektive;
  z. B.: high (hoch) – higher (höher) – highest (höchsten);
- zweisilbige Adjektive auf -er, -le, -ow, -y;
  z. B.: narrow (eng) – narrower (enger) – narrowest (engsten).

Besonderheiten in der Rechtschreibung
- y wird zu i;
  z. B.: easy – easier – easiest;
- Ausfall von -e;
  z. B.: large – larger – largest;
- Verdopplung des Endkonsonanten nach kurzem, betontem Vokal;
  z. B.: big – bigger – biggest.

Steigerung mit more/most

Mit more/most werden gesteigert
- zweisilbige Adjektive außer auf -er, -le, -ow, -y;
  z. B.: childish – more childish – most childish
  kindisch – kindischer – am kindischsten
- drei- und mehrsilbige Adjektive;
  z. B.: important – more important – most important
  wichtig – wichtiger – am wichtigsten

Unregelmäßige Steigerung

Einige Adjektive werden unregelmäßig gesteigert. Dazu gehören:
good – better – best
bad – worse – worst
ill – worse – worst
little (klein) – smaller – smallest
little (wenig) – less – least
much – more – most
many – more – most

Zwei Steigerungsmöglichkeiten

Manche Adjektive haben zwei Komparative/Superlative mit unterschiedlichen Anwendungsweisen. Dazu gehören:

old	older – oldest – (allgemein) elder – eldest (bei Familienmitgliedern)
near	nearer – nearest (örtlich) / – next (Reihenfolge)
late	later – latest (zeitlich) latter – last (Reihenfolge)

Der Vergleich

- zum Ausdruck der Gleichheit:
  as + (Positiv) + as;
  z. B.: Peter is as tall as Anne.
- Zum Ausdruck der Ungleichheit:
  not as + (Positiv) + as;
  z. B.: Peter is not as tall as Brian.
  oder
  less + (Positiv) + than;
  z.B.: Peter is less tall than Brian.
- Zum Ausdruck eines höheren Grades:
  (Komparativ) + than;
  z. B.: Brian is taller than Peter.

- Zum Ausdruck des höchsten Grades:
  the + (Superlativ);
  z. B.: This building is the highest.
- Zwei Komparative:
  the + (Komparativ) the + (Komparativ),
  dt. je + (Komparativ), desto + (Komparativ);
  z. B.: the sooner the better
  je eher, desto besser.

A-Übungen (Exercises)

I. Write down the comparative and superlative of the following adjectives.
(Schreibe Komparativ und Superlativ der folgenden Adjektive auf!)

1. new
2. comfortable
3. simple
4. difficult
5. friendly
6. large
7. thin
8. deep
9. characteristic
10. heavy
11. short
12. lazy
13. low
14. great
15. funny
16. polite
17. bad
18. interesting
19. cheap
20. hot

II. Translate the following expressions.
(Übersetze die folgenden Ausdrücke!)

1. lauter als (loud)
2. so jung wie (young)
3. am größten (big)
4. aktiver als (active)
5. am nettesten (nice)
6. netter als (nice)

7. am kleinsten (small)
8. schöner als (pretty)
9. so einfach wie (simple)
10. am niedrigsten (low)
11. so vorsichtig wie (careful)
12. berühmter als (popular)
13. reicher als (rich)
14. am aufregendsten (exciting)
15. genauer als (exact)
16. so lang wie (long)
17. neuer als (new)
18. stärker als (strong)
19. so heiß wie (hot)
20. am leichtesten (easy)

B-Übungen (Exercises)

Make up three sentences each.
(Bilde jeweils drei Sätze!)

Beispiel:
old: Mary (11 years) / Paul (12 years) / Susan (14 years)

1. Mary is not as old as Paul.
2. Paul is older than Mary.
3. Susan is the oldest.

1. expensive: book (£1)/record (£3)/album (£4)
2. fast: VW (60 mph)/Ford (80 mph)/Mercedes (120 mph)
3. comfortable: chair/armchair/couch
4. high: house/office building/Empire State Building
5. good at school: Peter (1)/Mary (2)/Maud (3)

The Adverb – das Adverb

Ähnlich wie im Deutschen gibt es ursprüngliche Adverbien (z. B. here, there, now usw.) und abgeleitete Adverbien (z. B. lovely, well usw.). Besondere Schwierigkeiten machen die abgeleiteten Adverbien, da diese im Deutschen meist die gleiche Form wie das entsprechende Adjektiv haben, sich im Englischen jedoch in ihrer Form vom Adjektiv unterscheiden.

Beispiel:
Er hat eine wunderbare Stimme.
(wunderbar/wonderful = Adjektiv)
He has a wonderful voice.

Er singt wunderbar.
(wunderbar/wonderfully = Adverb)
He sings wonderfully.

Bildungsweise von Adverbien

- Viele Adverbien werden mit der Endung -ly von Adjektiven abgeleitet;
  z. B.: loud – loudly.

Besonderheiten

- Bei mehrsilbigen Adjektiven wird y zu i;
  z. B.: happy – happily.
- Nach Konsonant entfällt -le;
  z. B.: simple – simply.
- das stumme -e entfällt bei due, true, whole;
  z. B.: true – truly.
- Endet ein Adjektiv bereits auf -ly, wird das Adverb durch 'in a ... way' gebildet;
  z. B.: friendly – in a friendly way.
- Das Adverb zu 'good' lautet 'well'.
- Bei Adjektiven auf -ic bildet man das Adverb mit -ally;
  z. B.: systematic – systematically.
- Adjektiv und Adverb haben manchmal gleiche Form und gleiche Bedeutung. Dazu gehören:
  daily, hourly, weekly, monthly, early, likely, fast, long, far.

- Adjektiv und Adverb haben manchmal gleiche Form aber unterschiedliche Bedeutung. Dazu gehören:

	als Adjektiv	als Adverb
well	gesund	gut
ill	krank	schlecht
still	still	noch
only	einzig	erst, nur

- Manche Adjektive haben zwei Adverbformen ($Adverb_1$, $Adverb_2$), die gleiche oder unterschiedliche Bedeutungen haben können. Dazu gehören:

Adjektiv	$Adverb_1$	$Adverb_2$
right (richtig)	right (richtig)	rightly (richtig)
slow (langsam)	slow (langsam)	slowly (langsam)
hard (hart)	hard (hart)	hardly (kaum)
fair (fair)	fair (fair)	fairly (ziemlich)
deep (tief)	deep (tief)	deeply (zutiefst)
pretty (hübsch)	pretty (ziemlich)	prettily (hübsch)
high (hoch)	high (hoch)	highly (höchst)
late (spät)	late (spät)	lately (in letzter Zeit)

Steigerung von Adverbien

- Ursprüngliche und mit Adjektiven formgleiche Adverbien werden mit -er/-est gesteigert;
  z. B.: soon – sooner – soonest
  fast – faster – fastest.
- Adverbien auf -ly werden mit more/most gesteigert;
  z. B.: quickly – more quickly – most quickly.

Adjektiv oder Adverb?

- Adjektiv
  Ein Adjektiv bezieht sich auf ein Substantiv.
  Beispiel:
  He is a nice boy.

  The house is small.

- Adverb
  Ein Adverb bezieht sich
  - auf ein Verb;
    z. B.: He sings nicely.
  - auf ein Adjektiv;
    z. B.: He is completely stupid.
  - auf ein anderes Adverb:
    z. B.: He sings absolutely beautifully.
  - auf einen ganzen Satz,
    z. B.: Unfortunately I didn't see him.

Beachte:

- Bei Verben, die einen Zustand – sein, werden oder fortbestehen – ausdrücken, steht kein Adverb. Dazu gehören:
  to be (sein)
  to become, to get, to grow (werden)
  to seem (scheinen)
  to remain (bleiben).
- Bei Verben der Sinneswahrnehmung steht kein Adverb, es sei denn, die Sinnesorgane tun wirklich etwas.

Dazu gehören:

Verb	ohne Adverb in der Bedeutung	mit Adverb in der Bedeutung
to look	aussehen	schauen
to feel	sich fühlen	fühlen = tasten
to smell	riechen (z. B. Fisch)	riechen (mit der Nase)
to taste	schmecken (z. B. eine Mahlzeit)	schmecken (mit dem Mund)
to sound	sich anhören, klingen wie	

Stellung von Adverbien

- Adverbien des Ortes und der bestimmten Zeit stehen am Satzanfang oder Satzende. Stehen beide unmittelbar zusammen, gilt Ort vor Zeit.
  Beispiel:
  I met him in London yesterday.
  Yesterday I met him in London.

- Adverbien der Art und Weise (z. B. quickly) und Adverbien der unbestimmten Zeit (z. B. sometimes, often) stehen vor dem Vollverb oder nach dem 1. Hilfsverb.
  Beispiel:
  He quickly came to the door.
  He sometimes opens the door.
  He has never opened the door.

Wenn kein Objekt folgt, stehen Adverbien der Art und Weise gewöhnlich hinter dem Verb;
z. B.: He opened quickly.

A-Übungen (Exercises)

I. Form the adverbs.
(Bilde die Adverbien!)

1. usual
2. dangerous
3. warm
4. full
5. gentle
6. whole
7. terrible
8. fresh
9. fast
10. thin
11. slow
12. lively
13. daily
14. heavy
15. fantastic
16. fluent
17. clever
18. good

19. serious
20. beautiful

II. Write down the comparatives and superlatives of the following adverbs. (Steigere die folgenden Adverbien!)

1. easily
2. early
3. quickly
4. hard
5. daily
6. quietly
7. comfortably
8. loudly
9. truly
10. slowly
11. terribly
12. wisely
13. angrily
14. generally
15. happily
16. awfully
17. prettily
18. extremely
19. secretly
20. silently

III. Decide whether to use adjectives or adverbs. (Entscheide, ob Adjektiv oder Adverb stehen muß!)

1. He (quick) wrote a letter.
2. He (quick) answered the questions.
3. This is an (easy) exercise.
4. You can (easy) open this tin.
5. Petra is a (pretty) girl.
6. She is always (pretty) dressed.
7. She's got (pretty) hair.
8. Edith dances (good).
9. She is a (good) dancer.
10. Paul speaks English (fluent).
11. His English is (fluent).
12. She always speaks (serious).
13. She's a very (serious) person.
14. She has a (soft) voice.

15. She always talks (soft).
16. It's a (terrible) day today.
17. Yesterday it rained (terrible).
18. The boys are (terrible) loud.
19. He was in a very (dangerous) situation.
20. Sometimes he behaves (dangerous).

B-Übungen (Exercises)

I. Put the adverbs or adverbial phrases in suitable positions.
(Setze die Adverbien oder adverbialen Bestimmungen an passende Stellen!)

1. He wrote a letter. (yesterday/in his office)
2. The baby drinks milk. (usually)
3. Mary writes dictations. (normally/well)
4. Susan reads a book. (often/in the evening)
5. We have lunch. (in this pub/sometimes)
6. I have met him. (never/before)
7. He works. (generally/quickly)
8. Mary wears a dress. (always)
9. Our dog is hungry. (always/in the morning)
10. She walked. (slowly/out of the room)

II. Put in adverbs or adjectives.
(Setze Adverb oder Adjektiv ein!)

1. When the old lady heard the noise, she remained (silent).
2. The fish smells (awful).
3. She (slow) opened the door, she was frightened.
4. You can (easy) give the (correct) answers, because the questions are not (difficult).
5. He seemed to be very (excited).
6. Mr. Miller attended the evening course (regular) and now he speaks Italian (fluent).
7. His spelling seems to be (correct).
8. He can't pronounce the words (correct).
9. The cake tastes (good).
10. Peter has got a cold. He can't smell very (good).
11. She (anxious) looked at the man.
12. This man looks (pretty) (old).
13. Mary is an (absolute) (clever) girl.
14. I hope the weather will remain (fine).
15. My grandmother is (serious) (ill).
16. It was (short) after 8 o'clock, when she (automatic) turned on the TV.

17. She came in (quiet), but her husband was already sleeping (deep).
18. Her body turned (cold), because she was so (frightened).
19. He (general) keeps the milk in the fridge to keep it (fresh), because he only likes (fresh) milk.
20. He is a (remarkable) (good) swimmer, but it looks as if he is getting (tired).

III. Translate the following sentences.
(Übersetze die folgenden Sätze!)

1. Der Mann am Telefon klang aufgeregt.
2. Ich bin erkältet. Ich kann nicht gut riechen, aber ich bin sicher, der Kuchen riecht gut.
3. Die Äpfel fühlen sich sehr weich an.
4. Die Suppe schmeckt wirklich gut.
5. Der Plan hört sich gut an.

The Pronouns – die Pronomen

Personal Pronouns – Personalpronomen

Personalpronomen stehen als Stellvertreter von Personen, Tieren oder Dingen. Ihre Form richtet sich danach, welche und wie viele Personen usw. sie vertreten und ob sie Subjekt oder Objekt eines Satzes sind.

Formen

a) Als Subjekt (auf die Frage „Wer oder was?"):

Singular
1. I = ich
2. you = du
3. he = er
   she = sie (für eine Frau)
   it = es (für ein Ding oder Tier ohne Namen)

Plural
1. we = wir
2. you = ihr
3. they = sie (für mehrere Personen/Dinge)

Beispiel:
She (Mary) goes to school. (Wer? → She)

b) Als Objekt (auf die Frage „Wem, wen oder was?"):

Singular
1. me
2. you
3. him
   her
   it

Plural
1. us
2. you
3. them

Beispiel:
Give him (Peter) the book! (Wem? → Him)
I saw her (Mary) yesterday. (Wen? → Her)

A-Übungen (Exercises)

Replace the underlined words by personal pronouns.
(Ersetze die unterstrichenen Wörter durch Personalpronomen!)

1. The children went to the zoo last week.
2. Peter met Mary in town.
3. The books are on the table.
4. The record is quite good.
5. Can't you see my brother?
6. The girls had a party.
7. I saw Mary in the restaurant.
8. The students are in a youth hostel.
9. Let's play with the boys.
10. I have known the girl for a long time.
11. The exercise is difficult.
12. The music is too loud.
13. I don't like these records.
14. Mr. Miller is paying the workers.
15. Give Peter this book.
16. I visited Aunt Mary last week.
17. Read the sentences carefully!
18. Don't open the window.
19. The boys and girls are playing.
20. He never talks about Peter.

Possessive Pronouns – Possesivpronomen

Es gibt zwei Arten von Possessivpronomen:
a) attributive (attributive), vor dem Substantiv stehende Possessivpronomen

Formen

Singular	1. my 2. your 3. his, her, its
Plural	1. our 2. your 3. their

Beispiel:
This is his (Peter's) book.
Das ist sein Buch.
Their (the Millers') room is on the 2nd floor.
Ihr Zimmer ist im 2. Stock.

Beachte:

Attributive Possessivpronomen werden abweichend vom Deutschen in Bezug auf Körperteile und Kleidungsstücke verwendet.

Beispiel:

He put his hands in his pockets.
Er steckte die Hände in die Taschen.

b) substantivische (nominal) Possessivpronomen

Formen

Singular	1. (of) mine 2. (of) yours 3. (of) his (of) hers
Plural	1. (of) ours 2. (of) yours 3. (of) theirs

Beispiel:

This book is mine.
Dieses Buch ist meins.
This book is one of mine.
Dieses Buch ist eines von meinen.

Die substantivischen Possessivpronomen stehen stellvertretend für ein attributives Possessivpronomen + Substantiv.

Beispiel:

This is my pen. →
This is mine.

Die substantivischen Possessivpronomen mit 'of' bedeuten 'one of my' usw. (einer, eine, eines von meinen usw.).

Beispiel:

a friend of mine = one of my friends.

A-Übungen (Exercises)

I. Replace the attributive possessive pronoun + noun by a nominal possessive pronoun.
(Ersetze das attributive Possessivpronomen + Substantiv durch ein substantivisches Possessivpronomen!)

1. This is my coat. It's . . .
2. Those are your books. They're . . .
3. This is their car. It's . . .
4. It's our room. It's . . .
5. This is their house. It's . . .
6. It's his football. It's . . .
7. This is her handbag. It's . . .
8. This is her bike. It's . . .
9. Take your book! Take . . .
10. Don't drink her lemonade! Don't drink . . .

II. Replace the underlined words by a possessive pronoun.
(Ersetze die unterstrichenen Wörter durch ein Possessivpronomen!)

1. He's a friend of Mr. Miller's.
2. This is Peter's room.
3. The girls' dresses are in the wardrobe.
4. These records are Paul's.
5. Mary's hat is in the car.
6. I like Susan's hairstyle.
7. The house over there is my parents' house.
8. Have you seen that brother of Mary's?
9. The boys' changing rooms are downstairs.
10. Where is my husband's key?
11. The secretary's office is rather small.
12. The children's toys are upstairs.
13. Have you seen my brother's new bike?
14. Peter's letter has already arrived.
15. Susan's and Colin's party was great.
16. Tom's father is not at home.
17. Did you find the teacher's key?
18. Don't use the children's towels!
19. He is a neighbour of Mrs. Baker's.
20. My father's pen was very expensive.

Interrogative Pronouns – Interrogativpronomen

Übersicht über die Interrogativpronomen

	Frage nach Personen	Frage nach Dingen
als Subjekt	who (= wer) Who wants to see me?	what (= was) What shall I do?
als Genitivobjekt (Besitzer)	whose (= wessen) Whose bike is this?	
als Objekt	who (whom im literarischen Stil) (= wem, wen) Who do you want to see?	what (= was) What do you want to do?
aus einer bestimmten Anzahl	which (= welche, welcher, welches) Which of the boys is Peter? Which of the books do you want?	
in der Bedeutung 'was für ...'	what (kind of) What (kind of) people were in the pub? What (kind of) records are these?	

Beachte:
Bei Fragen mit 'who' werden Präpositionen (z. B. for, with, of usw.) nachgestellt; z. B.: Who are you waiting for?

A-Übungen (Exercises)

I. Put in 'who', 'whose' or 'what'.
(Setze 'who', 'whose' oder 'what' ein!)

1. .... is the lady over there?
2. .... is waiting for me?
3. .... is in this box?
4. .... opened my letter?
5. .... records are these?
6. .... did you meet at the party?
7. .... house is this?
8. .... is next?
9. .... would you like to drink?
10. .... wanted to come at 7 o'clock?
11. .... bicycle did you repair last week?
12. .... car is this?
13. .... do you want to buy?

14. . . . . can do this exercise?
15. . . . . looks after the children?

II. Put in 'what' or 'which'.
(Setze 'what' oder 'which' ein!)

1. . . . . kind of boy is he?
2. . . . . of these books do you like?
3. . . . . house is yours, No. 10 or No. 11?
4. . . . . tube shall we take, Circle Line or Jubilee Line?
5. . . . . sort of flowers did you buy?
6. . . . . is your address?
7. . . . . dress do you prefer, the white one or the red one?
8. . . . . school do you go to?
9. . . . . kind of furniture do you prefer?
10. . . . . Mr. Miller do you mean, the elder or the younger one?
11. . . . . colour is your new blouse?
12. . . . . country is larger, England or Germany?
13. . . . . is your new teacher like?
14. . . . . do you prefer, walking or going by bus?
15. . . . . book is yours, the white one or the grey one?

B-Übungen (Exercises)

Ask for the underlined words.
(Frage nach den unterstrichenen Wörtern!)

1. Sheila goes to <u>Grammar School</u>.
2. I went to see <u>my uncle</u>.
3. I would like to talk to <u>the doctor</u>.
4. Paul would prefer to dance with <u>Maud</u>.
5. Her name is <u>Sheila</u>.
6. Mary is reading <u>an English book</u>.
7. They talked about <u>the boys</u>.
8. Peter is waiting for <u>Mr. Miller</u>.
9. The secretary wants to discuss the problem with <u>the boss</u>.
10. I lent my record to <u>Susan</u>.

Relative Pronouns – Relativpronomen

Relativpronomen leiten Relativsätze ein.

Übersicht über die Relativpronomen

	für Personen	für Dinge
Subjekt	who that	which that
besitzanzeigend	whose	whose, of which
Objekt	who(m) that	which that

Beispiele:

- Person/Subjekt:
  This is the man who (that) lives next door. –
  Das ist der Mann, welcher (der) nebenan wohnt.
- Ding/Subjekt:
  This is the book which (that) has 50 pages. –
  Das ist das Buch, welches (das) 50 Seiten hat.
- Person/besitzanzeigend:
  This is the man whose house is next to ours. –
  Das ist der Mann, dessen Haus neben unserem liegt.
- Ding/besitzanzeigend:
  This is the book whose (of which the) cover is damaged. –
  Das ist das Buch, dessen Umschlag beschädigt ist.
- Person/Objekt:
  This is the man whom I met before. –
  Das ist der Mann, den ich schon vorher getroffen habe.
- Ding/Objekt:
  This is the book which (that) I found. –
  Das ist das Buch, welches (das) ich gefunden habe.

Beachte:

'Which' kann sich auch auf einen ganzen Satz beziehen;
z. B.: He passed his exam, which made him very proud.
In diesem Fall steht vor dem Relativpronomen ein Komma.

Der Wegfall des Relativpronomens

Relativpronomen können in einem notwendigen Relativsatz weggelassen werden, wenn das Relativpronomen nicht Subjekt, sondern Objekt ist.

Beispiel:

This is the man (whom) I saw last week. –
Das ist der Mann, den ich letzte Woche sah.

Hilfestellung

Daß ein Relativpronomen Objekt ist, kann man daran erkennen, daß ihm ein Substantiv oder Personalpronomen im Nominativ folgt.

Beispiel:

These are photos of all the countries (which) I visited.
This is the wine (which) Mary likes best.
This is the man (whom) the police arrested.

A-Übungen (Exercises)

I. Put in 'who(m)' or 'which'.
(Setze 'who(m)' oder 'which' ein!)

1. Mr. Miller, . . . we are talking about, is not here now.
2. Billy, . . . was driving the car, was seriously injured.
3. Susan, . . . is my best friend, can't come.
4. Coffee, . . . is my favourite drink, is not very healthy.
5. Have you seen the beautiful flowers . . . grow in our garden?
6. There are a few things . . . I always forget.
7. I gave him the book . . . he wanted.
8. Mrs. Cooper is the lady . . . works for Mr. Parker.
9. The students, . . . were very tired, didn't learn much.
10. The house . . . belongs to my uncle will be pulled down soon.
11. The car . . . they are going to buy is quite expensive.
12. I can only learn words . . . I have written down.
13. This is the newspaper . . . I read yesterday.
14. Where are the magazines . . . I put on this desk?
15. My uncle, . . . is quite rich, has got a bungalow.

II. Put in 'who', 'which' or 'whose'.
(Setze 'who', 'which' oder 'whose' ein!)

1. Susan, . . . is my sister, goes to university.
2. The people . . . I admire most are doctors.
3. The film . . . I like best is 'Star Wars'.
4. Have you met Ralph, . . . sister is in your class?
5. London, . . . is the capital of England, is a very interesting city.
6. The man . . . you met last night is my boss.
7. Mr. White, . . . car was stolen, is our neighbour.
8. Paul, . . . parents are English, speaks English very well.
9. The girls . . . won the prize danced well.
10. Football is the game . . . I like best.

B-Übungen (Exercises)

Fill in the correct relative pronoun, but only where necessary!
(Setze das richtige Relativpronomen ein, aber nur wenn notwendig!)

1. Mr. Schulz was the man . . . had the accident.
2. It's difficult to find food . . . is typically English.
3. A lot of tourists . . . come to London want to go shopping.
4. Peter, . . . had good marks at school, thought that he could go to university.
5. Who was the first person . . . you saw this morning?
6. This is Mr. Cooper, . . . wife you met last week.
7. Mrs. Baker, . . . has just come home from work, is very tired.
8. I'd like to go to the restaurant . . . opened last week.
9. Have you seen the picture . . . Mary painted?
10. Ralph, . . . is always tired, likes to stay at home.
11. Mr. Miller, . . .is a mechanic, can repair his car himself.
12. Did you get the parcel . . . I sent you last week?
13. This is the most interesting film . . . I've ever seen.
14. I'd like to show you the pullover . . . my mother bought for me.
15. The girls . . . died in the accident were very young.
16. You have to do something . . . you really can do.
17. We ate all the strawberries . . . we could find.
18. The worker, . . . had worked very hard, stopped for a break.
19. The project . . . he had worked on for such a long time was a success.
20. The photo . . . the journalist took was really great.

Reflexive Pronouns – Reflexivpronomen

Reflexivpronomen können zwei Funktionen erfüllen:

a) Sie können reflexiv gebraucht werden, d. h., sie kennzeichnen eine Übereinstimmung von Subjekt und Objekt.

Beispiel:
I have hurt myself. –
Ich habe mich (selbst) verletzt.

b) Sie können verstärkend gebraucht werden, um ein Subjekt/Objekt besonders hervorzuheben.

Beispiel:
He saw the Queen himself. –
Er selbst sah die Königin.

Formen

Singular	1. myself 2. yourself 3. himself herself itself
Plural	1. ourselves 2. yourselves 3. themselves

Reflexivpronomen mit 'by' stehen in der Bedeutung „alleine".

Beispiel:
I must do that by myself. –
Ich muß das alleine machen.

Beachte:

- Nach Ortspräpositionen, wie above, after, before, behind, with usw., stehen anders als im Deutschen nur Personalpronomen und nicht Reflexivpronomen.
  Beispiel:
  Shut the door behind you. –
  Schließen Sie die Tür hinter sich!

– Einige Verben haben im Gegensatz zur deutschen Bedeutung <u>kein</u> Reflexivpronomen bei sich. Dazu gehören:

to remember	– sich erinnern
to approach	– sich nähern
to complain	– sich beschweren
to imagine	– sich vorstellen (geistig)
to lie down	– sich hinlegen
to move	– sich bewegen
to recover	– sich erholen
to rely on	– sich verlassen auf
to sit down	– sich setzen
to turn to	– sich wenden an
to hurry	– sich beeilen
to behave	– sich benehmen

A-Übungen (Exercises)

Put in the suitable reflexive pronoun.
(Setze das passende Reflexivpronomen ein!)

1. Roger made . . . a wooden desk.
2. I'd like to talk to the boss . . .
3. Did you bake that cake . . .?
4. The Queen . . . will open the new school.
5. He always repairs his car . . .
6. Lady Anne had to open the door . . .
7. I'd like to see the hotel . . ., not a photo.
8. Mrs. Clark can't paper the walls . . .
9. I said to . . . 'I must help him.'
10. She made the dress . . .
11. I introduced . . . to him.
12. Do you wash your curtains . . .?
13. We always clean our rooms . . .
14. You have to translate the exercise . . .
15. The boys cooked the meals . . .

B-Übungen (Exercises)

Put in the correct reflexive or personal pronoun if possible.
(Setze das richtige Reflexiv- oder Personalpronomen ein, wo dies möglich ist!)

1. Peter is old enough to go to the dentist by . . .
2. People should try to see . . . as others see them.

3. Can I speak to the boss . . . instead of speaking to his secretary?
4. Suddenly they heard a noise hehind . . .
5. As the secretary was on holiday, the boss had to write the letter . . .
6. He had no money with . . .
7. He ought to be ashamed of . . .
8. Did you speak to the director . . .
9. Have you got any matches on . . .?
10. She looked at . . . in the mirror.
11. She was sitting in the garden all by . . .
12. She could not remember . . . his name.
13. The children sat . . . down at the table.
14. He had his brother with . . .
15. Imagine . . . all the money!
16. She couldn't move . . .
17. They left Paul behind . . .
18. It's difficult to remember . . . everybody's birthday.
19. We introduced . . . to the new teacher.
20. Did you do this exercise . . .?

Demonstrative Pronouns – Demonstrativpronomen

Übersicht über die Demonstrativpronomen

für Personen und Dinge	
Singular	Plural
this = das hier that = das da / jenes	these = diese hier those = diese da / jene

'This'/'these' stehen für das räumlich/zeitlich Nähere.
'That'/'those' stehen für das räumlich/zeitlich Entferntere.

Beispiel:
Is that your coat over there? –
Ist das dein Mantel da drüben?
No, this is my coat. –
Nein, dieses (hier) ist mein Mantel.

A-Übungen (Exercises)

I. Put 'this' or 'these' in front of the nouns.
(Setze 'this' oder 'these' vor die Substantive!)

1. books
2. key
3. boy
4. days
5. records
6. flowers
7. hat
8. coat
9. girls
10. handbags

II. Translate the words in brackets ().
(Übersetze die Wörter in Klammern!)

1. Is (das) Patrick over there?
2. I like (jene) kind of books.
3. (Das hier) is your book.
4. Whose flowers are (das hier)?
5. Do you know all (diese) men?
6. (Dies) are my brothers, Paul and Simon.
7. (Das) is the warmest day of (dieses) month.
8. (Dieser) boy is older than (jener) boy.
9. You can either take (diesen) hat or (jenen) hat.
10. (Dieser) gentleman over there is Mr. Baker.

'Some' and 'any'

'Some' und **'any'** stehen beide in der Bedeutung ‚etwas/einige'. Sie unterscheiden sich in ihrer Anwendung.

some: +	any: – / ?
'some' steht im bejahten Satz; z. B.: Here ist some tea for you.	'any' steht im verneinten Satz; z. B.: There isn't any tea in the pot. 'any' steht im Fragesatz; z. B.: Is there any tea left?
<u>Ausnahmen:</u> 'some' steht in Fragesätzen, wenn eine bejahte Antwort erwartet wird (z. B. wenn man jemandem etwas anbietet); z. B.: Would you like some tea? und nach where, when, how usw.; z. B.: Where can I get something to eat?	<u>Ausnahmen:</u> 'any' steht in bejahten Sätzen in der Bedeutung ‚jeder x-beliebige'; z. B.: Any student can do this exercise. und in if-Sätzen: z. B.: If I had any money left, I'd buy this record.

Diese Regeln gelten auch für die Zusammensetzungen mit 'some' und 'any' (something/anything, somebody/anybody usw.)

A-Übungen (Exercises)

Put in 'some' or 'any'.
(Setze 'some' oder 'any' ein!)

1. I'd like . . . French wine.
2. I need . . . pullovers for cold weather.
3. Are there . . . students in the classroom?
4. There's . . . ice-cream for you.
5. You must buy . . . new exercise books.
6. I took . . . nice photographs.
7. There aren't . . . eggs in the fridge.
8. I'm sorry, we haven't got . . . English books at the moment.
9. Here are . . . letters for you.
10. Are there . . . sandwiches left?
11. I've seen . . . very nice shoes.
12. Have you read . . . good books lately?
13. There were . . . very nice people at the party.
14. Are there . . . apples in the basket?
15. Take . . . sugar in your tea!

16. Have you got . . . idea what I could do?
17. I haven't got . . . matches.
18. Are there . . . letters today?
19. I haven't got . . . stamps at home.
20. There is . . . money for you on the table.

B-Übungen (Exercises)

Put in 'some' or 'any'.
(Setze 'some' oder 'any' ein!)

1. If I had . . . stamps, I'd give you one.
2. Can I offer you . . . cake?
3. Would you give me . . . information about sailing?
4. Have you got . . . money?
5. Can I have . . . coffee?
6. . . . idiot parked his car in front of the gate.
7. You can take . . . bus to Baker Street.
8. Would you like . . . wine.
9. I bought . . . nice flowers.
10. . . . dictionary will tell you.
11. . . . students want to go to the theatre.
12. If Mary had . . . spare time, she'd help you.
13. Where can I get . . . good French books?
14. They sell . . . nice posters in this shop.
15. There are . . . biscuits in the tin.

'As', 'Like' and 'How'

a) **'As'** wird benutzt

- bei Gleichstellungen;

  Beispiel:

  He works as a mechanic. –
  Er arbeitet als Mechaniker. (= Er ist Mechaniker.)

- bei Vergleichen, wenn dem Substantiv/Pronomen <u>ein Verb</u> folgt;

  Beispiel:

  Drink your wine as they <u>do</u> in France. –
  Trinken Sie Ihren Wein, wie man es in Frankreich tut.

- bei gleichen Eigenschaften (Doppel-'as');

  Beispiel:

  He is as tall as his father. –
  Er ist genauso groß wie sein Vater.

b) **'Like'** wird benutzt

- vor einem Substantiv oder Pronomen bei einem bildlichen Vergleich;

  Beispiel:

  He works like a slave. –
  Er arbeitet wie ein Sklave. (= Er ist <u>kein</u> Sklave.)

- bei Vergleichen, wenn nur ein Substantiv/Pronomen folgt;

  Beispiel:

  Drink like a <u>king</u>! –
  Trinke wie ein König!

- in der Verbindung 'to look like' – aussehen wie.

c) **'How'** wird benutzt als Fragewort (wie?/auf welche Weise?/in welchem Maße?);

  Beispiel:

  How did you do that? –
  Wie hast du das gemacht?

Beachte:

Wie nennt man das?	– What do you call this?
Wie heißt du?	– What's your name?
Wie spät ist es?	– What's the time?
Wie wär's mit . . .?	– What about . . .?
Wie sieht dein Auto aus?	– What does your car look like?

A-Übungen (Exercises)

Put in 'as', 'like' or 'how'.
(Setze 'as', 'like' oder 'how' ein!)

1. . . . is your mother?
2. He looks . . . his brother.
3. We didn't know him. He came . . . a stranger.
4. He is . . . clever . . . Peter.
5. He works . . . a madman.
6. He did it . . . his father had done it.
7. . . . do you do?
8. He came . . . soon . . . possible.
9. He looks . . . a clergyman, but he isn't.
10. Does your mother make bread . . . they do in Germany?
11. . . . did it happen?
12. He works . . . a carpenter, it's his job.
13. He talks exactly . . . his brother.
14. She walks . . . a queen.
15. . . . did you manage to pass the test?

B-Übungen (Exercises)

Translate the following sentences.
(Übersetze die folgenden Sätze!)

1. Wie hast du die letzten Ferien verbracht?
2. Das Gebäude wird als Werkstatt benutzt.
3. Er fährt wie ein Idiot.
4. Sie spricht Englisch wie eine Engländerin.
5. Er arbeitet als Lehrer.
6. Sie hat Augen wie ein Adler.
7. Dieser Park ist schöner als unser Garten.
8. Er kämpfte wie ein Verrückter.
9. Er sieht aus wie ein Indianer.
10. Paul benimmt sich wie ein kleines Kind.

'Each' and 'Every'/'All' and 'Whole'

'Each', 'every', 'all' und 'whole' bereiten Schwierigkeiten in der Anwendung, da sie ähnliche Bedeutungen haben.

'Each' = jeder (einzelne)

Beispiel:
The teacher must ask each student in the class. –
Der Lehrer muß jeden (einzelnen) Schüler der Klasse fragen.
You must take a pill each day for two weeks. –
Du mußt jeden (einzelnen) Tag zwei Wochen lang eine Tablette nehmen.
You mean £10 each. –
Du meinst, jedes (kostet) 10 Pfund.

'Each' betont eine Person oder ein Ding aus einer begrenzten Anzahl. 'Each' steht vor einem Substantiv im Singular oder hinter einem Objekt.

'Every' = jeder (allgemein verstanden; alle)

Beispiel:
We go to the cinema every week. –
Wir gehen jede Woche ins Kino.
Every student must work hard. –
Jeder (alle) Schüler muß hart arbeiten.

'Every' und seine Zusammensetzungen (everybody, everyone = jeder/jede/jedes, everything = alles usw.) werden benutzt, wenn „jeder" (Person oder Ding) ganz allgemein gemeint ist.

'All' = alle, alles . . . (ohne Ausnahme)

- 'All' + Substantiv (im Plural!) hat eine allgemeine Bedeutung.
  Beispiel:
  All workers earn good money. –
  Alle Arbeiter verdienen gutes Geld.
- 'All' + the (my/his/. . .) + Substantiv (im Plural!) hat die Bedeutung „alle einer bestimmten Gruppe".
  Beispiel:
  All the workers in this firm earn good money. –
  Alle Arbeiter dieser Firma verdienen gutes Geld.

- 'all' + Verb;
  Beispiel:
  My friends will all come. –
  Meine Freunde werden alle kommen.
- 'all' + the (my/his/. . .) + Substantiv (im Singular!);
  z. B.: all the time – die ganze Zeit
- 'all' + the (my/his/. . .) + Substantiv (im Plural!);
  z. B.: All the girls in my class . . .
  aber: all morning/day/usw. – den ganzen Morgen/Tag/usw.
- 'all' + Adjektiv;
  z. B.: all dirty – ganz schmutzig

'Whole' = ganze/ganzes/usw.

z. B.: We drank the whole bottle.

A-Übungen (Exercises)

Put in 'every', 'each', 'all' or 'whole'.
(Setze 'every', 'each', 'all' oder 'whole' ein!)

1. . . . that could be done was to wait.
2. . . . the people in the village are farmers.
3. . . . child at the party got a present.
4. Give them 2 pence . . ..
5. . . . the people in the room clapped.
6. Those apples are 10 pence . . .
7. I gave him . . . he wanted.
8. . . . of them wanted to try the game.
9. He used his . . . energy.
10. . . . member was present.
11. . . . he said was 'Good-bye!'
12. Take . . . of them.
13. That's . . . wrong.
14. Tell me the . . . truth.
15. . . . the other boys came too late.
16. . . . I want is a rest.
17. He spent the . . . of his money on records.
18. The teacher gave . . . of the boys a ticket.
19. . . . Monday I attend an English course.
20. The best luck to . . . of you!
21. . . . our friends enjoyed the party.
22. We have three different flavours. . . . kind is delicious.
23. . . . tourist gets a free map.

„Lassen“

Für das deutsche „lassen“ gibt es im Englischen viele Wiedergabemöglichkeiten:

etwas erlauben/zulassen: to allow/to permit/to let

Beispiel:
The doctor allowed the patient to go home.
The doctor permitted the patient to go home. –
Der Arzt erlaubte dem Patienten, nach Hause zu gehen.
My father let me watch TV every evening. –
Mein Vater erlaubte mir, jeden Abend fernzusehen.

etwas vorschlagen: let's do something

Beispiel:
Let's go swimming. –
Laß uns schwimmen gehen.

jemanden zu etwas veranlassen: to make somebody do something

Beispiel:
The police made him open his bag. –
Die Polizei veranlaßte ihn, die Tasche zu öffnen.

veranlassen, daß etwas von jemandem anderen getan wird: to have/get something done

Beispiel:
Mr. Miller has his car repaired.
Mr. Miller gets his car repaired. –
Mr. Miller läßt sein Auto reparieren.

einen Zustand lassen, wie er ist; etwas zurück-, hinter-, belassen: to leave something/somebody; to keep somebody doing something

Beispiel:
Paul left his books at school. –
Paul ließ seine Bücher in der Schule.
Paul left the engine running. –
Paul ließ den Motor laufen.

Don't keep me waiting. –
Laß mich nicht warten!

Einige Redewendungen

Laß das!	– Stop it.
Laß den Arzt kommen!	– Send for the doctor!
Laß die Polizei kommen!	– Call the police!
Laß dir Zeit!	– Take your time!
Laß mir Zeit!	– Give me time!
Laß mich in Ruhe!	– Leave me alone!

B-Übungen (Exercises)

Translate the following sentences.
(Übersetze die folgenden Sätze!)

1. Wann wirst du dir die Haare schneiden lassen?
2. Der Lehrer ließ uns 20 Sätze schreiben.
3. Ich lasse meine Hemden immer bügeln.
4. Ich lasse das Fenster sofort reparieren.
5. Laß bitte den Hund in Ruhe!
6. Er ließ mich für sich arbeiten.
7. Laß uns ins Kino gehen!
8. Peter läßt sein Fahrrad meistens in der Garage.
9. Mr. Baker ließ den Wagen stehen.
10. Der Besitzer ließ die Kinder im Garten spielen.
11. Laß mich diesen Brief zu Ende schreiben!
12. Der Trainer ließ uns nach Hause gehen.
13. Laß die Briefe da liegen!
14. Peter ließ seine Freundin warten.
15. Könnte ich den Unterricht 10 Minuten früher verlassen?
16. Du kannst dein Auto nicht hier lassen.
17. Die Passagiere können das Schiff verlassen.
18. Mutter läßt uns ins Schwimmbad gehen.
19. Laß mir 5 Minuten Zeit!
20. Frau Becker läßt ihre Kleider machen.

Anhang 1: Lösungen zu den Übungen

Seite 13/14

A: 1. go; 2. reads; 3. like; 4. watch; 5. cleans; 6. listen to; 7. works; 8. stands; 9. opens, reads, sleeps; 10. play, write.

B: 1. The girls don't like . . .; 2. Do you play . . .? 3. Mr. Miller doesn't go . . .; 4. Does he stay . . .? 5. He sometimes doesn't spend . . .; 6. Mrs. Miller doesn't work. 7. Does Peter read . . .? 8. No, he doesn't like . . .; 9. Does Mary speak . . .? 10. No, she doesn't speak . . ., . . . speaks . . .

Seite 15/16

A/I: 1. are pulling down; 2. is repairing; 3. are playing; 4. am writing; 5. is wearing; 6. is running; 7. are playing; 8. is preparing; 9. is shouting; 10. is telephoning.

A/II: 1. At the moment Susan is visiting her grandmother. 2. John isn't at home. He is just playing tennis. 3. Mary is just doing (nicht: 'making'!) her homework. 4. The Millers are just sitting in the garden and (are) playing cards. 5. Give me my umbrella! It's raining. 6. Listen! Stephen is playing the piano. 7. I can't come. I'm helping my mother. 8. Let's go into the garden. The sun is shining. 9. Father is just watching TV and mother is reading a book. 10. Look! The doctor is coming.

A/III: 1. has breakfast/is lying; 2. goes/is having; 3. starts/is sitting; 4. makes/is arriving; 5. has/is working.

B/I: 1. gets/is; 2. is still sleeping; 3. is working/has; 4. goes/is dancing and having fun; 5. hates/has to stay/is cleaning; 6. are you doing; 7. plays/is cutting; 8. stand; 9. is playing/isn't playing; 10. is having.

B/II: 1. Look, the boys are playing football, though they normally don't like sports. 2. While Mr. Miller is reading a book, his wife is watching TV. 3. Frankfurt lies on the Main. 4. Every Saturday Mrs. Miller does her shopping. 5. Every day between 2 o'clock and 5 o'clock I do my homework, but today I'm listening to records. 6. Mr. Miller seldom smokes, but today he's smoking a cigar. 7. What are you doing? I'm washing my hair. 8. Our neighbour plays the piano daily. Listen! She's practising now. 9. Stephen usually goes to school by bus, but today he's taking the tube (underground)/going by tube. 10. I don't go to the cinema very often, but my brother goes almost every week.

Seite 18/19

A/I: 1. wrote; 2. met; 3. built; 4. bought; 5. got; 6. didn't come; 7. Did . . . give; 8. married; 9. had; 10. moved; 11. Did . . . see; 12. didn't do; 13. was; 14. spent; 15. were; 16. visited; 17. learned; 18. called; 19. were not; 20. discovered.

A/II: got up – went – washed – dressed – went – had – left – walked – took – sat – rang – rushed – had – didn't like – ate – were – had – was – left – got – arrived.

B/I: 1. The weather was fine yesterday. 2. Last month we didn't have (oder: had no) time. 3. We bought our house two years ago. 4. The Bergs moved house yesterday. 5. Last month we wrote 3 classtests. 6. I didn't have any bad mark in my last report. 7. I didn't get a letter from him last month. 8. Yesterday I saw the new film in the cinema. 9. My brother worked all day yesterday. 10. Three weeks ago the police caught the thief. 11. I lost my wallet 2 days ago. 12. Yesterday he forgot to pick up the book. 13. My friend didn't come in time yesterday evening. 14. Did you watch the football match yesterday? 15. When did you go to bed yesterday?

Seite 20/21

A/I: 1. Mrs. Peggy was doing . . .; 2. Paul was reading . . .; 3. Mary was drinking . . .; 4. Simon was sleeping . . .; 5. Peter and Mary were dancing; 6. Susan was making . . .; 7. His secretary was writing . . .; 8. Mr. Smith was flirting . . .; 9. Johnny and Stephen were telling . . .; 10. Jean was doing . . .

A/II: 1. was doing; 2. was cutting; 3. was playing; 4. was sleeping/was listening; 5. was working/was lying; 6. were getting up; 7. were playing/was writing/was knitting; 8. was sleeping/was trying; 9. was shining/were boating/were resting; 10. was telephoning/was making.

B: 1. was having/was telephoning; 2. was lying/heard; 3. came/was smoking; 4. entered/were not working; 5. were playing/was reading; 6. opened/sat/drank; 7. was watching/thought; 8. was explaining/were writing/didn't understand; 9. was sleeping/broke; 10. were doing/rang.

Seite 22–24

A/I: 1. He has already ironed . . . 2. He has already cleaned . . . 3. He has already made . . . 4. He has already washed . . . 5. He has already done . . . 6. He has already repaired . . . 7. He has already used . . . 8. He has already cut . . . 9. He has already cleared . . . 10. He has already cooked . . . 11. He hasn't cleared up . . . 12. He hasn't written . . . 13. He hasn't made . . . 14. He hasn't cleaned . . . 15. He hasn't repaired . . .

A/II: 1. haven't seen; 2. hasn't been; 3. has come; 4. has she lived; 5. Have you ever been; 6. Has anyone telephoned; 7. has asked; 8. has bought; 9. haven't visited; 10. have worked; 11. has just arrived; 12. has he gone; 13. have lost; 14. have never spoken; 15. have finished.

B: 1. He has already gone to school. 2. The Millers have lived in Germany since 1980. 3. I haven't met him for one month. 4. We haven't been to the cinema for 2 months. 5. Have you ever been to New York? 6. I have never eaten pizza. 7. Give the book back to me when you've read it. 8. Mr. Becker has already smoked 5 cigarettes since he has been here. 9. Stop talking! I've had enough of this nonsense. 10. How long have you known Jim?

Seite 25

A/I: 1. has been waiting; 2. have been discussing; 3. has been lying; 4. has been standing; 5. has been smoking; 6. have you been learning; 7. have been standing; 8. have been working; 9. has been typing; 10. has been snowing.

A/II: 1. has been dancing/has already danced; 2. has been reading/has already read; 3. have been waiting/have already waited; 4. has been taking/has already ruined; 5. has been talking/hasn't talked; 6. has been reading/has read; 7. has been writing/has already written; 8. have been taking/have taken; 9. has been making/has made; 10. have been doing/haven't learned.

Seite 26/27

A/I: 1. since; 2. since; 3. since; 4. since; 5. since; 6. since; 7. for; 8. for; 9. since; 10. for; 11. since; 12. since; 13. for; 14. since.

A/II: 1. for; 2. since; 3. for; 4. since; 5. for; 6. for; 7. since; 8. since; 9. for; 10. for.

Seite 27/28

A: 1. learned; 2. have not been; 3. visited; 4. moved in; 5. has worked/has been working; 6. have looked/have been looking/haven't found; 7. have not seen; 8. took; 9. spent; 10. left; 11. Have you ever been; 12. was; 13. has watched/has been watching; 14. have just arrived; 15. went skiing; 16. has not finished; 17. have you written; 18. has not worn; 19. understood; 20. wrote.

B: 1. I was in Hamburg yesterday. 2. I have not been in Frankfurt for 2 years. 3. He has never been in Mainz. 4. Have you ever eaten pizza? 5. Last week I bought a new record. 6. My grandfather has (already) been lying in hospital for 3 weeks. 7. My mother has (already) been going to this hairdresser for 2 years. 8. He arrived 2 hours ago. 9. I have been playing tennis for 3 years. 10. Last year Mr. Baker got his driving licence. 11. He has not worked for this firm for three months now. 12. I was born on 1st August 1962 and since then I have lived in Berlin. 13. I haven't spoken any Spanish since I was in Spain. 14. I have known him for 5 years, but I've never seen him smoking. 15. Two hours ago they started playing Monopoly and they have been playing ever since then. 16. When I saw him for the first time, I didn't know who he was. 17. For years I spent my holidays in France, but I haven't been there for two years now. 18. Since I watched a football match for the first time I have gone to the stadium every Sunday. 19. He has not heard from his brother for one year. 20. I have never been to England again since I had the accident.

Seite 30/31

A/I: 1. had checked; 2. had collected; 3. had prepared; 4. had repaired; 5. had listened; 6. had told; 7. had packed; 8. had told; 9. had bought; 10. had borrowed; 11. had had; 12. had asked; 13. had discussed; 14. had put; 15. had attended; 16. had not checked; 17. had not bought; 18. had not planned; 19. had not read; 20. had not asked.

A/II: 1. had been waiting for; 2. had been; 3. had seen; 4. had caught; 5. had been typing; 6. had learned/had been learning; 7. had won; 8. had known; 9. had already been trying; 10. had discovered

B/I: 1. had just had; 2. went/had finished; 3. had finished/drank; 4. took/had done; 5. had not seen/met; 6. asked/had learned; 7. had repaired/went; 8. had left/remembered; 9. had driven/had lost; 10. had gone/started.

B/II: 1. I had already read the book before I saw the film. 2. After I had done my shopping, I went home. 3. Did you see the film after he had (gone) left? 4. They celebrated after they had won the match. 5. After she had written the essay, she could go home.

Seite 34–36

A/I: 1. will get stuck; 2. won't (=will not) get out; 3. won't run; 4. will be; 5. will have to work; 6. will be; 7. will be; 8. won't start; 9. will clean; 10. will go; 11. will spend; 12. will sell; 13. won't be able to; 14. will have; 15. will be.

A/II: 1. is going to take; 2. is going to have; 3. is going to stay; 4. are going to visit; 5. are going to go; 6. am going to talk; 7. are going to walk; 8. are going to have; 9. are going to play; 10. is not going to eat; 11. is going to go; 12. are going to take; 13. are going to clear up; 14. is going to explain; 15. are going to cycle.

A/III: 1. will be swimming; 2. will be sunbathing; 3. will be reading; 4. will be sitting; 5. will be having; 6. will be playing; 7. will be writing; 8. will be visiting; 9. will be talking; 10. will be flirting; 11. will not (= won't) be swimming; 12. will be looking; 13. will be resting; 14. will be running; 15. will be working.

B: 1. will help; 2. are going to repair; 3. will come; 4. will be/is; 5. will be sitting; 6. are having; 7. am going to look; 8. is going to snow; 9. will be closing; 10. will not (won't) go; 11. is; 12. will be; 13. will go; 14. will be keeping; 15. is going to be.

Seite 37/38

A/Ia: 1. will have decorated; 2. will have washed; 3. will have cleaned; 4. will have made; 5. will have built; 6. will have prepared; 7. will have invited; 8. will have painted; 9. will have checked; 10. will have practised.

Ib: 1. will have been decorating; 2. will have been washing; 3. will have been cleaning; 4. will have been making; 5. will have been building; 6. will have been preparing; 7. will have been inviting; 8. will have been painting; 9. will have been checking; 10. will have been practising.

Seite 39

A/I: 1. would be; 2. would build; 3. would come; 4. would help; 5. would like; 6. would not (wouldn't) go; 7. would watch; 8. would read; 9. would be able to; 10. would go.

A/II: 1. Would you open the window, please! 2. I would like to drink tea. 3. Mary would like to dance. 4. Would you please turn down the radio! 5. They would like to go to England.

Seite 41

A: 1. would have worked; 2. would have passed; 3. would have seen; 4. would have tried; 5. would have finished; 6. would have asked; 7. would have caught; 8. would have met; 9. would not (wouldn't) have been; 10. would not (wouldn't) have done.

Seite 41–43

B: 1. spent/would never go; 2. was talking/had met/came; 3. has never seen/was; 4. will have been working/will still not be finished; 5. had seen/decided/rented; 6. is going to have/has already invited; 7. have been drinking/am still doing/am not going to stop; 8. has not seen/am going to take; · 9. came/had never thought; 10. doesn't smoke/smokes; 11. went/has not written; 12. was/had never been; 13. would never marry/did not learn; 14. has just promised/will never do; 15. have now been listening/didn't you tell/had never heard.

B/II: 1. Peter has never been to the cinema, but he watches TV every night. 2. He had never seen a picture of the Queen of England before he came to England. 3. I was reading the newspaper when Mary suddenly came in. 4. After Paul had lost his way last time, he said he would never go to London by car again. 5. Although I usually have a glass of wine with my dinner, today I'm having some beer. 6. After James had served the tea, he went back to the kitchen. 7. Tomorrow afternoon the baker will have made the sandwiches for our party. We are going to fetch them around 5 o'clock. 8. Since I came back/returned from my holiday, the sun hasn't shone at all. 9. Paul used to go to the cinema occasionally, but since he began working as a waiter he hasn't had any time. 10. While Paul was listening to records, his parents were watching TV. 11. Bill had been working in Spain for two years before he came to Germany. 12. Although Oliver has not yet been to England, he speaks English fluently. 13. Paul didn't want to go to school any longer because he didn't understand a word of what the teacher said. 14. Susan lived in England from 1975 to 1980, then she moved to Australia and since 1984 she has been living in the USA. 15. When I came in Paul and Susan were playing cards. 16. I would like to go to England, but I haven't had a holiday for two years. 17. The train leaves at 17.45. I hope we will be at the station in time. 18. When did you buy your new car? I haven't seen it yet.

Seite 45–47

A/I: 1. Our neighbours will be invited (by us). 2. The bill was paid (by us) last week. 3. The vegetables are being cooked by mother. 4. The sentence was explained by the teacher. 5. The book had been given away by my father. 6. The old lady has always been helped by the policeman. 7. The children are looked after by the lady. 8. My bike was repaired by my father last weekend. 9. The house was built by the company. 10. A new restaurant will be opened by Mr. Baker next week. 11. The sentences haven't yet been translated by him. 12. The street has already been cleaned by the workers. 13. The letter was posted by the secretary yesterday. 14. I am sent to the baker by my mother. 15. Ten letters are typed by Mrs. Cooper every morning.

A/II: 1. She was asked to open the window by Mr. Miller. 2. I was taken to school by my father. 3. He was invited by Mary. 4. He will be looked after by me. 5. She was always admired by her. 6. It was won by our class last year. 7. We were introduced to Mr. Baker by Mary. 8. It had been opened carefully by Mr. Cooper. 9. She was seen in Frankfurt by us yesterday. 10. They have been stolen by thieves.

B/I: 1. The rooms were shown to the visitors by Mr. Cooper. The visitors were shown the rooms by Mr. Cooper. 2. This house was built last year. 3. Animals mustn't be fed. 4. This box can't be opened. 5. His hat was blown down the street by the wind. 6. English is spoken all over the world. 7. The famous buildings will be described to us by the teacher. 8. The butter was passed to me by her. 9. A present has been promised to us by them. We have been promised a present by them. 10. A letter had been written to him by her. He had been written a letter by her. 11. A huge bottle was brought to us by the waiter. We were brought a huge bottle by the waiter. 12. The ball was thrown to me by him. 13. This building was used as a prison. 14. I have never been beaten at chess. 15. The answers must be written down.

B/II: 1. The paintings were stolen yesterday. 2. We were sent a letter. 3. He was offered a cup of tea. 4. The house will be painted next year. 5. We have been invited to the party.

Seite 48/49

A/I: 1. will have; 2. will take; 3. find; 4. comes; 5. visit; 6. will write/have; 7. get/will buy; 8. gets/will take; 9. meet/will tell; 10. will go/move.

A/II: 1. If I get my pocket money, I'll buy the record. 2. We'll go to London if we find a hotel. 3. If it rains, we'll play Monopoly. 4. If I find your book, I'll give it to you. 5. We'll move if we find a bigger flat.

B/I: 1. can afford/will buy; 2. learn/will be able; 3. send/will be glad; 4. will not be able to buy/doesn't lend; 5. will not be/don't work.

B/II: 1. If we get some extra money, we will able to buy new costumes. 2. If we have a free day on Saturday, we will work extremely hard on Monday. 3. If the performance is a success, the school will become famous. 4. If we put advertisements in the newspaper, a lot of people will come.

Seite 50/51

A/I: 1. had; 2. were; 3. had; 4. would be; 5. found/would go; 6. would call/saw; 7. had/would be; 8. would build/had; 9. phoned/would come; 10. came/would be.

A/II: 1. If I got 1000 DM, I would buy a motorbike. 2. If I were you, I wouldn't be so lazy. 3. If I found a wallet, I would take it to the police. 4. If I saw an accident, I would call the ambulance. 5. If I were in your situation, I would tell my parents.

B/I: 1. had/would not be able; 2. would not have/were; 3. would give up/built; 4. attacked/would be able; 5. were/would tell.

B/II: 1. If the city had no money to maintain the old people's homes, many old people would be helpless. 2. If I had a car, I would allow my brother to drive it/my brother would be allowed to drive it. 3. I would study mathematics if I didn't make so many mistakes. 4. We would be able to go out more often if we had more time.

Seite 52/53

A/I: 1. I would have seen . . .; 2. I would have watched . . .; 3. I would have spent . . .; 4. I would have seen . . .; 5. I would have gone . . .

A/II: 1. would have known; 2. had not forgotten; 3. had known; 4. had been/would have learned; 5. had come/would not have escaped; 6. would not have burned down/had arrived; 7. had met/would have liked; 8. had not been/would have come; 9. had had/would have bought; 10. would have sold/had had.

B: 1. If I hadn't stayed up late in the evenings, I wouldn't have been tired. 2. If I hadn't eaten too many sweets, I wouldn't have had to go to the dentist. 3. If I had had more money, I would have bought the nice dress. 4. If my father had allowed it, I would have gone to a disco. 5. If my parents hadn't told me to do my exam first, I would have left school and started working.

Seite 53

1. were; 2. had not run; 3. will get; 4. would never have come; 5. will call; 6. knew; 7. were; 8. would have opened; 9. will never learn; 10. would never have been able to come.

Seite 57/58

A/I: a) 1. . . . (that) she will be at home tomorrow. 2. . . . (that) Peter is watching TV. 3. . . . (that) she has breakfast at 7 o'clock every day. 4. . . . (that) he was ill yesterday. 5. . . . (that) he must sign these letters.

b) 1. . . . if I will be at home tomorrow. 2. . . . when I came. 3. . . . if Mr. Miller has arrived. 4. . . . who that lady is. 5. . . . where I parked my car.

c) 1. . . . to mind the steps. 2. . . . to write these sentences. 3. . . . not to eat chocolate in the living-room. 4. . . . not to play with the knife. 5. . . . to answer these letters at once.

A/II: a) 1. . . . (that) the Millers had had an accident a year ago. 2. . . . (that) they would have to learn a lot the following day. 3. . . . (that) his son never did his work properly. 4. . . . (that) after she had read the book, she had bought it. 5. . . . (that) the article had been published in their school magazine.

b) 1. . . . if I was leaving the following Sunday. 2. . . . what I did with all that money. 3. . . . why he didn't buy a dictionary. 4. . . . who had given me this present. 5. . . . when we were going to do our homework properly.

c) 1. . . . not to throw away this paper. 2. . . . to be in time. 3. . . . not to use her record-player. 4. . . . not to go out after 10 o'clock. 5. . . . not to feed the animals.

B: 1. . . . if I were going to come with him to the football stadium the following Saturday. 2. . . . not to write our homework in pencil, but in ink. 3. . . . what I would have done if I had not met John. 4. . . . why John had not gone to England the previous spring. 5. . . . (that) those rooms hadn't been used for three months. 6. . . . if I hadn't told her that I had washed up all the dishes. 7. . . . why I didn't use my books instead of using his. **8.** . . . why he had never told us that he had had problems before he had come here. **9.** . . . (that) her boy-friend had never bought any flowers for her. **10.** . . . (that) she is never going to sell her parrot. **11.** . . . if they didn't learn their new words, they would never pass the exam. **12.** . . . why he had not stolen the TV when he had found out that nobody had been at home. **13.** . . . if he had stolen the TV, he would not have been able to run away quickly. **14.** . . . (that) he would never understand those burglars. **15.** . . . if I thought it would rain the following day. **16.** . . . who had already finished. **17.** . . . (that) their most expensive bowl had been broken when she had been tidying up the room. **18.** . . . (that) he hoped she would succeed. **19.** . . . if the man had spoken Italian. **20.** . . . (that) it had to be done immediately.

Seite 62–64

A/I: **1.** Mr. Miller had to wait . . .; **2.** Susan was able to translate . . .; **3.** My parents had to sell . . .; **4.** Peter was allowed to go . . .; **5.** The children were not allowed to play . . .; **6.** The students had to write . . .; **7.** I had to be . . .; **8.** Mr. Baker had to pay . . .; **9.** The girls were not allowed to open . . .; **10.** You were not allowed to open . . .

A/II: **1.** He will be able to go . . .; **2.** Next year I will be able to speak . . .; **3.** She will not be allowed to come . . .; **4.** Tomorrow the old lady will be able to walk . . .; **5.** You will have to write . . .; **6.** The secretary will not (won't) be able to answer . . .; **7.** Next year the boys will be allowed to work . . .; **8.** You will not be allowed to go . . .; **9.** When will she be able to speak . . .? **10.** Why will you have to work . . .?

B/I: **1.** has not been able to spend; **2.** was not allowed to join; **3.** will be able to afford; **4.** could play; **5.** could not believe; **6.** had to work/couldn't come; **7.** to be allowed to go; **8.** would not be allowed to stay out; **9.** will be able to pass; **10.** would have to be; **11.** have not been able to speak; **12.** had been able to repair; **13.** will have to look for; **14.** had to move; **15.** must/has to practise.

B/II: **1.** You should/ought to read a few pages in your book every evening. **2.** They had to go home early, because their son was ill. **3.** Since when have you been able to play the guitar so well? **4.** You know (that) you are not allowed to do that! **5.** They will not/won't be allowed to go before 6 o'clock. **6.** Would you open the window, please! **7.** You are not allowed to tell her. **8.** You should/ought to stop smoking at last. **9.** You needn't help me if you are not able to. **10.** Could you please ask Mary if I may go with her. **11.** Would you tell me when he is able to come? **12.** When will Mr. Smith finally be able to speak French correctly? **13.** Why did you have to watch TV so long yesterday? **14.** You needn't give me an answer if you don't want to. **15.** If they/you are able to/can stay one hour longer today, they/you won't/will not have to come tomorrow.

Seite 66/67

A/I: **1.** He doesn't like . . .; **2.** Mr. Miller can't eat . . .; **3.** Mrs. Miller wasn't . . .; **4.** Mary didn't have . . .; **5.** Paul didn't write . . .; **6.** The children don't play . . .; **7.** The children are not playing . . .; **8.** I didn't do . . .; **9.** Peter doesn't play . . .; **10.** I didn't watch . . .; **11.** They won't/will not see . . .; **12.** Mother didn't buy . . .; **13.** He doesn't spend . . .; **14.** Peter doesn't come . . .; **15.** I don't clean . . .

A/II: 1.a) What did you do last week? b) When did you go on a climbing tour? c) Who went on a climbing tour last week? 2.a) Who works in an office in Frankfurt? b) Where does Mr. Baker work? 3.a) What does Susan do at 7 o'clock every day? b) When does Susan get up? c) Who gets up at 7 o'clock every day? 4.a) Who sat in class from 8 to 12 o'clock? b) When did the boys sit in class? c) Where did the boys sit? 5.a) When did Peter win a prize in London? b) What did Peter win in London? c) Who won a prize in London? d) Where did Peter win a prize?

B/I: 1. When did you wake up last night; 2. Where do your parents always spend their holidays? 3. Who works very hard? 4. What did the students write last week? 5. What does he always do? 6. When did the workers go on strike? 7. What does this lady clean every day? 8. What did your brother sell last week? 9. Who(m) did you meet two weeks ago? 10. Who works as a mechanic?

B/II: 1. When do you get up in the morning? 2. Do you often watch TV? 3. I don't go to the cinema. 4. Did you learn your words yesterday? 5. Do you know my brother? 6. I don't read comics. 7. How do I get to the High Street/to Main Street? 8. Why don't you buy a new bike? 9. Do you still go to the bus stop every morning? 10. Don't you recognize your old friend?

Seite 70/71

A/I: 1. go; 2. go; 3. to work; 4. come; 5. to pass; 6. to see; 7. not talk; 8. to go; 9. to go; 10. clean.

A/II: 1. how to write; 2. first to come; 3. tool to repair; 4. girl to take; 5. first to reach; 6. where to put; 7. how to type; 8. last to arrive; 9. nothing to give; 10. whether to call.

B: 1. It's difficult for an Indian to find a good job. 2. The boss expects his workers to have finished the work by 5 o'clock. 3. The boy is old enough to look after himself. 4. It was too late to go to the cinema. 5. Remind me to shut the windows. 6. I want him to do his homework properly. 7. The house is too small for such a big family to live in.

Seite 73/74

A: 1. taking; 2. waiting; 3. (your) smoking; 4. watching TV; 5. seeing you; 6. reading; 7. travelling; 8. dancing; 9. winning; 10. speaking; 11. smoking; 12. reading; 13. cleaning; 14. getting; 15. speaking.

B: 1. lending/to buy; 2. having; 3. trying to repair; 4. to start looking for (to look for); 5. to stop playing (to play); 6. getting up; 7. to come; 8. to start eating/waiting/to come; 9. not to be nervous; 10. singing (to sing)/practising; 11. to visit; 12. driving; 13. meeting; 14. going out; 15. to remind/to tell/not to come.

Seite 75/76

A: 1. isn't he? 2. don't you? 3. did he? 4. didn't they? 5. hadn't I? 6. won't she? 7. doesn't he? 8. aren't they? 9. could he? 10. didn't he? 11. aren't you? 12. hasn't he? 13. haven't you? 14. did she? 15. weren't you? 16. will you? 17. didn't he? 18. do you? 19. isn't she? 20. is she? 21. oughtn't I? 22. will you? 23. didn't you? 24. can you? 25. don't you?

Seite 77

A: 1. he can; 2. I don't; 3. she has; 4. they have; 5. I needn't; 6. she does; 7. he isn't; 8. you can; 9. I'm not; 10. she didn't; 11. she won't; 12. I haven't; 13. he has; 14. he isn't; 15. she had; 16. he was; 17. they weren't; 18. I couldn't; 19. I wasn't; 20. I did; 21. I haven't; 22. I did; 23. she doesn't; 24. I would; 25. I can.

Seite 80/81

A: 1. cars; 2. ladies; 3. houses; 4. fishermen; 5. desks; 6. lamps; 7. roses; 8. wishes; 9. hats; 10. matches; 11. tomatoes; 12. copies; 13. garages; 14. classes; 15. teachers; 16. bridges; 17. apples; 18. children; 19. days; 20. students; 21. bicycles; 22. drivers; 23. dresses; 24. cups; 25. dogs; 26. suitcases; 27. records; 28. policemen; 29. women; 30. tickets.

B: 1. passers-by; 2. ideas; 3. theses; 4. commanders-in-chief; 5. sit-ins; 6. mice; 7. merry-go-rounds; 8. women-clerks; 9. heroes; 10. teeth; 11. woman-haters; 12. chairmen; 13. grown-ups; 14. songwriters; 15. aircraft; 16. lookers-on; 17. ideals; 18. men-servants; 19. roots; 20. broadcasting-stations; 21. thieves; 22. chimneys; 23. horsemen; 24. chimney-sweepers; 25. bacilli; 26. cities; 27. lives; 28. mothers-in-law; 29. negroes; 30. halves.

Seite 82/83

A: 1. are; 2. is; 3. are; 4. is; 5. take; 6. is; 7. are; 8. come; 9. are; 10. are; 11. put; 12. seems; 13. is; 14. costs; 15. are; 16. are; 17. promises; 18. is; 19. talk; 20. work.

B: 1. His binoculars were very expensive. 2. Mathematics is his favourite subject. 3. The firm are building a new office block. 4. Billiards is often played in pubs. 5. This is the 10 o'clock news. 6. Paul's trousers are very modern. 7. The police are looking for the thief. 8. The furniture is from the 18th century. 9. These stairs are very dangerous. 10. The cutlery consists of 24 pieces. 11. Great damage was caused. 12. This information wasn't very useful. 13. Where are the scales? 14. The staff have already left. 15. These scissors are a present from my aunt.

Seite 84–86

A/I: 1. the girls'; 2. Mr. Miller's; 3. Sally's; 4. the boy's; 5. Mr. Harris'; 6. the lady's; 7. the men's; 8. my brother's; 9. my sister's; 10. the Millers'; 11. my father's; 12. The student's; 13. Anne's; 14. the teacher's; 15. the woman's; 16. the women's; 17. five minutes'; 18. my sister's; 19. the clerk's; 20. the secretaries'.

A/II: 1. Susan's; 2. the rooms of the house; 3. our dog's blanket; 4. the size of the book; 5. my uncle's; 6. three days' work; 7. the killing of the animals; 8. the director's; 9. an hour's rest; 10. the bosses'; 11. the roof of the house; 12. the baby's; 13. the door of the room; 14. a glass of milk; 15. the end of the road; 16. the men's; 17. John's; 18. my friend's; 19. the Browns'; 20. the page of the newspaper.

B: 1. my little brother's ball; 2. Mr. Smith's secretary; 3. my sister's birthday; 4. a six months' course; 5. the pages of the book; 6. the pupils' test; 7. today's paper; 8. the children's toys; 9. the price of the car; 10. the morning's post; 11. the melody of the song; 12. Paul's friends; 13. my brother's wife; 14. Fred's and Paul's uncle; 15. the cost of living.

Seite 89–91

A/I: 1. a; 2. a; 3. an; 4. an; 5. an; 6. a; 7. a; 8. an; 9. a; 10. a; 11. a; 12. an; 13. a; 14. an; 15. a; 16. a; 17. a; 18. a; 19. a; 20. an.

A/II: 1. a; 2. a; 3. a; 4. a; 5. a; 6. a; 7. an/a; 8. a; 9. a; 10. -.

A/III: 1. -; 2. the; 3. -; 4. -; 5. the; 6. -; 7. -; 8. -/the; 9. the/the; 10. -.

B/I: 1. an; 2. an; 3. -/a; 4. the; 5. -; 6. -/-; 7. -/-; 8. a/the; 9. a; 10. the/-; 11. the; 12. a; 13. -; 14. a; 15. a; 16. -; 17. the/the; 18. the/a; 19. a/a; 20. -.

B/II: 1. quite a lot; 2. such a; 3. too cold a day; 4. All the houses; 5. double the time; 6.Both the ladies; 7. such a; 8. rather a bad cold; 9. half a bottle; 10. Half an hour.

Seite 93/94

A/I: 1. many; 2. much; 3. much; 4. many; 5. many; 6. many; 7. much; 8. many; 9. many; 10. much; 11. much; 12. many; 13. many; 14. many; 15. many; 16. many; 17. much; 18. many; 19. much; 20. many.

A/II: 1. a few; 2. little; 3. a few; 4. a little; 5. a little; 6. a few; 7. a few; 8. a few; 9. little; 10. a few; 11. a few; 12. a little; 13. a few; 14. a few; 15. a few; 16. a few; 17. a few; 18. a few; 19. a little; 20. a few.

B: 1. many flowers; 2. less money; 3. the fewest children; 4. the most hand-bags; 5. fewer books; 6. more tea; 7. the most hamburgers; 8. fewer fields; 9. more subjects; 10. the most friends; 11. the fewest letters; 12. more rooms; 13. more luck; 14. fewer cars; 15. much rubbish/garbage; 16. less sugar; 17. less art; 18. much peace; 19. the most energy; 20. the fewest accidents.

Seite 97/98

A/I: 1. newer / newest; 2. more comfortable / most comfortable; 3. simpler / simplest; 4. more difficult/most difficult; 5. friendlier/friendliest; 6. larger/largest; 7. thinner/thinnest; 8. deeper/deepest; 9. more characteristic/most characteristic; 10. heavier/heaviest; 11. shorter/shortest; 12. lazier/laziest; 13. lower/lowest; 14. greater/greatest; 15. funnier / funniest; 16. more polite / most polite; 17. worse / worst; 18. more interesting/most interesting; 19. cheaper/cheapest; 20. hotter/hottest.

A/II: 1. louder than; 2. as young as; 3. the biggest; 4. more active than; 5. the nicest; 6. nicer than; 7. the smallest; 8. prettier than; 9. as simple as; 10. the lowest; 11. as careful as; 12. more popular than; 13. richer than; 14. the most exciting; 15. more exact than; 16. as long as; 17. newer than; 18. stronger than; 19. as hot as; 20. the easiest.

B/I: 1.a) The book is not as expensive as the record. b) The record is more expensive than the book. c) The album is the most expensive. 2.a) The VW is not as fast as the Ford. b) The Ford is faster than the VW. c) The Mercedes is the fastest. 3.a) The chair is not as comfortable as the armchair. b) The armchair is more comfortable than the chair. c) The couch is the most comfortable. 4.a) The house is not as high as the office building. b) The office building is higher than the house. c) The Empire State Building is the highest. 5.a) Maud is not as good at school as Mary. b) Mary is better at school than Maud. c) Peter is the best.

Seite 102–105

A/I: 1. usually; 2. dangerously; 3. warmly; 4. fully; 5. gently; 6. wholly; 7. terribly; 8. freshly; 9. fast; 10. thinly; 11. slowly; 12. in a lively way; 13. daily; 14. heavily; 15. fantastically; 16. fluently; 17. cleverly; 18. well; 19. seriously; 20. beautifully.

A/II: 1. more easily/most easily; 2. earlier/earliest; 3. more quickly/most quickly; 4. harder/hardest; 5. -/-; 6. more quietly/most quietly; 7. more comfortably/most comfortably; 8. more loudly/most loudly; 9. more truly/most truly; 10. more slowly/most slowly; 11. more terribly/most terribly; 12. more wisely/most wisely; 13. more angrily/most angrily; 14. more generally/most generally; 15. more happily/most happily; 16. more awfully/most awfully; 17. more prettily/most prettily; 18. more extremely/most extremely; 19. more secretly/most secretly; 20. more silently/most silently.

A/III: 1. quickly; 2. quickly; 3. easy; 4. easily; 5. pretty; 6. prettily; 7. pretty; 8. well; 9. good; 10. fluently; 11. fluent; 12. seriously; 13. serious; 14. soft; 15. softly; 16. terrible; 17. terribly; 18. terribly; 19. dangerous; 20. dangerously.

B/I: 1. He wrote a letter in his office yesterday./Yesterday he wrote a letter in his office. 2. The baby usually . . .; 3. Mary normally writes dictations well. 4. Susan often reads a book in the evening./In the evening Susan often reads a book. 5. We sometimes have lunch in this pub./In this pub we sometimes . . .; 6. I have never met him before. 7. He generally works quickly. 8. Mary always . . .; 9. Our dog is always hungry in the morning./In the morning our dog is always hungry. 10. She slowly walked out of the room.

B/II: 1. silent; 2. awful; 3. slowly; 4. easily/correct/difficult; 5. excited; 6. regularly/fluently; 7. correct; 8. correctly; 9. good; 10. well; 11. anxiously; 12. pretty old; 13. absolutely clever; 14. fine; 15. seriously ill; 16. shortly/automatically; 17. quietly/deeply; 18. cold/frightened; 19. generally/fresh/fresh; 20. remarkably good/tired.

B/III: 1. The man on the phone sounded excited. 2. I have got a cold. I can't smell well, but I'm sure the cake smells good. 3. The apples feel very soft. 4. The soup really tastes good. 5. The plan sounds good.

Seite 106/107

A: 1. They; 2. He/her; 3. They; 4. It; 5. him; 6. They; 7. her; 8. They; 9. them; 10. her; 11. It; 12. It; 13. them; 14. He/them; 15. him; 16. her; 17. them; 18. it; 19. They; 20. him.

Seite 109

A/I: 1. mine; 2. yours; 3. theirs; 4. ours; 5. theirs; 6. his; 7. hers; 8. hers; 9. yours; 10. hers.

A/II: 1. his; 2. his; 3. Their; 4. his; 5. Her; 6. her; their; 7. their; 8. hers; 9. Their; 10. his; 11. Her; 12. Their; 13. his; 14. His; 15. Their; 16. His; 17. his/her; 18. their; 19. hers; 20. His.

Seite 110/111

A/I: 1. Who; 2. Who; 3. What; 4. Who; 5. Whose; 6. Who(m); 7. Whose; 8. Who/What; 9. What; 10. Who; 11. Whose; 12. Whose; 13. What; 14. Who; 15. Who.

A/II: 1. What; 2. Which; 3. Which; 4. Which; 5. What; 6. What; 7. Which; 8. What; 9. What; 10. Which; 11. What; 12. Which; 13. What; 14. Which; 15. Which.

B: 1. Where; 2. Who(m); 3. Who(m); 4. Who(m); 5. What; 6. What; 7. Who(m)/What; 8. Who(m); 9. Who(m); 10. Who(m).

Seite 113/114

A/I: 1. who(m); 2. who; 3. who; 4. which; 5. which; 6. which; 7. which; 8. who; 9. who; 10. which; 11. which; 12. which; 13. which; 14. which; 15. who.

A/II: 1. who; 2. who(m); 3. which; 4. whose; 5. which; 6. who(m); 7. whose; 8. whose; 9. who; 10. which.

B: 1. who; 2. which; 3. who; 4. who; 5. -; 6. whose; 7. who; 8. which; 9. -; 10. who; 11. who; 12. -; 13. -; 14. -; 15. who; 16. -; 17. -; 18. who; 19. -; 20. -.

Seite 116/117

A: 1. himself; 2. himself/myself; 3. yourself/yourselves; 4. herself; 5. himself; 6. herself; 7. itself; 8. herself; 9. myself; 10. herself; 11. myself; 12. yourself/yourselves; 13. ourselves; 14. yourself/yourselves; 15. themselves.

B: 1. himself; 2. themselves; 3. himself; 4. them; 5. himself; 6. him; 7. himself; 8. himself/yourself/yourselves; 9. you; 10. herself; 11. herself; 12. -; 13. -; 14. him; 15. -; 16. -; 17. -; 18. -; 19. ourselves; 20. yourself/yourselves.

Seite 118

A/I: 1. these; 2. this; 3. this; 4. these; 5. these; 6. these; 7. this; 8. this; 9. these; 10. these.

A/II: 1. that; 2. that; 3. This; 4. these; 5. these; 6. These; 7. This/this; 8. This/that; 9. this/that; 10. That.

Seite 119/120

A: 1. some; 2. some; 3. any; 4. some; 5. some; 6. some; 7. any; 8. any; 9. some; 10. any; 11. some; 12. any; 13. some; 14. any; 15. some; 16. any; 17. any; 18. any; 19. any; 20. some.

B: 1. any; 2. some; 3. some; 4. any; 5. some; 6. some; 7. any; 8. some; 9. some; 10. any; 11. some; 12. any; 13. any; 14. some; 15. some.

Seite 122

A: 1. How; 2. like; 3. as; 4. as. . . as; 5. like; 6. as; 7. How; 8. as. . . as; 9. like; 10. as; 11. How; 12. as; 13. like; 14. like; 15. How.

B: 1. How did you spend your last holiday? 2. The building is used as a garage. 3. He drives like an idiot. 4. She speaks English like an Englishwoman. 5. He works as a teacher. 6. She has eyes like an eagle. 7. This park is more beautiful than our garden. 8. He fought like a madman. 9. He looks like an Indian. 10. Paul behaves like a little child.

Seite 124

A: 1. All; 2. All; 3. Each; 4. Each; 5. All; 6. each; 7. all; 8. All/Each; 9. whole; 10. Every; 11. All; 12. all/each; 13. all; 14. whole; 15. All; 16. All; 17. whole; 18. each; 19. Every; 20. all; 21. All; 22. Each; 23. Each.

Seite 126

B: 1. When will you get your hair cut? 2. The teacher made us write 20 sentences. 3. I always have my shirts ironed. 4. I'll have the window repaired at once. 5. Leave the dog alone, please! 6. He made me work for him. 7. Let's go to the cinema. 8. Peter mostly leaves his bike in the garage. 9. Mr. Baker left his car behind. 10. The owner allowed the children to play in the garden. 11. Let me finish this letter! 12. The trainer allowed us to go home. 13. Leave the letters there! 14. Peter kept his girl-friend waiting. 15. Could I leave the lesson 10 minutes earlier? 16. You can't leave your car here. 17. Passengers are allowed to leave the ship. 18. Mother lets us go to the swimming-pool. 19. Give me 5 minutes! 20. Mrs. Baker has her dresses made.

Anhang 2: Grammatische Ausdrücke

Englisch	Fremdwort	Deutsch
accusative	Akkusativ	4. Fall/Wenfall
active voice	Aktiv	Tatform
adjective	Adjektiv	Eigenschaftswort
adverb	Adverb	Umstandswort
article	Artikel	Geschlechtswort
auxiliary verb	Hilfsverb	Hilfszeitwort
case	Kasus	Fall
collective nouns	——	Sammelbegriffe
command	Imperativsatz	Befehlssatz
comparative	Komparativ	Steigerungsstufe
comparison	——	Steigerung
conditional I	Konditional I	Zukunft in der Vergangenheit
conditional clause	Konditionalsatz	Bedingungssatz
conditional II	Konditional II	vollendete Zukunft in der Vergangenheit
consonant	Konsonant	Mitlaut
continuous form	——	Verlaufsform
dative	Dativ	3. Fall/Wemfall
declension	Deklination	Beugung
definite article	bestimmter Artikel	bestimmtes Geschlechtswort
demonstrative pronoun	Demonstrativpronomen	hinweisendes Fürwort
direct object	Akkusativobjekt	Satzergänzung im 4. Fall/Wenfall
direct speech	direkte Rede	wörtliche Rede
finite verb	finites Verb	gebeugtes Tätigkeitswort
future	Futur I	Zukunft
future perfect	Futur II	vollendete Zukunft
genitive	Genitiv	2. Fall/Wesfall
gerund	Gerundium	Tätigkeitswort als Hauptwort
imperative	Imperativ	Befehlsform
indefinite article	unbestimmter Artikel	unbestimmtes Geschlechtswort
indirect objekt	Dativobjekt	Satzergänzung im 3. Fall/Wemfall
infinite verb	infinites Verb	ungebeugtes Tätigkeitswort

infinitive	Infinitiv	Grundform/1. Verbform
interrogative pronoun	Interrogativpronomen	Fragefürwort
main clause	——	Hauptsatz
modal auxiliaries	unvollständige Hilfsverben	unvollständige Hilfszeitwörter
nominative	Nominativ	1. Fall/Werfall
noun	Substantiv/Nomen	Hauptwort
object	Objekt	Satzergänzung
participle	Partizip	Mittelwort
passive voice	Passiv	Leideform
past participle	Partizip Perfekt	Mittelwort der Vergangenheit
past perfect	Plusquamperfekt	vollendete Vergangenheit/ Vorvergangenheit
past tense	Imperfekt/Präteritum	Vergangenheit
personal pronoun	Personalpronomen	persönliches Fürwort
plural	Plural	Mehrzahl
positive	Positiv	Grundstufe
possessive pronoun	Possessivpronomen	besitzanzeigendes Fürwort
predicate	Prädikat	Satzaussage
preposition	Präposition	Verhältniswort
present perfect	Perfekt	vollendete Gegenwart
present tense	Präsens	Gegenwart
primary auxiliaries	vollständige Hilfsverben	vollständige Hilfszeitwörter
pronoun	Pronomen	Fürwort
question	Interrogativsatz	Fragesatz
question tag	——	Frageanhängsel
reflexive pronoun	Reflexivpronomen	rückbezügliches Fürwort
relative pronoun	Relativpronomen	bezügliches Fürwort
relative clause	Relativsatz	Bezugswortsatz
reported speech	indirekte Rede	abhängige Rede
short answer	——	Kurzantwort
singular	Singular	Einzahl
statement	——	Aussagesatz
subject	Subjekt	Satzgegenstand
superlative	Superlativ	Höchststufe
tense	Tempus	Zeit
verb	Verb	Tätigkeitswort
vowel	Vokal	Selbstlaut
word order	——	Satzstellung

NÜTZLICHE RATGEBER

EINE AUSWAHL

Stand: Frühjahr 1994

Hobby und Freizeit

Falken-Handbuch
Zeichnen und Malen
(**4167**-5) Von B. Bagnall, 336 S., 1154 Farbzeichnungen, Pappband. ●●●●●

Kreativ Zeichnen
(**4688**-X) Von B. Bagnall, 176 S., zahlr. Farbabb., Pappband. ●●●●

Punkt, Punkt, Komma, Strich
Zeichnen leicht gemacht
(**4721**-5) Von H. Witzig, 144 S., 512 s/w-Zeichnungen, Pappband. ●●

Punkt, Punkt, Komma, Strich
Zeichenstunde für Kinder
(**0564**-4) Von H. Witzig, 144 S., über 250 Zeichnungen, kart. ●

Einmal grad und einmal krumm
Zeichenstunde für Kinder
(**0599**-7) Von H. Witzig, 144 S., 363 Abb., kartoniert. ●

Figürliches Zeichnen
leicht gemacht
(**1010**-9) Von H. Witzig, 112 S., 462 Figuren, kartoniert. ●

Airbrush
Kreatives Gestalten mit dem Luftpinsel
(**1133**-4) Von C. M. Mette, 80 S., 145 Farbfotos, 40 Farbzeichnungen, kartoniert. ●●

Kalligraphie
Die Kunst des schönen Schreibens
(**4263**-9) Von C. Hartmann, 120 S., 44 Farbvorlagen, 29 s/w-Vorlagen, 2 s/w-Zeichnungen, 38 Farbfotos, Pappband. ●●●●

Gestalten mit Schrift
Kalligraphie
(**1044**-3) Von I. Schade, 80 S., 2 Farb- und 1 s/w-Foto, 143 Farbzeichnungen, kart. ●●

Hobby Aquarellmalen
Landschaft und Stilleben
(**0876**-7) Von I. Schade, A. Brück, 80 S., 111 Farbabb., kart. ●●

Technik · Gestaltung · Ausdruck
Aquarellmalerei
Von der Realität zum Bild
(**4529**-8) Von Prof. W. Wrisch, 136 Seiten, 172 farb. Abbildungen, 5 s/w-Abbildungen, 46 Zeichnungen, Pappband. ●●●●

Hobby Ölmalerei
Landschaft und Stilleben
(**0875**-9) Von H. Kämper, I. Becker, 80 S., 93 Farbabb., kart. ●●

FALKEN
Lexikon der Seidenmalerei
Mit großer Farbmischtabelle
(**4737**-1) Von K. Huber, 208 S., 192 Farbfotos, Pappband. ●●●●

Seidenmalerei in Vollendung
(**4414**-3) Hrsg. von R. Smend, 160 S., 227 Farbfotos, 36 s/w-Fotos, geprägter Leineneinband mit Schutzumschlag, im Schuber. ●●●●●

Seidenmalerei
Westen · Blusen · Hosen
(**1455**-4) Von C. Köhl, ca. 64 Seiten, durchgehend vierfarbig, zahlreiche Abbildungen, mit Vorlagebogen, kartoniert. ●●

Seidenmalerei und Modedesign
Modelle · Techniken · Schnittmuster
(**4476**-3) Von B. Hansen, 176 S., 140 Farbf.93 Farb-, 68 s/w-Zeichn., Pappband. ●●●●

Seidenmalerei Exklusive Tücher
(**1303**-5) Von E. Schwinge, 80 S., 79 Farbfotos, 6 Zeichnungen, kart. ●●

Kreative Seidenmalerei
Motive · Muster · Farbenspiel
(**4720**-7) Von M. Neubacher-Fesser, ca. 136 S., zahlr. Farbabb., Pappband. ●●●●

Seidenmalerei
Muster über Muster
20 Künstlerinnen präsentieren 120 Ideen
(**4744**-4) 128 S., 188 Farbabbildungen, Pappband. ●●●●

Seidenmalerei
Die wichtigsten Techniken Schritt für Schritt
(**1357**-4) Von B. Hansen, 64 S., 97 Farbfotos, kartoniert. ●●

Seidenmalerei als Kunst und Hobby
(**4264**-7) Von S. Hahn, 136 S., 256 Farbfotos, 1 s/w-Foto, Pappband. ●●●●

Neue zauberhafte Seidenmalerei
Motive und Anregungen aus der Natur
(**0924**-0) Von R. Henge, 80 S., 148 Farbfotos, 27 s/w-Zeichnungen, kart. ●●

Krawatten, Tücher und Fliegen individuell gestalten
Seidenmalerei
(**1242**-X) Von A. Reichmann, 64 S., durchgehend vierfarbig, kart. ●●

Aquarellieren auf Seide
Materialien · Techniken · Motive
(**0917**-8) Von I. Demharter, 32 S., 41 Farbfotos, Pappband. ●

Airbrush auf Seide
(**1342**-6) Von I. Demharter, 64 S., zahlreiche Farbabbildungen, kart. ●●

Airbrush Seidenmalerei
Mit Vorlagen für Schablonen
(**1356**-6) Von C. M. Mette, 80 S., 129 Farbf., kartoniert. ●●●

Seidenmalerei Bäume und Blätter
(**5249**-9) Von D. Kosik, 32 S., 5 Farbfotos, 23 Farb- u. 13 s/w-Zeichungen, kart. ●

Seidenmalerei Landschaften
(**5153**-0) Von D. Kosik, 32 S., 50 Farbfotos, 12 Zeichnungen, mit Vorlagebogen in Originalgröße, kart. ●

Seidenmalerei Kissen
(**5151**-4) Von I. Demharter, 32 S., 42 Farbfotos, 2 Zeichnungen, mit Vorlagebogen in Originalgröße, kart. ●

Seidenmalerei Blusen und T-Shirts
(**5184**-0) Von A. Keller, 32 S., 28 Farbfotos, 12 Zeichnungen, mit Vorlagebogen in Originalgröße, kartoniert. ●

Seidenmalerei Tücher und Schals
(**5152**-2) Von R. Henge, 32 S., 36 Farbfotos, 1 Zeichnungen, mit Vorlagebogen in Originalgröße, kart. ●

Seidenmalerei Tiermotive
(**5204**-9) Von A. Keller, 32 S., 37 Farbfotos, mit Vorlagebogen in Originalgröße, kart. ●

Serti Designo
Seidenmalerei mit Kreidestiften
(**5208**-1) Von S. Tichy-Gibley, 32 S., 46 Farbfotos, mit Vorlagebogen in Originalgröße, kart. ●

Seidenmalerei Lampenschirme
(**5154**-9) Von I. Walter-Ammon, 32 S., 47 Farbfotos, 1 Zeichnung, mit Vorlagebogen in Originalgröße, kart. ●

Seidenmalerei Blüten, Blätter, Ranken
(**5165**-4) Von D. Kosik, 32 S., 35 Farbfotos, 4 Zeichnungen, mit Vorlagebogen in Originalgröße, kart. ●

Seidenmalerei Schmuckkarten und Miniaturbilder
(**5166**-2) Von I. Walter-Ammon, 32 S., 37 Farbfotos, 2 Zeichnungen, mit Vorlagebogen in Originalgröße, kart. ●

Akzente mit Perlen, Pailetten und Straß
Seidenmalerei
(**5248**-0) Von A. Keller, 32 S., ca. 50 Farbf., mit Vorlagebogen in Originalgröße, kart. ●

Seidenmalerei Bilder in Konturentechnik
(**5182**-4) Von I. Demharter, 32 S., 28 Farbfotos, 2 Zeichnungen, mit Vorlagebogen in Originalgröße, kart. ●

Seidenmalerei Applikationen
(**5224**-3) Von J. Bressau, 32 S., 50 Farbfotos, mit Vorlagebogen in Originalgröße, kart. ●

Apartes aus bemalter Seide
(**5274**-X) Von E. Möller, 48 Seiten, durchgehend vierfarbig, kartoniert. ●

Malen auf Seide
kinderleicht
(**5218**-9) Von R. Henge, 32 S., 11 Farbfotos, 44 Farbzeichn., Vorlagebogen, kartoniert. ●

Moderne Stoffmalerei
(**1358**-2) Von H. Sander, 64 S., 73 Farbf., 50 s/w-Zeichn., kart. ●●

Perfekt Stricken
Mit Sonderteil Häkeln.
(**4250**-7) Von H. Jaacks, 256 S., 703 Farbfotos, 169 Farb- und 121 s/w-Zeichnungen, Pappband. ●●●●

Das moderne Standardwerk
Nähen
(**4709**-6) Von S. von Rudzinski, 176 S., vierfarbig, Pappband. ●●●●

Stoffpuppen
nach alten Vorbildern
(**5281**-2) Von M. Meinesz, 48 S., durchgehend vierfarbig, mit Vorlagebogen, kart. ●

Heißgeliebte Teddys
Selbermachen · Sammeln · Restaurieren
(**0900**-3) Von H. Nadolny und Y. Thalheim, 80 Seiten, 118 Farbfotos, kartoniert. ●●●

Die hier vorgestellten Bücher, Videokassetten und Software sind in folgende Preisgruppen unterteilt:

● Preisgruppe bis DM 10,–/S 79,–/SFr 11,–
●● Preisgruppe über DM 10,– bis DM 20,– / S 80,– bis S 160,– / SFr 10,– bis SFr 21,–
●●● Preisgruppe über DM 20,– bis DM 30,– / S 161,– bis S 240,– / SFr 21,– bis SFr 30,–
●●●● Preisgruppe über DM 30,– bis DM 50,– / S 241,– bis S 400,– / SFr 30,– bis SFr 50,–
●●●●● Preisgruppe über DM 50,–/S 401,–/SFr 50,–
* (unverbindliche Preisempfehlung)

Die Preise entsprechen dem Status beim Druck dieses Verzeichnisses (s. Seite 1) – Änderungen, im besonderen der Preise, vorbehalten –

Falken-Verlag GmbH · Postfach 1120 FALKEN D-65521 Niedernhausen/Ts. · Tel.: 0 61 27 / 70 20

Marionetten
selbst bauen und führen
(**1043**-5) Von D. Köhnen, 80 S., 150 Farbfotos, mit Schnittmusterbogen, kartoniert. ●●

Hampelmänner
Basteln mit Kindern ab 5 Jahren
(**5240**-5) Von F. Michalski, 32 S., ca. 50 Farbabb., mit Vorlagebg. in Originalgröße, kart. ●

Künstlerpuppen
im 20. Jahrhundert
(**4719**-3) Hrsg. R. Höckh, 160 S., 192 Farbfotos, 26 s/w-Fotos, Pappband. ●●●●●

Charakterpuppen
aus Cernit und Porzellan selbst gestalten
(**1156**-3) Von S. Becker, 64 S., 143 Farbfotos, 30 Zeichnungen, 13 Vignetten, mit Schnittmusterbogen, kartoniert. ●●

Puppen zum Liebhaben
(**5199**-9) Von B. Wehrle, 32 S., 27 Farbfotos, 9 s/w-Zeichnungen, mit Vorlagebogen in Originalgröße, kartoniert. ●

Basteln mit Kindern
Moosgummi
(**5271**-5) Von A. und R. Schurr, 48 S., durchgehend vierfarbig, mit Vorlagebogen, kart. ●

Neue zauberhafte Salzteig-Ideen
(**0719**-1) Von I. Kiskalt, 80 S., 324 Farbfotos, 12 Zeichnungen, Schablonen, kart. ●●

Salzteig kinderleicht
(**0973**-9) Von I. Kiskalt, 80 S., 224 Farbfotos, 8 Zeichnungen, kartoniert. ●●

Hobby Salzteig
(**0662**-4) Von I. Kiskalt, 80 S., 150 Farbfotos, 5 Zeichnungen und Schablonen, kart. ●●

Kreatives gestalten mit Ton
Töpfern ohne Scheibe – Aufbaukeramik
(**0896**-1) Von A. Riedinger, 80 S., 207 Farbfotos, 16 Zeichnungen, 7 Vignetten, kart. ●●

Kreatives Gestalten mit Ton
Töpfern auf der Scheibe
(**0971**-2) Von A. Riedinger, 80 S., 28 Farb- und 3 s/w-Zeichnungen, 178 Farbf., kart. ●●

Kneten und Modellieren
kinderleicht
(**5217**-0) Von V. Ettelt, 32 S., 12 Farbtafeln, 72 Farbzeichnungen, Vorlagebogen, kart. ●

Hobby Glaskunst in Tiffany-Technik
(**0781**-7) Von N. Köppel, 80 S., 194 Farbfotos, 6 s/w-Abbildungen, kartoniert. ●●

Tiffany-Technik
und andere kunstvolle Arbeiten in Glas
(**0972**-0) Von D. Köhnen, 80 S., 176 Farbfotos, 5 s/w-Zeichnungen, kartoniert. ●●

Ikebana
Grundstile und Variationen
(**4749**-5) Von E. Schwalm, 112 Seiten, ca. 165 Farbfotos, 43 Grafiken, 2 Tabellen, gebunden. ●●●●

Dekorieren und Gestalten mit Naturmaterialien
rund ums Jahr
(**4748**-7) Von E. Dommershausen u.a., 128 S., ca. 200 Farbf. und -zeichnungen, geb. ●●●

Masken
phantasievoll dekorieren
(**5155**-7) Von Chr. Familler, 32 S., 48 Farbf., mit Vorlagebg. in Originalgröße, kart. ●

Laubsägearbeiten für das Kinderzimmer
(**5245**-6) Von H.-P. Krafft, 32 S., ca. 50 Farbf., mit Vorlagebg. in Originalgröße, kartoniert. ●

Schwingtiere aus Holz gestalten
(**5222**-7) Von der Arbeitsgem. Werken, 32 S., 50 Farbfotos, mit Vorlagebogen in Originalgröße, kartoniert. ●

FALKEN Video
Drachen
bauen und fliegen
(**6141**-2) VHS, ca. 45 Min., in Farbe, mit Broschüre. ●●●●*

Drachen
bauen und steigen lassen.
(**0767**-1) Von W. Schimmelpfennig, 80 Seiten, 1 dreiseitige Ausklapptafel, 55 Farbfotos, 139 Zeichnungen, kart. ●●●

Lenkdrachen
bauen und fliegen
(**1011**-7) Von W. Schimmelpfennig, 64 Seiten, 51 Farbf. und 126 Zeichnungen, kart. ●●

Neue Lenkdrachen und Einleiner
bauen und fliegen
(**1353**-1) Von W. Schimmelpfennig, 80 Seiten, 54 Farbf., 95 Farbzeichn., kart. ●●●

Drachen
Einfache Modelle für Kinder
(**5156**-5) Von W. Schimmelpfennig, 32 Seiten, 11 Farbfotos, 31 Zeichnungen, mit Vorlagebogen, kartoniert. ●

Basteln mit Kleinkindern
ab 3 Jahren
(**4747**-9) Von W. Kottke und I. Hübers-Kemink, 128 Seiten, über 200 Farbabbildungen, mit Vorlagebogen, gebunden. ●●●

Das goldene Bastelbuch für Kinder
(**4769**-X) Von U. Barff (Hrsg.), 336 Seiten, durchg. vierf., mit 2 Vorlagebogen, geb. ●●●

Basteln mit Kindern
Dinos & Drachen
(**5279**-0) Von G. Reinscheid, 48 Seiten, durchgehend vierfarbig, mit Vorlagebogen, kart. ●

Basteln mit Kindern
Fensterbilder Ritter und Burgen
(**5284**-7) Von D. Köhnen, 48 Seiten, durchgehend vierfarbig, mit Vorlagebogen, kart. ●

Das große farbige
Bastelbuch für Kinder
(**4254**-X) Von U. Barff, I. Burkhardt, J. Maier, 224 S., 157 Farbf., 430 Farb- und 60 s/w-Zeichn., m. Schnittmusterbg., Pappband. ●●●

Origami
Tiere aus aller Welt
(**5250**-2) Von J. Maier, 32 Seiten, 19 Farbfotos, 68 Farb- u. 16 s/w-Zeichnungen, kartoniert. ●

Hobby Origami
Papierfalten für groß und klein
(**0756**-6) Von Z. Aytüre-Scheele, 80 Seiten, 820 Farbfotos, kartoniert. ●●

Neue zauberhafte Origami-Ideen
Papierfalten für groß und klein
(**0805**-8) Von Z. Aytüre-Scheele, 80 Seiten, 720 Farbfotos, kartoniert. ●●

Zauberwelt Origami
Tierfiguren aus Papier
(**1045**-1) Von Z. Aytüre-Scheele, 80 Seiten, 660 Farbfotos, kartoniert. ●●

Kreatives Gestalten mit **Papiermaché**
(**5246**-4) Von B. Jetzek-Berkenhaus, 32 S., ca. 50 Farbfotos, mit Vorlagebogen in Originalgröße, kartoniert. ●

Marmorieren
Muster · Techniken · Gestaltungsideen
(**5247**-2) Von T. Hartel, 32 S., ca. 50 Farbfotos, mit Vorlagebg. in Originalgröße, kart. ●

Heut basteln wir mit Pappe und Papier
(**4413**-5) Von U. Barff, J. Maier, 224 Seiten, 117 Farbfotos, 480 Farbzeichn., 25 s/w-Abb., mit Schnittmusterbogen, Pappband. ●●●

Das große farbige Bastel- und Werkbuch
(**4439**-9) Von D. Rex, 256 S., 999 Farbfotos, 33 Farbzeichnungen, Pappband. ●●●●

Mein liebstes Spiel- und Bastelbuch
Die Welt der Dinosaurier
Tiere und Landschaften zum Selbermachen Ausbrechen, aufstellen, spielen
(**4478**-X) Von B. Burkart, 8 Blatt mit herauslösbaren Motiven, 280-g-Karton mit Stanzung, 8 S. Bastelanl. und Sachinformation. ●●

Das große farbige
Dinosaurierbastelbuch
(**4686**-3) Von S. Koter, 128 S., 87 Farbfotos, 71 Farbzeichn., Vorlagebogen, Pappbd. ●●●

Fensterbilder in Scherenschnitt
(**5169**-7) Von A. Hahn, 32 Seiten, 52 Farbfotos, 3 s/w-Fotos, mit Vorlagebogen in Originalgröße, kartoniert. ●

Fensterbilder
Meine Lieblingstiere
(**5197**-2) Von Y. Thalheim, H. Nadolny, 32 Seiten, 38 Farbfotos, mit Vorlagebogen in Originalgröße, kartoniert. ●

Fensterbilder Enten und Gänse
(**5278**-2) Von D. Köhnen, 48 Seiten, durchgehend vierfarbig, mit Vorlagebogen, kart. ●

Fensterbilder Lustige Tiere
(**5210**-3) Von F. Michalski, 32 S., 47 Farbfotos, mit Vorlagebogen in Originalgröße, kart. ●

Fensterbilder Bauernhof
(**5264**-2) Von D. Köhnen, 48 Seiten, 44 Farbfotos, Vorlagebogen, kartoniert. ●

Fensterbilder Dinosaurier
(**5260**-X) Von C. Hüfner, 32 S., 8 Farbfotos, 47 Farbzeichnungen, Bastelbogen, kart. ●

Basteln mit Kindern
Fensterbilder Ritter und Burgen
(**5284**-7) Von D. Köhnen, 48 Seiten, durchgehend vierfarbig, mit Vorlagebogen, kart. ●

Mit Farben und Papieren
Fenster dekorieren
(**5255**-3) Von K. Groß, 32 Seiten, 8 Farbfotos, 59 Farbzeichnungen, kartoniert. ●

Basteln mit Kindern
Große Fensterbilder
(**5276**-6) Von D. Köhnen, 48 Seiten, durchgehend vierfarbig, mit Vorlagebogen, kart. ●

Originelle Fensterbilder
aus Tonpapier und Tonkarton
(**1305**-1) Von D. Köhnen, 64 Seiten, 70 Farbfotos, kartoniert. ●●

Die schönsten Fensterbilder
(**1066**-4) Von C. Kimmerle, 64 S., 100 Farbfotos, 7 Zeichnungen, kartoniert. ●●

Das Fensterbilder-Alphabet
Basteln mit Kindern ab 5 Jahren
(**5242**-1) Von E. Bohne, 32 S., ca. 50 Farbabb., mit Vorlagebogen in Originalgröße, kart. ●

Märchenhafte Fensterbilder
(**5185**-9) Von J. Maier, 32 S., 37 Farbfotos, mit Vorlagebogen in Originalgröße, kart. ●

Fensterbilder Blumen und Tiere
(**5186**-7) Von M. Twachtmann, 32 Seiten, 41 Farbfotos, 3 Zeichnungen, mit Vorlagebogen in Originalgröße, kartoniert. ●

Fensterbilder rund um die Welt
(**1411**-2) Von D. Köhnen, 64 Seiten, Vorlagebogen, 66 Farbfotos, kartoniert. ●●

Fensterbilder Zahlen
(**5268**-5) Von E. Bohne, 32 S., zahlr. Farbabbildungen, Vorlagebogen, kartoniert. ●

Fensterbilder Strand und Meer
(**5266**-9) Von B. Alex, 32 S., 57 Farbfotos, Vorlagebogen, kartoniert. ●

Fensterschmuck
Originelle Ideen für Dekorationen und Fensterbilder
(**1241**-1) Von D. Köhnen, 64 S., ca. 70 Farbfotos, Vorlagebogen, kartoniert. ●●

Klassisches Origami
Asiatische Faltkunst für Fortgeschrittene
(**1454**-6) Von P. D. Tuyen, ca. 80 Seiten, ca. 600 farbige Abbildungen, kartoniert. ●●

Sticker
Bastelspaß mit bunten Bildern
(**5270**-7) Von D. Dieterle und J. Reick, 48 S., 73 Farbfotos, mit Vorlagebogen, kartoniert. ●

Papierflieger
(**5157**-3) Von T. Gött, 32 S., 73 Farbf., 19 Zeichn., mit Vorlagebogen in Originalgröße, kart. ●

Windspielzeug
Bastelspaß mit Kindern ab 5 Jahren
(**5241**-3) Von D. Köhnen, 32 S., ca. 50 Farbabb., mit Vorlagebg. in Originalgröße, kart. ●

Flieger und Schiffe aus Papier
falten, ausbalancieren und steuern
(**1410**-4) Von C. Hüfner, ca. 80 Seiten, zahlr. Farbabbildungen, kartoniert. ●●

Faltschnitte
(**5257**-X) Von B. Blankenburg, 32 S., 12 Farbf., 42 Farbzeichn., Vorlagebogen, kartoniert. ●

Laternen und Lampions
(**5206**-5) Von C. Hüfner, 32 S., 60 Farbfotos, mit Vorlagebogen in Originalgröße, kart. ●

Mobiles aus Papier
(**5183**-2) Von J. Maier, 32 S., 17 Farbfotos, 35 Farbzeichnungen, mit Vorlagebogen in Originalgröße, kartoniert. ●

Tiermobiles
(**5258**-8) Von C. Hüfner, 32 Seiten, 57 Farbzeichnungen, Vorlagebogen, kartoniert. ●

Sonne, Mond und Sterne
Motive und Geschenkideen
(**5282**-0) Von D. Köhnen, 48 Seiten, durchgehend vierfarbig, mit Vorlagebogen, kart. ●

Bastelideen für Indianerspiele
(**5252**-9) Von B. Nelich, D. Velte, 32 Seiten, 38 Farbfotos, Vorlagebogen, kartoniert. ●

Der große Verkleidungsspaß
Kinderkostüme
(**1304**-3) Von C. Baumgarten, 53 Farbfotos, 183 Farbzeichn., Vorlagebogen, kart. ●●

Lustige Geschenk- und Schultüten
(**5263**-4) Von F. Michalski, 32 Seiten, 26 Farbfotos, Vorlagebogen, kartoniert. ●

Deco Art
Die Kunst, Geschenke zu verpacken
(**0949**-6) Von B. Niermann, 80 S., 78 Farbfotos, 191 Zeichnungen, kartoniert. ●●

Geschenke wunderschön verpacken
(**1113**-X) Von P. Jansen, 80 S., 79 Farbfotos, 166 Farbzeichnungen, kartoniert. ●●

Geschenke umweltfreundlich verpacken
(**1240**-3) Von P. Jansen, 64 S., vierfarbige Fotos und Illustrationen, kartoniert. ●●

Geldgeschenke
phantasievoll gestalten
(**5251**-0) Von P. Jansen, 32 Seiten, 49 Farbfotos, Vorlagebogen, kartoniert. ●

Geldgeschenke · Gutscheine · Geschenkanhänger
originell gestalten und verpacken
(**1115**-6) Von S. Haenitsch-Weiß, A. Weiß, 80 Seiten, 176 Farbfotos, kartoniert. ●●

Geschenke verpacken für Kinderfeste
(**5195**-6) Von C. Netolitzky, 32 S., 43 Farbfotos, mit Vorlagebogen in Originalgröße, kart. ●

Originelles Ambiente für Gäste
Festdekorationen
(**1049**-4) Von B. Niermann, 80 S., 125 Farbfotos, 59 Farbzeichn., kartoniert. ●●

Origineller Bastelspaß rund ums Herz
Motive und Geschenkideen
(**5272**-3) Von D. Köhnen, 48 Seiten, durchgehend vierfarbig, mit Vorlagebogen, kart. ●

Dekorative Schleifen
aus Bändern und Papier
(**5205**-7) Von M. Schorege, 32 S., 28 Farbfotos, 31 Farbzeichnungen, mit Vorlagebogen in Originalgröße, kartoniert. ●

Dekorieren und Arrangieren mit
Seidenblumen
(**5200**-6) Von M. L. Sprang, 32 S., 37 Farbfotos, 14 Farbzeichnungen, mit Vorlagebogen in Originalgröße, kartoniert. ●

Schmuck- und Glückwunschkarten
Papierarchitektur · Collagen · Faltschnittkarten
(**1114**-8) Von C. Sanladerer, 64 S., 55 Farbfotos, 31 Zeichnungen, kartoniert. ●●

Einladungs-, Tisch- und Menükarten
selbst gestalten
(**1302**-7) Von S. Haenitsch-Weiß, 80 Seiten, zahlreiche Farbabbildungen, kartoniert. ●●

Basteln mit Kindern
Moosgummi
(**5271**-5) Von A. und R. Schurr, 48 Seiten, durchgehend vierfarbig, mit Vorlagebogen, kartoniert. ●

Originell und Modern
Moosgummi
(**1354**-X) Von S. Boczkowski-Sigges, 56 Seiten, 92 Farbfotos, kartoniert. ●●

Osterschmuck
Neue Ideen für Kränze, Sträuße, Gestecke
(**5267**-7) Von I. Gleim, ca. 32 Seiten, zahlr. Farbabbildungen, kartoniert. ●

Basteln mit Kindern für
Ostern
(**5283**-9) Von V. Ettelt u.a., 48 Seiten, 12 Farbf., 83 Farbzeichnungen, mit Vorlagebg., kart. ●

Ostereier originell dekorieren
(**5219**-7) Von W. Velte, 32 S., 44 Farbfotos, mit Vorlagebogen in Originalgröße, kart. ●

Fensterbilder für die Osterzeit
(**5244**-8) Von R. Lübke, D. Lübke, 32 S., ca. 50 Farbf., mit Vorlagebg. in Originalg., kart. ●

Basteln für Ostern
(**5164**-6) Von Chr. Adjano, 32 S., 47 Farbfotos, mit Vorlagebogen in Originalgröße, kart. ●

Ostereier
Basteln mit Kindern ab 5 Jahren
(**5243**-X) Von Vera Ettelt, 32 Seiten, mit Spielebogen, kartoniert. ●

Tischdekorationen für Ostern
(**5220**-0) Von Chr. Adjano, 32 S., 49 Farbfotos, mit Vorlagebogen in Originalgröße, kart. ●

Basteln und dekorieren für
Advent und Weihnachten
(**4446**-1) Von G. Teusen, C. Netolitzky, 176 S., 285 Farbf., mit Bastelvorlagebg., Pappb. ●●●

Kinderbastelbuch
für Advent und Weihnachten
(**4687**-1) Von S. Wetzel-Maesmanns, 104 S., ca. 120 Farbfotos, ca. 300 Anleitungsillustrationen, Vorlagebogen, Pappband. ●●

Lustige Bastelideen für die
Weihnachtszeit
(**5256**-1) Von B. Löschenkohl, 32 S., 8 Farbfotos, 69 Farbzeichn., Vorlagebogen, kart. ●

Basteln für Weihnachten
(**5162**-X) Von Chr. Adjano, 32 S., 44 Farbfotos, mit Vorlagebogen in Originalgröße, kart. ●

Fensterbilder Winter und Weihnachten
(**5275**-8) Von F. Michalski, 48 S., 57 Farbfotos, Vorlagebogen, kartoniert. ●

Fensterdekorationen für die Weihnachtszeit
(**5181**-6) Von Y. Thalheim, H. Nadolny, 32 S., 33 Farbfotos, mit Vorlagebogen in Originalgröße, kartoniert. ●

Fensterbilder für Advent und Weihnachten
(**5211**-1) Von M. Schorege, 32 S., 24 Farbf., 15 Zeichn., mit Vorlagebg. in Originalg., kart. ●

Strohsterne
in bunter Vielfalt
(**5273**-1) Von M. Schorege, 48 S., 46 Farbfotos, Vorlagebogen, kartoniert. ●

Duftender Weihnachtsschmuck
aus Tonpapier und Potpourris
(**5254**-1) Von S. Wetzel-Maesmanns, 32 Seiten, 38 Farbfotos, Vorlagebogen, kartoniert. ●

Duftsträuße und Potpourris
(**1239**-X) Von A. Effelsberg, 80 Seiten, ca. 200 vierfbg. Abbildungen, kartoniert. ●●

Potpourris
Rezepturen und Geschenkideen
(**5265**-0) Von U. Altmann, 32 Seiten, 53 Farbfotos, kartoniert. ●

Trockenblumen
Gewürzsträuße, Gestecke, Kränze, Buketts
(**0643**-8) Von R. Strobel-Schulze, 88 Seiten, 170 Farbfotos, kartoniert. ●●

Phantasievolles Schminken
Verzauberte Gesichter für Maskeraden, Laienspiele und Kinderfeste
(**0907**-0) Hrsg.: H. u. Y. Nadolny, 64 Seiten, 227 Farbfotos, kartoniert. ●●

Schminken für Kinder
(**5177**-8) Von Y. Thalheim, H. Nadolny, 32 S., 68 Farbfotos, mit Vorlagebogen in Originalgröße, kartoniert. ●

Do it yourself und Technik

Moderne Fotopraxis
(**4401**-1) Von G. Koshofer, Prof. H. Wedewardt, 224 S., 363 Farbfotos, 106 s/w-Fotos, 5 Farb- und 24 s/w-Zeichnungen, Pappband. ●●●●

So macht man bessere Fotos
(**1158**-X) Von G. Koshofer, 144 S., 259 Farbfotos, 25 s/w-Fotos, kartoniert. ●●

So macht man bessere Kinderfotos
(**1459**-7) Von G. Koshofer, ca. 120 Seiten, ca. 260 farbige Abbildungen, kartoniert. ●●●

Kodak Photo CD
Bilder archivieren, bearbeiten, präsentieren
(**4388**-0) Von H. Freund, ca. 176 Seiten, durchgehend vierfarbig, kartoniert. ●●●

Videografieren
Filmen mit Video 8. Technik – Bildgestaltung – Schnitt – Vertonung.
(**0843**-0) Von M. Wild, K. Möller, 120 Seiten, 101 Farbfotos, 22 s/w-Fotos, 52 Zeichnungen, kartoniert. ●●●

Videografieren perfekt
Profitricks für Aufnahmetechnik und Nachbearbeitung
(**0969**-0) Von W. Schild, 120 S., 144 Farbabbildungen, 5 s/w-Zeichnungen, kart. ●●●

Besser VIDEOfilmen
Moderne Technik für perfekte Videos
(**1458**-9) Von W. Schild, ca. 160 Seiten, zahlreiche Farbabbildungen, kartoniert. ●●●

Videofilmen wie ein Profi
Technik · Motive · Filmaufbau · Nachbearbeitung
(**4506**-9) Von T. Pehle, 232 S., 444 Farbfotos, 61 zweifbg. Zeichnungen, Pappband. ●●●●

Do it yourself
Heimwerken
(**4117**-9) Von T. Pochert, 456 S., 1103 Farbfotos, 100 Farbabb., Pappband. ●●●●

Drechseln
Material · Technik · Beispiele
(**1306**-X) Von O. Maier, 72 S., 195 Farbabbildungen, 14 s/w-Zeichnungen, kartoniert. ●●

Do it yourself
Dachgeschoß- und Innenausbau
(**1243**-8) Von M. Maurer, 96 S., 314 Farbfotos, 35 Zeichn., kartoniert. ●●

Do it yourself
Sanitärinstallationen
(**1118**-0) Von W. Kawlath, 96 Seiten, 214 Farbabbildungen, kartoniert. ●●

Do it yourself
Metall bearbeiten
(**1119**-9) Von O. Maier, 96 S., 230 Farbfotos, 6 s/w-Zeichnungen, kartoniert. ●●

Do it yourself
Elektroarbeiten
(**0975**-5) Von K. H. Schubert, 120 S., 193 Farbfotos, 40 Zeichnungen, kartoniert. ●●

Möbel im Designer-Stil
entwerfen und bauen
(**1360**-4) Von H.-W. Bastian, ca. 64 Seiten, zahlr. Farbabbildungen, kartoniert. ●●●

Möbel für Kinderzimmer und Wohnbereich
(**1456**-2) Von H.-W. Bastian, 80 Seiten, vierfarbig, kartoniert. ●●

Schnitzen
Hölzer · Muster · Werkzeuge
(**1414**-7) Von O. Maier, ca. 64 Seiten, zahlr. Farbabbildungen, kartoniert. ●●

Modellbauelektronik
Fernsteuerungen für Autos, Schiffe, Flugzeuge
(**1361**-2) Von W. Kawlath, 80 Seiten, zahlr. Farbabbildungen, kartoniert. ●●

Alarmanlagen
für Wohnung, Haus, Auto
(**1308**-6) Von H.-W. Bastian, 64 Seiten, 81 Farbfotos, 32 Zeichnungen kartoniert. ●●

Solarstromanlagen
bauen und installieren
(**1457**-0) Von P. Röbke-Doerr, E. Steffens, ca. 80 Seiten, ca. 200 farbige Abbildungen, kartoniert. ●●

Hifi-Boxen
(**1307**-8) Von U. Hilgefort, 96 S., 160 Farbfotos, 49 Zeichnungen, kartoniert. ●●

Technik im Garten
Pumpen · Filter · Beleuchtung
(**1238**-1) Von H.-W. Bastian, 64 S., 90 Farbfotos, 17 Farbzeichnungen, kartoniert. ●●

Restaurieren von Möbeln
Stilkunde, Materialien, Techniken, Arbeitsanleitungen in Bildfolgen.
(**4120**-9) Von E. Schnaus-Lorey, 152 S., 37 Farbf., 75 s/w-Fotos, 352 Zeichn., Pappbd. ●●●●

Elektronik als Hobby
Von der Grundlagenschaltung zum integrierten Schaltkreis
Mit 8 wichtigen Universalplatinen
(**4293**-0) Von W. Priesterath, 264 S., 80 s/w-Fotos, 128 Zeichn., Pappband. ●●●●

Die Super-Sportwagen der Welt
(**4423**-2) Von H. G. Isenberg, 194 S., 184 Farbfotos, 4 farbige Ausklapptafeln, 32 s/w-Fotos, Pappband. ●●●●

Die Super-Rennwagen der Welt
(**4707**-X) Von H. G. Isenburg, 194 Seiten, 189 Farbf., 31 s/w-Fotos, Pappband. ●●●●

Die Super-Trucks der Welt
(**4257**-4) Von H. G. Isenberg, 194 Seiten, 205 Farbfotos, 87 s/w-Fotos, 7 Farbzeichn., 4 farbige Ausklapptafeln, Pappbd. ●●●●

Die Super-Motorräder der Welt
(**4193**-4) Von H. G. Isenberg, 192 Seiten, 170 Farb- und 100 s/w-Fotos, 8 Zeichnungen, Pappband. ●●●●

Die Super-Eisenbahnen der Welt
(**4287**-6) Von W. Kosak, H. G. Isenberg, 224 S., 269 Farbfotos, 79 s/w-Fotos, 8 Vignetten, 5 farbige Ausklapptafeln, Pappband. ●●●●

Die Super-Dampfloks der Welt
(**4480**-1) Von H. Faust, H. G. Isenberg, 194 Seiten, 193 Farbfotos, mit vier Ausklapptafeln, Pappband ●●●●

Plastikmodellbau
Autos, Schiffe, Flugzeuge in vollendeter Technik.
(**1116**-4) Von W. Kawlath, 96 Seiten, 272 Farbabbildungen, kartoniert. ●●

Spiele und Denksport

Spielbare Witze für Kinder
(**0824**-4) Von H. Schmalenbach, 112 Seiten, 30 Zeichnungen, kartoniert. ●

Neue spielbare Witze für Kinder
(**1173**-3) Von H. Schmalenbach, 96 Seiten, 31 Zeichnungen, kartoniert. ●

Scherzfragen, Drudel und Blödeleien
gesammelt von Kindern.
(**0506**-7) Hrsg. von W. Pröve, 80 Seiten, 57 Zeichnungen, kartoniert. ●

Spiele mit Papier und Bleistift
(**2044**-9) Von K.-H. Koch, ca. 96 Seiten, kartoniert. ●

Der Elefant in meiner Hand …
Fingerspiele
für Kinder vom Baby – bis zum Grundschulalter
(**2043**-0) Von G. Falkenberg, 72 Seiten, 146 Farbzeichnungen, kartoniert. ●

Kinderspiele
die Spaß machen
(**2009**-0) Von H. Müller-Stein, 104 Seiten, 28 Abbildungen, kartoniert. ●

Kinderspiele mit Buchstaben und Wörtern
(**1041**-9) Von Dr. U. Vohland, 96 Seiten, 54 Zeichnungen, kartoniert. ●

Spiel und Spaß am Krankenbett
für Kinder und die ganze Familie
(**2035**-X) Von H. Bücken, 96 Seiten, 97 Zeichnungen, kartoniert. ●

Spiele im Freien
(**2038**-4) Von G. Wagner, 88 S., 20 zweifbg.-Zeichnungen, kartoniert. ●

Spiel und Spaß zu Hause
(**2039**-2) Von U. Geißler, 80 S., 90 zweifbg. Abbildungen, kartoniert. ●

Spiel und Spaß auf Reisen
Für Kinder und die ganze Familie
(**1085**-0) Von U. Geißler, 80 S., 107 zweifbg.-Zeichnungen, kartoniert. ●

Kleine Spiele ganz groß
(**1330**-2) Von U. Vohland, 80 Seiten, 93 s/w-Zeichnungen, kart. ●

Entdeckungsspiele für die ganze Familie
Rallyes zu Fuß und mit dem Fahrrad
(**1393**-0) Von U. Vohland, 96 S., 117 Zeichnungen, kartoniert. ●●

Kinder spielen Theater
(**4696**-0) Von G. Walter, 160 S., 48 Farbfotos, 229 Farbzeichnungen, Pappband. ●●●

Guten Tag, Kinder!
Neue Texte mit Spielanleitungen fürs Kasperletheater.
(**0861**-9) Von U. Lietz, 96 S., 18 s/w-Zeichnungen, kartoniert. ●

Kasperletheater
Spieltexte und Spielanleitungen · Basteltips für Theater und Puppen.
(**0641**-1) Von U. Lietz, 114 Seiten, 4 Farbtafeln, 12 s/w-Fotos, 39 Zeichnungen, kartoniert. ●●

Kindergeburtstage, die keiner vergißt
Planung, Gestaltung, Spielvorschläge.
(**0698**-5) Von G. und G. Zimmermann, 104 S., 80 Vignetten, kartoniert. ●

Kindergeburtstag
Vorbereitung, Spiel und Spaß.
(**0287**-4) Von Dr. I. Obrig, 136 S., 40 Abb., 11 Zeichn., 9 Lieder mit Noten, kart. ●●

Unvergeßliche Kindergeburtstage
(**4705**-3) Von G. Hennekemper, 176 S., 116 Farbfotos, 134 Farbzeichn., Pappband. ●●●

Unvergeßliche Kinderpartys
Tolle Ideen für Einladungen, Dekorationen und Spiele
(**4756**-8) Von V. Mirschel, 112 S., zahlreiche Farbfotos und -zeichnungen, gebunden. ●●●

Unvergeßliche Kinderfeste
Tolle Dekorationen, Spiele, Sketche für drinnen und draußen
(**4457**-7) Von Dr. G. Hennekemper, 192 S., 111 Farbfotos, 214 Farb- und 14 s/w-Zeichnungen, 4 S. Schnittmuster, Pappband. ●●●

Spielen mit den Allerkleinsten
(**4691**-X) Von S. Horak, 128 S., 47 Farbfotos, Pappband. ●●●

Lauter tolle Sachen, die Kinder gerne machen
(**4731**-2) Hrsg. U. Barff., 352 S., 117 Farbfotos, 778 Farbzeichnungen, Pappband. ●●●●

Das große bunte Spielebuch
für Kinder von 2 bis 6 Jahren
(**4543**-3) Von R. Grabbet, 160 S., 312 Farbabbildungen, Pappband. ●●●

Mein kunterbuntes Ratebuch
Rätselspiele mit Bildern und Wörtern für Kinder von 7 bis 10 Jahren
(**4697**-9) Von D. und R. Zey, ca. 144 Seiten, durchgehend vierfarbig, gebunden. ●●●

Neues Buch der siebzehn und vier Kartenspiele
(**0095**-2) Von K. Lichtwitz, 96 S., kartoniert. ●

Alles über Pokern
Regeln und Tricks.
(**2024**-4) Von C. D. Grupp, 112 S., 29 Kartenbilder, kartoniert. ●

Rommé und Canasta
in allen Variationen.
(**2025**-2) Von C. D. Grupp, 88 S., 24 Zeichnungen, kartoniert. ●

Doppelkopf, Schafkopf, Binokel, Cego, Tarock und andere Stammtischspiele.
(**2015**-5) Von C. D. Grupp, 112 S., kartoniert. ●

Das Skatspiel
Eine Fibel für Anfänger
(**0206**-8) Von K. Lehnhoff, 96 S., kartoniert. ●

Spielend Skat lernen
unter freundlicher Mitarbeit des Deutschen Skatverbandes
(**2005**-8) Von Th. Krüger, 120 Seiten, 181 s/w-Fotos, 22 Zeichnungen, kart. ●●

Patiencen
in Wort und Bild. (**2003**-1) Von I. Wolter-Rosendorf, 120 Seiten, kartoniert. ●

Neue Patiencen
(**2036**-8) Von H. Sosna, 160 Seiten, 43 Farbtafeln, kartoniert. ●●

Spielend Bridge lernen
(**2012**-0) Von J. Weiss, 96 Seiten, 58 Zeichnungen, kartoniert. ●

Spieltechnik im Bridge
(**2004**-X) Von V. Mollo und N. Gardener, dt. Adaption von D. Schröder, 152 S., kart. ●●●

Neue Kartentricks
(**2027**-9) Von K. Pankow, 104 Seiten, 20 Abbildungen, kartoniert. ●

Das japanische Brettspiel Go
(**2020**-1) Von W. Dörholt, 104 S., 182 Diagramme, kart. ●

Spielend Go lernen
(**2041**-4) Von H. Otake, S. Futakuchi, 192 S., 615 s/w-Zeichnungen, kartoniert. ●●

Mah-Jongg
Das chinesische Glücks-, Kombinations- und Gesellschaftsspiel. (**2030**-9) Von U. Eschenbach, 80 S., 30 s/w-Fotos, 5 Zeichn., kart. ●

Backgammon
für Anfänger und Könner. (**2008**-2) Von G. W. Fink und G. Fuchs, 104 S., 41 Abb., kart. ●

Einführung in das Schachspiel
(**0104**-5) Von W. Wollenschläger und K. Colditz, 112 S., 116 Diagramme, kartoniert. ●

Schach, das königliche Spiel
Von den Grundzügen zum strategischen Spiel.
(**1105**-9) Von T. Schuster, 192 S., 302 Diagramme, kart. ●●

Spielend Schach lernen
(**2002**-3) Von T. Schuster, 96 S., , kartoniert. ●

Kinder- und Jugendschach
Offizielles Lehrbuch des Deutschen Schachbundes zur Erringung der Bauern-, Turm- und Königsdiplome.
(**0561**-X) Von B. J. Withuis, H. Pfleger, 144 S., 220 Zeichnungen und Diagramme, kart. ●●

Zug um Zug
Schach für jedermann 1
Offizielles Lehrbuch des Deutschen Schachbundes zur Erringung des Bauerndiploms.
(**0648**-9) Von H. Pfleger, E. Kurz, 80 Seiten, 24 s/w-Fotos, 8 Zeichnungen, 60 Diagramme, kartoniert. ●●

Zug um Zug
Schach für jedermann 2
Offizielles Lehrbuch des Deutschen Schachbundes zur Erringung des Turmdiploms.
(**0659**-4) Von H. Pfleger, E. Kurz, 128 Seiten, 7 s/w-Fotos, 13 Zeichnungen, 78 Diagramme, kartoniert. ●●

Zug um Zug
Schach für jedermann 3
Offizielles Lehrbuch des Deutschen Schachbundes zur Erringung des Königsdiploms.
(**0728**-0) Von H. Pfleger, G. Treppner, 128 S., 4 s/w-Fotos, 84 Diagr., 10 Zeichn., kart. ●●

Schach für Fortgeschrittene
Taktik und Probleme des Schachspiels
(**0219**-X) Von R. Teschner, 88 Seiten, 85 Diagramme, kartoniert. ●

Neue Schacheröffnungen
(**0478**-8) Von T. Schuster, 104 Seiten, 100 Diagramme, kartoniert. ●

Würfelspiele
für jung und alt. (**2007**-4) Von F. Pruss, 112 S., 21 s/w-Zeichnungen, kartoniert. ●

Roulette richtig gespielt
Systemspiele, die Vermögen brachten.
(**0121**-5) Von M. Jung, 96 S., zahlreiche Tabellen, kartoniert. ●

Spiele für Party und Familie
(**2014**-7) Von Rudi Carrell, 80 S., 22 Zeichnungen, kartoniert. ●

Neue Spiele für Ihre Party
(**2022**-8) Von G. Blechner, 120 S., 54 Zeichnungen, kartoniert. ●

Lustige Tanzspiele und Scherztänze
für Partys und Feste.
(**0165**-7) Von E. Bäulke, 80 S., 53 Abb., kart. ●

Das Spiel mit der Schwerkraft
Jonglieren
Mit Bällen, Keulen, Ringen und Diabolo.
(**1009**-5) Von S. Peter, 80 S., 149 Farbfotos, kartoniert. ●

Zaubern
einfach – aber verblüffend.
(**2018**-X) Von D. Bouch, 84 Seiten, 41 Zeichnungen, kartoniert. ●

Tips, Tricks und Gewinnstrategien für Game-Boy-Spiele
(**1235**-7) Von René Zey, 176 Seiten, 100 Zeichnungen, kartoniert. ●●

Neue Game-Boy-Spiele
Sport, Action und Adventure
(**1325**-6) Von R. Zey, 176 Seiten, 21 s/w-Zeichnungen, kartoniert. ●●

Alles über Super-Nintendo-Spiele
Technik, Tips und Facts
(**1340**-X) Von D. Mark, 104 S., zahlreiche Farbabbildungen, kartoniert. ●●

Das 3. Glücksrad Rätselbuch
(**1391**-4) 160 Seiten, kartoniert. ●●

Rätselspiele
Quiz- und Scherzfragen für gesellige Stunden
(**1270**-5) Von K. H. Schneider, ca. 80 Seiten, ca. 80 s/w-Abbildungen, kartoniert. ●

Knobeleien und Denksport
(**2019**-8) Von K. Rechberger, 142 Seiten, 105 Zeichnungen, kartoniert. ●

So feiert man Feste fröhlicher
Heitere Vorträge und Gedichte
(**0098**-7) Von Dr. Allos, 96 Seiten, 15 Abbildungen, kartoniert. ●

Die große Lachparade
Neue Texte für heitere Vorträge und Ansagen
(**0188**-6) Von E. Müller, 80 S., kartoniert. ●

Rat und Wissen

Der gute Ton
in Gesellschaft und Beruf.
(**0063**-4) Von I. Wolter, 80 S., 42 s/w-Fotos, 7 Zeichnungen, kartoniert. ●

Der gute Ton
im Privatleben.
(**1111**-3) Von I. Wolter, bearbeitet von Wolf Stenzel, 104 S., 42 s/w-Abbildungen, kart. ●

Umgangsformen heute
Die Empfehlungen des Fachausschusses für Umgangsformen.
(**4015**-6) 252 S., 108 s/w-Fotos, 17 Zeichnungen, Pappband. ●●●

Abc der modernen Umgangsformen
(**4754**-1) Von I. Wolff, ca. 300 Seiten, zahlreiche Abbildungen, gebunden. ●●●

Benehmen bei Tisch
(**0988**-7) Von I. Cording, 80 S., 90 Farbfotos, 5 s/w-Zeichnungen, kartoniert. ●●

Krawatten
Fliegen, Schals und Tücher gekonnt binden
(**1072**-9) Von Y. Thalheim, H. Nadolny, 48 S., 129 Farbfotos, 1 s/w-Foto, Pappband. ●

freundin
Farbberatung
Alle Farben, die Ihnen wirklich stehen
(**4520**-4) Von Chr. Buscher, 128 Seiten, 175 Farbfotos, Pappband. ●●●●

freundin
Das perfekte Make-up
(**4727**-4) Von M. Rüdiger, H. Kirchberger, G. Mergenburg, 128 Seiten, 271 Farbfotos, Pappband. ●●●●

freundin
Der große Ratgeber
Body Fitness
Diät · Pflege · Bräune · Gymnastk · Anti-Cellulite-Programm
(**4758**-4) Von M. Bückmann u.a., ca. 128 S., durchgehend vierfarbig, gebunden. ●●●●

freundin Ratgeber
Hochzeit feiern
(**4702**-2) Von C. von Hoerner-Nitsch, I. Weber, K. Riebartsch, C. von Bernuth, 128 Seiten, 188 Farbfotos., 28 s/w-Fotos, Pappbd. ●●●●

freundin
Typ & Frisur
(**4695**-2) Von E. Bolz, 128 S., 219 Farbfotos, Pappband. ●●●●

Gedichte, Reden und Sketche
für grüne, silberne u. goldene Hochzeitstage
(**1269**-1) Von F. Rieder, 160 S., durchgehend vierfarbig, Pappband. ●●

Von der Verlobung zur Goldenen Hochzeit
(**0393**-5) Von E. Runge, 112 Seiten, kartoniert. ●

Hochzeitszeitungen
Tolle Ideen für Leute von heute
(**1379**-5) Von Y. Thalheim, 80 S., 160 zweifbg. Abbildungen, kartoniert. ●●

Die Silberhochzeit
Vorbereitung · Einladung · Geschenkvorschläge · Dekoration · Festablauf · Menüs · Reden · Glückwünsche: (**0542**-3) Von K. F. Merkle, 112 S., 41 Zeichnungen, kartoniert. ●

Geburtstagsfeiern für jedes Alter
Planung und Festgestaltung
(**1382**-5) Von S. Ahrndt, 120 S., 145 Farbfotos, 28 Farbzeichnungen, kartoniert. ●●

Geburt und Taufe feiern
Planung und Festgestaltung
(**1443**-0) Von S. Ahrendt, 112 Seiten, 46 Farbzeichn., kartoniert. ●●

Wie soll es heißen?
(**0211**-4) Von D. Köhr, 136 S., kartoniert. ●

Unsere beliebtesten Vornamen
(**1023**-0) Von A. F. W. Weigel, 160 Seiten, 75 s/w-Fotos, Pappband. ●●

Die schönsten Vornamen
(**4755**-X) Hrsg. Dr. D. Voorgang, ca. 208 Seiten, über 100 Farbzeichnungen, gebunden. ●

Kindergedichte, Lieder und Sketche für Hochzeitsfeiern
(**1112**-1) Von B. Lins, 72 Seiten, 26 farbige Abbildungen, 15 Lieder, kartoniert. ●

Neue Kindergedichte und Lieder für Hochzeitsfeste
(**1431**-7) Von A. Schweiggert, 80 S., 27 s/w-Zeichnungen, kartoniert. ●

Kindergedichte rund ums Jahr
(**1040**-0) Von A. Schweiggert, 80 Seiten, 49 Zeichnungen, 6 Vignetten, kartoniert. ●

Kindergedichte für alle Tage und Feste
Freu dich, daß noch Blumen sprießen …
(**1489**-9) Von G. Rudolf, 160 S., durchgehend zweifarbig, gebunden. ●●

Ins Gästebuch geschrieben
(**0576**-8) Von K. H. Trabeck, 96 Seiten, 24 Zeichnungen, kartoniert. ●

Der Verseschmied
Kleiner Leitfaden für Hobbydichter.
(**0597**-0) Von T. Parisius, 96 Seiten, 28 Zeichnungen, kartoniert. ●

Mach' dir einen Reim
Der moderne Verseschmied
(**1433**-3) Von G. Rudorf, 192 S., Pappband. ●●

Die schönsten Volkslieder
(**0432**-X) Hrsg. D. Walther, 128 S., mit Noten und Zeichnungen, kartoniert. ●

Alte und neue
Wanderlieder
(**1268**-3) Von P. G. Walter, 96 S., zweifarbig, kartoniert. ●●

Neue Glückwunschfibel
für groß und klein.
(**0156**-8) Von R. Christian-Hildebrandt, 96 S., 13 Vignetten, kartoniert. ●

Großes Buch der Glückwünsche
(**0255**-6) Hrsg. von O. Fuhrmann, 176 S., 77 Zeichnungen und viele Gestaltungsvorschläge, kartoniert. ●●

Wetter und Wind ändern sich geschwind
Beliebte Bauernregeln
(**1267**-5) Von G. Haddenbach, ca. 80 Seiten, ca. 30 zweifarbige Illustrationen, kart. ●

Beliebte Verse fürs Poesiealbum
Rosen, Tulpen, Nelken …
(**0431**-1) Von W. Pröve, 96 Seiten, 11 Faksimile-Abbildungen, kartoniert. ●

Verse fürs Poesiealbum
(**0241**-6) Von I. Wolter, 120 Seiten, 20 Abbildungen, kartoniert. ●

Heiter und besinnliche
Verse fürs Poesiealbum
(**1069**-9) Von B. H. Bull, 160 Seiten, 70 zweifarbige Illustrationen, Pappband. ●●

Klassische Verse und Zitate
Für Glückwünsche, Briefe, Reden und Poesiealben
(**1223**-3) Von P. Motzan, 224 Seiten, 40 Abbildungen, Pappband. ●●

Die Kunst der freien Rede
Ein Intensivkurs mit vielen Übungen, Beispielen und Lösungen.
(**4189**-6) Von G. Hirsch, 232 Seiten, 11 Zeichnungen, Pappband. ●●●

Trinksprüche, Gästebuchverse, Richtsprüche
(**0224**-6) Von D. Kellermann, 96 Seiten, kartoniert. ●

Glückwünsche, Toasts und Festreden zu Polterabend und Hochzeit
(**0264**-5) Von I. Wolter, 112 Seiten, 18 Zeichnungen, kartoniert. ●

Trinksprüche und Festreden
(**1321**-3) Von L. Metzner, 144 S., 13 zweifarbige Zeichnungen, Pappband. ●●

Grußworte
für Gemeindefeiern, Vereinsjubiläen und andere offizielle Anlässe
(**4741**-X) Von M. Adam, 192 S., Pappbd. ●●

Moderne Reden und Ansprachen
(**4742**-8) Von M. Adam, 464 Seiten, Pappband. ●●●●

Reden zu Familienfesten
(**0675**-6) Von G. Georg, 112 S., kartoniert. ●

Reden im Verein
Musteransprachen für viele Gelegenheiten
(**0703**-5) Von G. Georg, 112 S., kartoniert. ●

Reden zum Jubiläum
Musteransprachen für viele Gelegenheiten
(**0595**-4) Von G. Georg, 112 S., kartoniert. ●

Reden und Sprüche zu Grundsteinlegung, Richtfest und Einzug
(**0598**-0) Von A. Bruder, G. Georg, 96 Seiten, kartoniert. ●

Die überzeugende Rede
Mehr Erfolg durch bessere Rhetorik
(**0076**-6) Von K. Wolter, G. Kunz, 96 Seiten, kartoniert. ●

Moderne Korrespondenz
Handbuch für erfolgreiche Briefe
(**4014**-8) Von H. Kirst und W. Manekeller, 544 Seiten, Pappband. ●●●●

Musterbriefe
für alle Gelegenheiten.
(**0231**-9) Hrsg. von O. Fuhrmann, 240 Seiten, kartoniert. ●●

Der moderne Brief
Geschäfts- und Privatkorrespondenz empfängerorientiert schreiben
(**1440**-6) Von Dr. G. Reinert-Schneider, 112 S., 44 s/w-Zeichn., kartoniert. ●●

Geschäftsbriefe
zeitgemäß und stilsicher
(**1323**-X) Von G. Briese-Neumann, 152 S., kartoniert. ●●

Geschäftliche Briefe
für Privatleute, Handwerker und Kaufleute
(**0041**-3) Von G. Briese-Neumann, ca. 120 S., kartoniert. ●

Einladungen texten und gestalten
(**1484**-8) Von R. Zey und A. Bellingen, ca. 80 S., kartoniert. ●

Privatbriefe
Muster für alle Gelegenheiten.
(**0114**-2) Von I. Wolter-Rosendorf, 112 S., kart. ●

Erfolgstips für den Schriftverkehr
Briefgestaltung · Rechtschreibung · Zeichensetzung · Stil. (**0678**-0) Von U. Schoenwald, 112 Seiten, kartoniert. ●

Behördenkorrespondenz
Musterbriefe · Anträge · Einsprüche
(**0412**-5) Von E. Ruge, 112 S., kartoniert. ●

Worte und Briefe der Anteilnahme
(**0464**-8) Von E. Ruge, M. Adam, 88 Seiten, mit vielen Abbildungen, kartoniert. ●

Briefe zu Geburt und Taufe
Glückwünsche und Danksagungen. (**0802**-3) Von H. Beitz, 96 S., 12 Zeichnungen, kart. ●

FALKEN Rechtsberater
Fallbeispiele · Musterbriefe · Gerichtsurteile
(**4734**-7) Hrsg. S. von Hasseln, 756 Seiten, Pappband. ●●●●

Alles, was man über Erziehungsgeld, Mutterschutz, Erziehungsurlaub wissen muß
Das neue Recht für Eltern
(**0835**-X) Von K. Möcks, A. Schmitt, 144 S., kartoniert. ●●

Alles, was man über die nichteheliche Lebensgemeinschaft wissen muß
(**1071**-0) Von T. Drewes, 104 Seiten, 8 s/w-Zeichnungen, kartoniert. ●●

Scheidung und Unterhalt
nach dem neuen Eherecht.
(**0403**-6) Von T. Drewes, 112 S., mit Kosten und Unterhaltstabellen, kartoniert. ●●

Alles, was man über
Eheverträge
wissen muß
(**1483**-X) Von T. Münster, 128 Seiten, kartoniert. ●●

Alles, was man über Scheidung und Unterhalt wissen muß
(**1264**-0) Von T. Drewes, 128 Seiten, kartoniert. ●●

Alles, was man über Renten wissen muß
Mit Rentenreformgesetz 1992
(**1265**-9) Von K. Möcks, A. Schmitt, 112 Seiten, kartoniert. ●●

Rasthaus-Ratgeber
Kinder haben keine Bremse
Verkehrserziehung für Kinder ab 3 Jahren
(**1497**-X) Von H.-D. Barth, 80 S, durchgehend vierfarbig, kartoniert. ●●

Rasthaus-Ratgeber
Stop dem Autoklau
Die wirksamsten Methoden gegen Autodiebstahl
(**1485**-6) Von M. Maurer, 64 Seiten, durchgehend vierfarbig, kartoniert. ●●

Rasthaus-Ratgeber
Gebrauchtwagenkauf
Auswahl · Bewertung · Kaufvertrag
(**1498**-8) Von U. Traub, 80 Seiten, durchgehend vierfarbig, kartoniert. ●●

Wolfgang Büsers Erfolgstips
Rentenreform '92
(**1244**-6) Von W. Büser, 80 S., kartoniert. ●

Wolfgang Büsers Erfolgstips
Teilzeitarbeit
(**1266**-7) Von W. Büser, 80 S., kartoniert. ●●

Wolfgang Büsers Erfolgstips
(Lohn-) Einkommensteuer '92
Aktuell: Zinssteuer '93
(**1324**-8) Von W. Büser, 176 S., kartoniert. ●●

Vermögensbildung mit System
Anlageformen · Strategien · Praxistips
(**1445**-7) Von W. Schwanfelder, 160 Seiten, kartoniert. ●●

Alles, was man über BAföG wissen muß
(**1387**-6) Von A. Mengeringhausen, 144 Seiten, kartoniert. ●●

Testament und Erbschaft
Erbfolge, Rechte und Pflichten der Erben, Erbschafts- und Schenkungssteuer, Mustertestamente. (**4139**-X) Von T. Drewes, R. Hollender, 304 Seiten, Pappband. ●●●

Erbrecht und Testament
(**0046**-4) Von H. Wandrey, 124 S., kart. ●

Alles, was man über Testament und Erbschaft wissen muß
(**0939**-9) Von T. Drewes, 136 Seiten, 9 s/w-Zeichnungen, kartoniert. ●●

Mietrecht
Leitfaden für Mieter und Vermieter
(**0479**-6) Von J. Beuthner, 196 S., kart. ●●

Haushaltstips
praktisch und umweltfreundlich
(**1046**-X) Von K. Winkell, 96 Seiten, 36 Zeichnungen, kartoniert. ●

Texte für den Anrufbeantworter
(**1389**-2) Von G. Kunz, 80 S., 12 s/w-Zeichnungen, kartoniert. ●

Alles, was man über den Umgang mit Behörden wissen muß
(**1390**-6) Von K. Möcks, A. Schmitt, 132 Seiten, kartoniert. ●●

Wege zum Börsenerfolg
Aktien · Anleihen · Optionen
(**4275**-2) Von H. Krause, 252 S., 4 s/w-Fotos, 86 Zeichnungen, Pappband. ●●●●

Wörter und Unwörter
Sinniges und Unsinniges der deutschen Gegenwartssprache
(**1401**-7) Hrsg. Gesellschaft für deutsche Sprache, 176 Seiten, kartoniert. ●●●

Richtige Groß- und Kleinschreibung
durch neue, vereinfachte Regeln. Erläuterungen der Zweifelsfragen anhand vieler Beispiele.
(**0897**-X) Von Prof. Dr. Ch. Stetter, 96 Seiten, kartoniert. ●

Gutes Deutsch schreiben und sprechen
(**4432**-1) Von W. Manekeller, Dr. G. Reinert-Schneider, 416 S., durchgehend zweifarbig, Pappband. ●●●●

Mehr Erfolg in der Schule
Deutsche Rechtschreibung und Grammatik
Übungen und Beispiele für die Klassen 5–10.
(**4407**-0) Von K. Schreiner, 256 S., durchgehend zweifarbig, Pappband. ●●●●

Diktate besser schreiben
Übungen zur Rechtschreibung für die Klassen 4 bis 8
(**0469**-9) Von K. Schreiner, 152 S., 31 Zeichnungen, kartoniert. ●●

Deutsche Grammatik
Ein Lern- und Übungsbuch
(**0704**-3) Von K. Schreiner, 122 S., kart. ●●

Aufsätze besser schreiben
Förderkurs für die Klassen 4 – 10
(**0429**-X) Von K. Schreiner, 144 Seiten, 31 Abb., kartoniert. ●●

Mehr Erfolg in der Schule
Der Deutschaufsatz
Übungen und Beispiele für die Klassen 5 – 10.
(**4271**-X) Von K. Schreiner, 240 S., 4 s/w-Fotos, 51 Zeichnungen, Pappband. ●●●●

Mehr Erfolg in der Schule
Deutsch
Textinterpretation, Literaturgeschichte und Stilkunde
(**4483**-6) Von K. Schreiner, 272 S., 43 zweifarbige Zeichnungen, Pappband. ●●●●

Gedächtnistraining mit Eselsbrücken
(**1388**-4) Von W. Ettig, 96 S., 36 s/w-Zeichnungen, kartoniert. ●

Geschichte
Von der Französischen Revolution bis zur Gegenwart
(**4723**-1) Von K. Schreiner, 256 S., 50 s/w-Fotos, 10 Farbzeichnungen, 6 zweifarbige Landkarten, Pappband. ●●●●

Geographie
Natürliche Grundlagen · Gestaltung der Umwelt · Die Staaten der Erde
(**4724**-X) Von V. Disch, 256 S., ca. 40 Karten und Grafiken, Pappband. ●●●●

Mehr Erfolg in der Schule
Mathematik 1
Arithmetik und Algebra. Übungen, Beispiele und Lösungen für die Klassen 5 bis 10.
(**4420**-8) Von R. Müller-Fonfara, 256 Seiten, 193 Zeichn., 2 s/w-Fotos, Pappband. ●●●●

Mehr Erfolg in der Schule
Mathematik 2
Geometrie, Statistik, Wahrscheinlichkeitsrechnung und kaufmännisches Rechnen
(**4456**-9) Von R. Müller-Fonfara, W. Scholl, 256 Seiten, 6 s/w-Fotos, 304 Zeichnungen, Pappband. ●●●●

Mathematische Formeln für Schule und Beruf
Mit Beispielen und Erklärungen.
(**0499**-0) Von R. Müller-Fonfara, 156 Seiten, 210 Zeichnungen, kartoniert. ●●

Schülerlexikon der Mathematik
Formeln, Übungen und Begriffserklärungen für die Klassen 5 – 10
(**0430**-3) Von R. Müller-Fonfara, 176 Seiten, 96 Zeichnungen, kartoniert. ●●

Mehr Erfolg in der Schule
Mathematik 3
Analysis, analytische Geometrie und lineare Algebra
(**4541**-7) Von R. Müller-Fonfara, W. Scholl, 240 Seiten, 140 zweifarbige Grafiken, Pappband. ●●●●

Mehr Erfolg in der Schule
Mathematik 4
Für die Klassen 11 bis 13
(**4701**-0) Von R. Müller-Fonfara, W. Scholl, 240 Seiten, 91 Zeichnungen, 3 s/w-Fotos, Pappband. ●●●●

Mathematik-Textaufgaben leicht gelöst
Aufgaben · Lösungsstrategien · Anwendungsbeispiele
(**1022**-2) Von R. Müller-Fonfara, 128 Seiten, 4 Zeichnungen, kartoniert. ●●

Rechnen aufgefrischt für Schule und Beruf.
(**0100**-2) Von H. Rausch, 144 S., kartoniert. ●

Besseres Englisch
Grammatik und Übungen für die Klassen 5 bis 10.
(**0745**-0) Von E. Henrichs, 144 S., kart. ●●

Mehr Erfolg in der Schule
Englisch
Textinterpretationen
(**4518**-2) Von E. Heinrichs-Kleinen, 256 S., Pappband. ●●●●

Mehr Erfolg in der Schule
Englische Grammatik
Regeln und Übungen für die Klassen 5 bis 13
(**4431**-3) Von E. Henrichs-Kleinen, 256 S., durchgehend zweifarbig, Pappband. ●●●●

Besseres Französisch
Grammatik und Übungen für die Klassen 9 bis 11
(**1039**-7) Von R. Lübke, 114 S., durchgehend zweifarbig, kartoniert. ●●

Mehr Erfolg in der Schule
Französische Grammatik
Für die Klassen 7 bis 13
(**4703**-7) Von R. Lübke, ca. 256 S., durchgehend zweifarbig, Pappband. ●●●●

Schnell und sicher zum Führerschein
Tips und Tricks aus 30jähriger-Fahrlehrer-Praxis.
(**1232**-2) Von O. Einert, 152 S., 156 Farbfotos, 161 z.T. farb. Zeichnungen, kartoniert. ●●

Die aktuellen Prüfungsfragen und Prüfungsbogen für den Führerschein Klasse 3
(**1490**-2) 104 Seiten, 371 Farbfotos, kart. ●●

Der Test-Knacker bei Führerscheinverlust
(**1262**-4) Von T. Rieh, 128 S., kartoniert. ●●

Erfolgreiche Bewerbung um einen Ausbildungsplatz
(**0715**-9) Von H. Friedrich, 128 S., kartoniert. ●

Bewerbungsstrategien
Erfolgreiche Konzepte für Karrierebewußte
(**1027**-3) Von Dr. W. Reichel, 128 S., kart. ●●

Karriereplanung mit System
Bewerbungsstrategien für Frauen
(**4455**-0) Von R. Ibelgaufts, 144 Seiten, 20 Cartoons, Pappband. ●●

Die Bewerbung
Der moderne Ratgeber für Bewerbungsbriefe, Lebenslauf und Vorstellungsgespräche.
(**4138**-1) Von W. Manekeller, 264 Seiten, Pappband. ●●●

Die erfolgreiche Bewerbung
Bewerbung und Vorstellung
(**0173**-8) Von W. Manekeller, U. Schoenwald, 144 Seiten, kartoniert. ●●

Lebenslauf und Bewerbung
Beispiele für Inhalt, Form und Aufbau
(**0428**-1) Von H. Friedrich, 112 S., kartoniert. ●

Bewerbungsbriefe und Stellengesuche
Für handwerkliche, gewerblich-technische und kaufmännische Berufe
(**0138**-X) Von Dr. W. Reichert, 96 S., kart. ●

Das überzeugende
Vorstellungsgespräch
Erfolgreiche Strategien für den ersten Eindruck
(**1261**-6) Von R. Ibelgaufts, 144 S., kart. ●●

Vorstellungsgespräche
sicher und erfolgreich führen.
(**0636**-5) Von H. Friedrich, 144 Seiten, kart. ●

Einstellungstests und andere Methoden der Bewerberauswahl
(**1263**-2) Von Dr. R. Hilke, H. Hustedt, 160 S., 27 Zeichnungen, kartoniert. ●●

Keine Angst vor Einstellungstests
Ein Ratgeber für Bewerber.
(**0793**-6) Von Ch. Titze, 120 Seiten, 67 Zeichnungen, kartoniert. ●

Assessment Center
Erfolgstips und Übungen für Bewerber
(**1385**-X) Von H. Beitz und A. Loch, ca. 128 S., kartoniert. ●●

Berufsstart für Hochschulabsolventen
Erfolgsstrategien für Bewerbung und Vorstellung
(**1482**-1) Von Dr. W. Reichel, ca. 144 S., kart. ●●

freundin Ratgeber
Psychoterror am Arbeitsplatz
Mobbing
(**1434**-1) Von B. Huber, 160 S., kartoniert. ●●

freundin Ratgeber
Frau mit Kind
Leitfaden für Alleinerziehende
(**1476**-7) Von G. Teusen, ca. 144 S., kart. ●●

freundin
Kind und Beruf: (K)ein Problem
(**1322**-1) Von I. Weber, 168 Seiten, 14 Zeichnungen, kartoniert. ●●

freundin Ratgeber
Neu im Job: So überzeugen Sie
(**1259**-4) Von G. Teusen, 160 S., kart. ●●

Die ersten Tage am neuen Arbeitsplatz
Ratschläge für den richtigen Umgang mit Kollegen und Vorgesetzten
(**0855**-4) Von H. Friedrich, 104 Seiten, kart. ●

Zeugnisse im Beruf
richtig schreiben, richtig verstehen
(**0544**-X) Von H. Friedrich, 112 Seiten, kart. ●

Arbeitszeugnisse
verstehen und interpretieren
(**1444**-9) Von A. Nasemann, 136 S., kart. ●●

So lernt man leicht und schnell
Maschinenschreiben
Lehrbuch für Schulen, Lehrgänge und Selbstunterricht. (**0568**-7) Von M. Kempkes, 112 S., 48 Zeichnungen, kartoniert. ●●

FALKEN-Software
Maschinenschreiben und Tastaturtraining für Computer
(**7009**-8) Von B. Hoppius, Diskette 5 1/4" u. 3 1/2" für IBM-PC + Kompatible, mit Begleitheft. ●●●●●*

Leicht und schnell gelernt
Maschinenschreiben im Selbstunterricht
(**0170**-3) Von O. Fonfara, 88 S., kartoniert. ●

Buchführung leicht gemacht
Ein methodischer Grundkurs für den Selbstunterricht (**4238**-8) Von D. Machenheimer, R. Kersten, 252 Seiten, Pappband. ●●●●

Buchführung leicht gefaßt
Für Handwerker, Gewerbetreibende und freiberuflich Tätige.
(**0127**-4) Von R. Pohl, 104 S., kartoniert. ●

Stenografie leicht gelernt
im Kurus oder Selbstunterricht
(**0266**-1) Von H. Kaus, 64 S., kartoniert. ●

Gitarre spielen
Ein Grundkurs für den Selbstunterricht
(**0534**-2) Von A. Roßmann, 96 S., 1 Schallfolie, 150 Zeichnungen, kartoniert. ●●●

FALKEN & HOHNER: Workshop Musik
Gitarre spielen
Folk, Blues, Pop, Rock auf der akustischen Gitarre
Für Anfänger und Wiedereinsteiger
(**1437**-6) Von W. Ruß, ca. 80 S., Begleit-CD ca. 60 Min. Spieldauer, zahlreiche Illustrationen und Fotos, kartoniert. ●●●●

FALKEN & HOHNER: Workshop Musik
Keyboard spielen
Pop & Rock
Für Anfänger und Wiedereinsteiger
(**1435**-X) Von M. Lonardoni, ca. 80 Seiten, Begleit-CD, ca. 60 Min. Spieldauer, zahlreiche Illustrationen und Fotos, kartoniert. ●●●●

FALKEN & HOHNER: Workshop Musik
Singen
In Chor, Singgruppe und solo
Für Anfänger und Wiedereinsteiger
(**1436**-8) Von W. Layer, ca. 80 S., Begleit-CD ca. 60 Min. Spieldauer, zahlreiche Illustrationen und Fotos, kartoniert. ●●●●

Faszinierendes Erlebnis
Tierwelt
(**4706**-1) Von U. und W. Dolder, 196 Seiten, 314 Farbzeichnungen, Pappband. ●●●●

Das große Buch der
Antworten auf Kinderfragen
(**4477**-1) Von H. Hofmann, U. Kopp, G. Jankovics u.a., 192 Seiten, 308 Farbzeichnungen, Pappband. ●●●

FALKEN LEXIKON
Das Wissen unserer Zeit
(**4736**-3) Hrsg. Lexikographisches Institut, 1008 Seiten, 681 Farbfotos, 1142 Farbzeichn., Pappband. ●●●●

Das neue, farbige
Jugendlexikon
(**4472**-0) Von J. Frey, D. Rex, 304 Seiten, 269 und 52 s/w-Fotos, 6 Farbzeichnungen, Pappband. ●●●●

Das große farbige Kinderlexikon
(**4195**-0) Von U. Kopp, 320 S., 493 Farbabbildungen, 17 s/w-Fotos, Pappband. ●●●●

Kinder-Überraschung
(**1499**-6) Von M. Semmel, ca. 80 Seiten, durchgehend vierfarbig, kartoniert. ●●

Briefmarken sammeln
(**0481**-8) Von D. Stein, 120 S., 4 Farbtafeln, 98 s/w-Abbildungen, kartoniert. ●

Telefonkartenlexikon für Sammler
(**1406**-6) Von M. Burzan, ca. 160 Seiten, zahlreiche Farbabbildungen, kartoniert. ●●●

Telefonkarten sammeln
Serien · Preise · Sammeltips
(**1326**-4) Von M. Burzan, 128 S., 251 Farbfotos, kartoniert. ●●

Die Handschrift als Spiegel des Charakters
Graphologie
(**1025**-7) Von Dr. W. Busch, 104 S., 87 Schriftproben, kartoniert. ●

Familienforschung · Ahnentafel · Wappenkunde
Wege zur eigenen Familienchronik
(**0744**-2) Von P. Bahn, 128 S., 8 Farbtafeln, 30 Abbildungen, kartoniert. ●●

Familienforschung und Wappenkunde
(**4485**-2) Von P. Bahn, 224 S., 114 zweifarbige Abbildungen, Pappband. ●●●●●

freundin Ratgeber
Frauen allein auf Reisen
(**1260**-8) Von H. Guilino, 192 S., 7 Zeichnungen, kartoniert. ●●

Brain Building
Das Supertraining für Gedächtnis, Logik, Kreativität
(**4704**-5) Von M. vos Savant, 256 Seiten, Pappband. ●●●

Traumdeutung
Die Bildersprache unserer Traumwelt entschlüsseln
(**4486**-0) Von G. Fink, 384 Seiten, 74 zweifarbige Fotos, Pappband. ●●●●

Kinderträume
Ein Ratgeber für Eltern
(**4505**-0) Von G. Fink, 176 S., 6 s/w-Zeichnungen, Pappband. ●●●

Wahrsagen
mit den Karten der Madame Lenormand
(**1328**-0) Von B. A. Mertz, 108 Seiten, 39 s/w-Abbildungen, kartoniert. ●●

Die 12 Tierzeichen
Chinesisches Horoskop
(**0423**-0) Von G. Haddenbach, 88 Seiten, kartoniert. ●

Partnerschaftshoroskop
Glück und Harmonie mit Ihrem Traumpartner.
(**0587**-3) Von G. Haddenbach, 112 Seiten, 11 Zeichnungen, kartoniert. ●

Im Zeichen der Sterne
(**0951**-8) Der feurige Widder
(**0952**-6) Der willensstarke Stier
(**0953**-4) Die vielseitigen Zwillinge
(**0954**-2) Der feinfühlige Krebs
(**0955**-0) Der königliche Löwe
(**0956**-9) Die zuverlässige Jungfrau
(**0957**-7) Die charmante Waage
(**0958**-5) Der leidenschaftliche Skorpion
(**0959**-3) Der temperamentvolle Schütze
(**0960**-7) Der treue Steinbock
(**0961**-5) Der selbstbewußte Wassermann
(**0962**-3) Die romantischen Fische
Von G. Haddenbach, 64 Seiten, 35 Farbfotos, Pappband. ●

Das neue FALKEN
Computerlexikon
(**4356**-2) Von Dr. B. Kopp, 336 S., 121 s/w-Fotos, 184 Computergrafiken, Pappbd. ●●●●

Computer-Grundwissen
Eine Einführung in Funktion und Einsatzmöglichkeiten
(**4359**-7) Von Chr. T. Wolff, 176 S., 182 Farbfotos, kartoniert.●●●●
(**4358**-9) Pappband.●●●●

Der PC
(**4732**-0) Von U. u. H. Freund, 336 Seiten, 386 Farbfotos, Pappband. ●●●●●

freundin
Das Computerbuch für Frauen
(**4372**-4) Von M. Thiel, 176 S., 102 Farbfotos, 73 Zeichnungen, Pappband. ●●●●

Desktop Publishing: Typografie und Layout Seiten gestalten am PC · für Einsteiger und Profis
(**4330**-9) Von Dr. H. D. Baumann, M. Klein, 320 S., zahlreiche zweifarbige Abbildungen, Pappband. ●●●●●

PC HELP!
Wissenschaftliche Texte mit Word 5.5
(**4360**-0) Von P. Vogel, 80 S., 34 zweifarbige Screenshots, kartoniert. ●●

PC HELP!
Praktische Computernutzung mit Works 2.0
(**4369**-4) Von A. Görgens, 72 Seiten, 64 zweifarbige Screenshots, kartoniert. ●●

PC HELP!
DFÜ mit dem PC
(**4370**-8) Von M. Hofmann, 88 Seiten, 41 zweifarbige Screenshots, kartoniert. ●●

PC HELP!
Zeichnen mit dem PC
(**4361**-9) Von M. Hofmann, 88 S., 57 zweifarbige Screenshots, kartoniert. ●●

PC HELP!
Präsentation mit dem PC
(**4368**-6) Von M. Hofmann, 96 S., 47 zweifarbige screenshots, kartoniert. ●●

PC HELP!
CONFIG. SYS. und AUTOEXEC. BAT
Optimale Systemkonfiguration
(**4338**-4) Von A. Görgens, 64 S., ca. 50 s/w-Abbildungen und Grafiken, kartoniert. ●●

PC HELP!
DOS-Kommandos richtig nutzen
(**4339**-2) Von A. Görgens, 64 S., ca. 50 s/w-Abbildungen und Grafiken, kartoniert. ●●

PC HELP!
Die ersten Schritte mit dem PC
(**4344**-9) Von P. Vogel, H. Ebsen, 64 S., ca. 50 s/w-Abb. und Grafiken, kartoniert. ●●

PC HELP!
Mehr Speicher unter DOS nutzen
(**4345**-7) Von K. O. Kuhl, 64 S., ca. 50 s/w-Abbildungen und Grafiken, kartoniert. ●●

PC HELP!
Viren erkennen und beseitigen
(**4346**-5) Von M. Hofmann, 64 S., ca. 50 s/w-Abbildungen und Grafiken, kartoniert. ●●

DTP-Lexikon für die Praxis
(**4373**-2) 136 S., 55 s/w-Fotos, kart. ●●●

Gestalten mit Pagemaker für Windows
(**4375**-9) Von M. Hofmann, R. Titius, 116 S., 53 zweifbg. screenshots, kartoniert. ●●

Präsentationsprogramme richtig nutzen
(**4376**-7) Von M. Hofmann, 96 S., 60 zweifarbige screenshots, kartoniert. ●●

Datenaustausch 1
(**4378**-3) Von M. Hofmann, 104 Seiten, 63 zweifarbig. screenshots, kartoniert. ●●

Datenaustausch 2
(**4379**-1) Von M. Hofmann, 96 S., 34 zweifarbige screenshots, kartoniert. ●●

Update
MS-DOS 6.0
Beilage: Kurzreferenz
(**4385**-6) Von M. Hofmann, 136 S., 55 s/w-Fotos, kartoniert. ●●●

PC-Pannen selbst beheben
Hardware · Software
(**4383**-X) Von M. Hofmann, 144 S., kart. ●●●

Windows für Workgroups
(**4381**-3) Von P. Vogel, 80 S., 40 Screenshots, kartoniert. ●●

Essen und Trinken

Rezepte für 1 Person
(**1294**-2) Hrsg. M. Sauerborn, 64 S., 75 Farbfotos, kartoniert. ●

Schnell und individuell
Die raffinierte Single-Küche
(**4266**-3) Von F. Faist, 160 S., 151 Farbfotos, Pappband. ●●●●

Frischer Fang aus Fluß und Meer
Fisch
(**0964**-X) Von L. Grieser, 48 S., 52 Farbfotos, Pappband. ●●

Fischgerichte
(**1448**-1) Hrsg.: S. Koch, 64 S., ca. 50 Farbfotos, kartoniert. ●

Zart und edel
Lachs
(**1403**-1) Von H. Imhof, 64 S., 49 Farbfotos, Pappband. ●●

Geflügelgerichte
(**1348**-5) Hrsg. E. Meyer zu Stieghorst, 64 S., 71 Farbfotos, kartoniert. ●

Gaumenfreuden Tag für Tag
Pfannengerichte
(**1007**-9) Von S. Fabke, 64 S., 54 Farbfotos, Pappband. ●●

Köstliches für Genießer
Fleischgerichte
(**4699**-5) Von F. Stein, 144 S., ca. 100 Farbfotos, gebunden. ●●●

Schnitzel, Steaks & Co.
(**1417**-1) Von N. Frank, 64 Seiten, 68 Farbfotos, kartoniert. ●

Köstliches aus dem Tontopf
(**1332**-9) Hrsg. S. Kieslich, 64 Seiten, 55 Farbfotos, kartoniert. ●

Suppen und Eintöpfe
(**1449**-X) Hrsg.: S. Koch, 64 S., ca. 50 Farbfotos, kartoniert. ●

Aus eigener Küche
Gute Wurst
(**0948**-8) Von J. Bessel, G. Quaas, 80 Seiten, 8 Farbtafeln, kartoniert. ●

Aus lauter Lust und Liebe
Knoblauch
(**0867**-8) Von L. Reinirkens, 64 S., 45 Farbfotos, Pappband. ●●

Bintje, Irmgard und Sieglinde
Kartoffeln
(**1032**-X) Von S. Fabke, 64 S., 43 Farb- und 1 s/w-Foto, Pappband. ●

Kartoffelgerichte
(**1297**-7) Hrsg. I. Feldhaus, 64 S., 64 Farbfotos, kartoniert. ●

Nudelgerichte
(**1293**-4) Hrsg. E. Fuhrmann, 64 S., 66 Farbfotos, kartoniert. ●

Pasta in Höchstform
Nudeln
(**0884**-8) Von M. Kirsch, 64 S., 62 Farbfotos, Pappband. ●●

Spezialitäten unter knuspriger Decke
Aufläufe
(**0882**-1) Von C. Adam, 48 S., 33 Farbfotos, Pappband. ●●

Aufläufe
(**1295**-0) Hrsg. E. Fuhrmann, 64 S., 62 Farbfotos, kartoniert. ●

Die Krönung der feinen Küche
Saucen
(**0817**-1) Von G. Cavestri, 48 S., 40 Farbfotos, Pappband. ●●

Gemüsegerichte
(**1347**-7) Hrsg. E. Fuhrmann, 64 S., 58 Farbfotos, kartoniert. ●

Gemüseaufläufe
(**1365**-5) Hrsg. E. Fuhrmann, 64 S., 58 Farbfotos, kartoniert. ●

Die schönsten Rezepte für
Frühstück und Brunch
(**1063**-X) Von K. Kruse-Schorling, 80 Seiten, 8 Farbtafeln, kartoniert. ●

Schnelle Küche
Für 2 Personen
(**4718**-5) freundin-Kochstudio, 80 Seiten, 105 Farbf., Pappband. ●●

Kochen auf der richtigen Welle im
Grill-Mikrowellengerät
(**1395**-7) Von T. Peters, 96 S., 79 Farbfotos, kartoniert. ●●

Fritieren
(**1350**-7) Hrsg. I. Teitge, 64 S., 62 Farbf., kart. ●

Schnell auf den Tisch gezaubert
Kochen mit Mikrowellen
(**0818**-X) Von A. Danner, 64 S., 52 Farbfotos, Pappband. ●

Italienische Vorspeisen **Antipasti**
(**1006**-0) Von S. Reiter-Westphal, 64 Seiten, 47 Farbfotos, Pappband. ●●

Mexikanische Küche
(**1439**-2) Von C. Zingerling, 64 S., ca. 50 Farbfotos, kartoniert. ●

Italienische Küche
(**1299**-3) Hrsg. E. Fuhrmann, 64 S., 65 Farbfotos, kartoniert. ●

Schlemmerreise durch die
Italienische Küche
(**4172**-1) Von V. Pifferi, 160 S., 109 Farbfotos, Pappband. ●●●●

Spaghetti, Tagliatelle + Co.
Pasta all'Italiana
(**1004**-4) Von I. Seyric, 64 S., 57 Farbfotos, Pappband. ●●

Pizza
(**1352**-3) Hrsg. M. Sauerborn, 64 S., 72 Farbfotos, kartoniert. ●

Tradition mit Charme
Wiener Spezialitäten
(**1343**-4) Von G. Scolik, 64 S., 46 Farbfotos, Pappband. ●●

Schlemmerreise durch die
Französische Küche
(**4296**-5) Von H. Imhof, 160 S., 147 Farbfotos, 3 s/w-Fotos, Pappband. ●●●●

Schlemmerreise durch die
Spanische Küche
(**4500**-X) Von A. Puente, 160 S., ca. 120 Farbfotos, Pappband. ●●●●

Vom Bosporus zum Ararat
Türkische Spezialitäten
(**1191**-1) Von S. Dogan, 64 S., 44 Farbfotos, Pappband.●●

Indische Küche
(**1404**-X) Von C. Zingerling, 64 S., 64 Farbfotos, kartoniert. ●

Schlemmerreise durch die
Thailändische Küche
(**4722**-3) Von C. Zingerling, 144 Seiten, 164 Farbfotos, Pappband. ●●●●

Köstlich fernöstlich
Asiatische Spezialitäten
(**1286**-1) Von M. Carroll, E. Mognol, 64 S., 49 Farbfotos, Pappband. ●●

Chinesische Küche
(**1289**-6) Hrsg. M. Sauerborn, 64 S., 73 Farbfotos, kartoniert. ●

Schlemmerreise durch die
Chinesische Küche
(**4184**-5) Von K. H. Jen, 160 S., 117 Farbfotos, Pappband. ●●●

Gerichte aus dem
Wok
(**1291**-8) Hrsg. M. Sauerborn, 64 S., 76 Farbfotos, kartoniert. ●

Mit Lust und Liebe **Chinesisch Kochen**
(**4441**-0) Von Ho Fu-Lung, Uli Franz, 176 Seiten, 189 Farbfotos, 29 Zeichnungen, Pappband. ●●●●

Fernöstliche Küche
(**1384**-1) Hrsg. R. Faller, 64 S., 73 Farbfotos, kartoniert. ●

Rezepte für Tisch- und Gartengrill
(**1351**-3) Hrsg. V. Müller, 64 S., 59 Farbfotos, kartoniert.●

Braten auf dem heißen Stein
(**1300**-0) Hrsg. R. Donhauser, 64 S., 56 Farbfotos, kartoniert. ●

Rezepte rund um Raclette und Doppeldecker
(**0420**-6) Von J.W. Hochscheid, 72 S., 8 Farbtafeln, kartoniert. ●

Schlemmen in geselliger Runde
Fleischfondues
(**0966**-6) Von M. Spötter, 64 S., 62 Farbfotos, Pappband. ●●

Fondues und Raclettes
(**4253**-1) Von F. Faist, 160 S., 125 Farbfotos, Pappband. ●●●●

Fondues
(**1298**-5) Hrsg. E. Meyer zu Stieghorst, 64 S., 69 Farbfotos, kartoniert. ●

Rezepte fürs Raclette
(**1290**-X) Hrsg. S. Kieslich, 64 Seiten, 59 Farbfotos, kartoniert. ●

Raclette-Spezialitäten
(**0881**-3) Von F. Faist, 48 S., 33 Farbfotos, Pappband. ●

Knackige Salate
(**1441**-4) Hrsg.: S. Kieslich, 64 S., ca. 50 Farbfotos, kartoniert. ●

Gartenfrisch genießen
Feine Salate
(**4450**-X) Von P. Nikolay, 160 S., 122 Farbfotos, Pappband. ●●●●

Köstliche Salate
zum Verwöhnen
(**0222**-X) Von Chr. Schönherr, 96 S., 8 Farbtafeln, 30 Zeichnungen, kartoniert. ●

Salate
(**1346**-9) Hrsg. E. Furhmann, 64 S., 62 Farbfotos, kartoniert.●

Frisch und leicht als Hauptgericht
Schlemmersalate
(**0934**-8) Von C. Adam, 64 S., 49 Farbfotos, Pappband. ●●

Gesund und vielseitig **Alles mit Joghurt**
täglich selbstgemacht, mit vielen Rezepten
(**0382**-6) Von G. Volz, 64 S., 8 Farbtafeln, kartoniert. ●

Marmeladen, Gelees und Kompotte
(**1442**-2) Hrsg.: F. Stein, 64 S., ca. 50 Farbfotos, kartoniert. ●

Gesunde Ernährung für mein Kind
(**0776**-6) Von M. Bustorf-Hirsch, 112 Seiten, 8 Farbtafeln, 5 s/w-Zeichnungen, kartoniert. ●●

Eßschule
Gesunde Ernährung für Kinder im Grundschulalter
(**1314**-0) Von A. Roßmeier, 80 Seiten, 44 Farbfotos, 50 farbige Vignetten, Pappband. ●●

Lieblingsgerichte für Kinder
Mit Sonderteil: Gesunde Kost für Babys ab 6 Monaten
(**4497**-6) Von G. Righi-Spanfellner, 112 S., 27 Farbzeichnungen, Pappband. ●●●

Das essen Kinder gern
(**1405**-8) Hrsg. S. Faust, 64 S., 80 Farbfotos, kartoniert. ●

Mit Lust und Liebe ...
Vollwertküche für Genießer
(**4412**-4) Von Prof. Dr. C. Leitzmann, H. Million, 256 Seiten, 329 Farbfotos, Pappband. ●●●●

Vegetarisch kochen und genießen
Alle Gerichte für 2 Personen
(**4715**-0) Von Prof. Dr. C. Leitzmann, K. Dittrich, C. u. G. Kurz, 128 S., 132 Farbfotos, Pappband. ●●●●

Das große FALKEN
Vitaminkochbuch
für Genießer
(**4714**-2) Von Prof. Dr. troph. M. Hamm, A. Roßmeier, 208 S., 224 Farbfotos, Pappband. ●●●●

Schmackhafte Vollwertkost ohne tierisches Eiweiß
(**0993**-3) Von M. Bustorf-Hirsch, 96 Seiten, 54 Farbfotos, kartoniert. ●●

Cholesterinarm kochen und genießen
(**4442**-9) Von R. Unsorg, 168 S., 132 Farbfotos, kartoniert. ●●●●

Die aktuelle **Cholesterintabelle**
(**1088**-5) Von Dr. H. Oberritter, 84 Seiten, 12 zweifarbige Grafiken, kartoniert. ●

Die aktuelle Vitamin- und Mineralstofftabelle
Mit Angaben zu den wichtigsten Vitaminen und Mineralstoffen
(**1110**-5) Von Dr. H. Oberritter, 88 Seiten, 1 zweifarbige Grafik, kartoniert. ●

Die aktuelle E-Zusatzstoff-Tabelle
Über 750 Angaben zu Herkunft, Verwendung und möglichen Nebenwirkungen
(**1233**-0) Von T. Pilgram, E.Dahl, 80 Seiten, zweifarbig, kartoniert. ●

Vollwertküche für Diabetiker
Köstlich kochen und backen für die ganze Familie
(**4473**-9) Von Prof. Dr. C. Leitzmann, Prof. Dr. H. Laube, H. Million, 168 S., 172 Farbfotos, 8 Zeichnungen, Pappband. ●●●●

Kochen und backen für Diabetiker
Gesund und schmackhaft für die ganze Familie
(**4467**-4) Von Dr. med. M. Toeller, W. Schumacher, A. Groote, Dr. troph. A. Klischan, 176 S., 182 Farbfotos, Pappband. ●●●●

Die Sojaküche
Gesund und abwechslungsreich essen
(**0553**-9) Von U. Kolster, 80 S., 8 Farbtafeln, kartoniert. ●

Gesund kochen mit Keimen und Sprossen
(**0794**-9) Von M. Bustorf-Hirsch, 96 S., 4 Farbtafeln, 13 s/w-Zeichnungen, kartoniert. ●

Waffeln
Hörnchen, Pfannkuchen und Crêpes.
(**0522**-9) Von C. Stephan, 64 S., 8 Farbtafeln, kartoniert. ●

Waffeln
(**1296**-9) Hrsg. L. Steiger, 64 S., 73 Farbfotos, kartoniert. ●

Fruchtige Pfannkuchen und Crêpes
(**1446**-5) Von S. Fabke, 64 S., ca. 50 Farbfotos, kartoniert. ●

Mehr Freude und Erfolg beim
Brotbacken
(**4148**-9) Von A. und G. Eckert, 160 Seiten, 177 Farbfotos, Pappband. ●●●●

Meine Vollkornbackstube
Brot · Kuchen · Aufläufe. (**0616**-0) Von R. Raffelt, 96 S., 4 Farbtafeln, 12 Zeichnungen, kartoniert. ●

Mit Honig, Nuß und Mandelkern
Weihnachtsplätzchen
(**1287**-X) Von H. Jaacks, 64 S., 48 Farbfotos, Pappband. ●●

Backen ohne Zucker
(**1234**-9) Von H. Erkelenz, 80 S., 8 Farbtafeln, kartoniert. ●

Süße Geheimnisse eiskalt gelüftet
Eis und Sorbets
(**0870**-8) Von H. W. Liebheit, 48 S., 38 Farbfotos, Pappband. ●●

Haltbarmachen in der Öko-Küche
Gesunde Konservierungsmethoden für Obst, Gemüse, Kräuter und Pilze. (**0923**-2) Von M. Bustorf-Hirsch, 120 S., 92 Farbabbildungen, kartoniert. ●●

Komm, koch und back mit mir
Kunterbuntes Kochvergnügen für Kinder.
(**4285**-X) Von S. und H. Theilig, illustriert von B. v. Hayek, 112 S., 45 Farbabbildungen, Pappband. ●●

Lieblingsgerichte für Kinder
Kerngesund und kunterbunt
(**4497**-6) Von G. Righi-Spanfellner, 112 Seiten, 27 Farbzeichnungen, Pappband. ●●●

Lirum, larum, Löffelstiel ...
Kinder kochen mit Knuddel
(**1094**-X) Von U. Bültjer, 80 S., 27 zweifarbige Zeichnungen, kartoniert. ●

Backe, backe Kuchen ...
Kinder backen mit Knuddel
(**1301**-9) Von U. Bültjer, 64 S., 34 Farbfotos, 60 Farbzeichn., kartoniert. ●

Mit Lust und Liebe
Garnieren und Verzieren
Dekoratives zu vielen Anlässen
(**4496**-8) Von M. Müller, E. Pratsch, H. Krieg, 160 Seiten, ca. 100 Farbfotos, Pappband. ●●●●

Mit Lust und Liebe **Kalte Platten & Buffets**
Anrichten und Garnieren
(**4427**-5) Von P. Grotz, 176 S., 228 Farbfotos, Pappband. ●●●●

Köstliches ganz leicht gezaubert
Raffinierte Rezepte rund um den Stabmixer
(**1453**-8) Von U. Kochendörfer, 96 Seiten, 84 Farbfotos, kartoniert. ●●

Garnieren und Verzieren
(**4236**-1) Von R. Biller, 160 S., 329 Farbfotos, 57 Zeichnungen, Pappband. ●●●●

Köstlichkeiten für Gäste und Feste
Kalte Platten
(**4200**-0) Von I. Pfliegner, 160 S., 130 Farbfotos, Pappband. ●●●●

Sandwich, Toasts & Co.
(**1331**-0) Von F. Faist, 64 Seiten, 62 Farbfotos, kartoniert. ●

Quiches, Tartes
und andere pikante Kuchen
(**1407**-4) Hrsg. I. Teitge, 64 S., 70 Farbf., kart. ●

freundin
Snacks
(**4521**-2) Von V. Müller, 80 S., 87 Farbfotos, Pappband.●●●

Kochen und backen mit Käse
(**1451**-1) Hrsg.: F. Stein, 64 S., ca. 50 Farbfotos, kartoniert. ●

Raffiniert kombiniert, schön dekoriert
Käseplatten
(**1192**-X) Von S. Carlsson, 64 S., 57 Farbfotos, Pappband.●●

FALKEN
Festival der schön gedeckten Tische
(**4738**-X) Von A. F. Endress, 204 S., 116 Farbfotos, 83 Farbzeichnungen, Pappbd. ●●●●

Der perfekt gedeckte Tisch
(**1028**-1) Von H. Tapper, 80 S., 161 Farbfotos, 13 Zeichnungen, kartoniert. ●●

Der schön gedeckte Tisch
Vom einfachen Gedeck bis zur Festtafel stimmungsvoll und perfekt arrangiert.
(**4246**-1) Von H. Tapper, 112 S., 206 Farbfotos, 21 s/w-Abbildungen, Pappband. ●●●

Servietten falten
80 Ideen für schön gedeckte Tische
(**1042**-7) Von M. Müller, O. Mikolasek, 80 S., 289 Farbfotos, 50 Zeichnungen, kart. ●●

Phantasievolle Tischdekorationen selber machen
(**0984**-4) Von Y. Thalheim, H. Nadolny, 80 S., 174 Farbfotos, 21 Zeichnungen, kart. ●●

Servietten dekorativ falten
Geschmackvolle Anregungen aus Stoff und Papier. (**0804**-X) Von H. Tapper, 32 Seiten, 134 Farbfotos, Pappband. ●

Weine und Säfte, Liköre und Sekt
selbstgemacht.
(**0702**-7) Von P. Arauner, 232 S., 76 Abb., kartoniert. ●●●

Was Weinfreunde wissen wollen
Fragen und Antworten rund um den Wein
(**1224**-1) Von Prof. Dr. K. Röder, H.-G. Dörr, ca. 224 Seiten, kartoniert. ●●

FALKEN Mixbuch
(**4733**-9) Hrsg. P. Bohrmann, 560 Seiten, 227 Farbfotos, Pappband. ●●●●

Vitamindrinks
(**1408**-2) Von H. Reith, W. Hubert, 64 Seiten, 68 Farbfotos, kartoniert. ●

Köstlich, cremig, sahnig, frisch
Mixen mit Milch
(**1151**-2) Von S. Carlsson, 64 S., 45 Farbfotos, Pappband.●

Milchmixgetränke
(**1450**-3) Von S. Carlsson, 64 S., ca. 50 Farbfotos, kartoniert. ●

Cocktails und Drinks
(**1292**-6) Hrsg. S. Kieslich, 64 S., 70 Farbfotos, kartoniert. ●

Bowlen und Punsche
(**1447**-3) Hrsg.: F. Brandl, 64 S., ca. 50 Farbfotos, kartoniert. ●

Fruchtig, spritzig, eisgekühlt
Mixen ohne Alkohol
(**0935**-6) Von S. Späth, 64 S., 44 Farbfotos, Pappband. ●●

Longdrinks
(**1345**-0) Hrsg. E. Meyer zu Stieghorst, 64 S., 79 Farbfotos, kartoniert. ●

Light Drinks
Mixen mit und ohne Alkohol
(**1222**-5) Von S. Edelberg, Heike Reith, 64 S., 48 Farbfotos, Pappband. ●●

Cocktails
(**4267**-1) Von W. R. Hoffmann, W. Hubert, U. Lottring, 160 S., 164 Farbfotos, 1 s/w-Foto, Pappband. ●●●●

Cocktails und Mixereien
für häusliche Feste und Feiern. (**0075**-8) Von J. Walker, 96 S., 4 Farbtafeln, kartoniert. ●

Das Fitmacher-Kochbuch
(**4698**-7) Von Prof. Dr. troph. M. Hamm, 112 S., ca. 100 Farbfotos, gebunden. ●●●

Schlank und gesund nach Dr. Hay
Schnelle Trennkostküche
(**4746**-0) Von H. Harper, 80 S., ca. 80 Farbfotos, kartoniert. ●●

Schlank werden nach Dr. Hay **Trennkost**
Die bewährten Vollwert-Rezepte von Ursula Summ. (**4298**-1) Von U. Summ, 96 Seiten, 54 Farbfotos, 1 Zeichnung, kartoniert. ●●

Das große Buch der Trennkost
Neue Rezepte von Ursula Summ
(**4498**-4) Von U. Summ, 144 S., ca. 100 Farbfotos, Pappband. ●●●

Gesund leben nach Dr. Hay
Cholesterinarme Trennkost
Neue Vollwert-Rezepte von Ursula Summ
(**4475**-5) Von U. Summ, 96 Seiten, 52 Farbfotos, kartoniert. ●●

Die neue Trennkost
(**4685**-5) Von U. Summ, 96 Seiten, 71 Farbfotos, kartoniert. ●●●

Das kleine 1 x 1 der Trennkost
(**1428**-7) Von S. Carlsson, 64 S., ca. 50 Farbfotos, kartoniert. ●

Schlank nach Maß
mit der Diät-Computerwaage
(**1064**-8) Von K. Alisch, 104 S., 8 Farbtafeln, kartoniert. ●

Gesundes Essen für Berufstätige
Die 4-Wochen-Vollwertkur (**1065**-6) Von M. Weber, ca. 80 S., 8 Farbtafeln, kart. ●

Garten

FALKEN Gartenjahr
(**4730**-4) Von K. Greiner, A. Weber, P. Michaeli-Achmühle, 320 Seiten, 380 Farbabbildungen, Pappband. ●●●●

Garten heute
Der moderne Ratgeber · Über 1000 Farbbilder. (**4283**-3) Von H. Jantra, 384 S., über 1000 Farbabbildungen, Pappband. ●●●●

Helmut Jantras Gartenbuch
Obst · Gemüse · Blumen
(**4522**-0) Von H. Jantra, 200 S., 395 Farbfotos, 123 Farbzeichnungen, 25 Tabellen, Pappband. ●●

1000 ganz bewährte Garten-Tips
(**4453**-4) Von H. Jantra, 320 S., 288 zweifbg. und 62 s/w-Zeichn., , Pappband. ●●●

Obst, Gemüse, Blumen, Gras
Gärtnern macht den Kindern Spaß
(**4517**-4) Von U. Krüger, 96 S., 85 Farbfotos, 180 Farbzeichznungen, Pappband. ●●

Rosen
(**4692**-8) Von H. Steinhauer, ca. 144 S., zahlr. Farbabbildungen Pappband. ●●●●●

Rosen
Auswahl · Pflege · Gestaltung
(**1183**-0) Von H. Jantra, 120 S., 200 Farbfotos, 20 Farbzeichnungen, 8 Bepflanzungspläne, kartoniert. ●●

Bunte Pracht der Stauden
Auswahl · Pflege · Gestaltung
(**1376**-0) Von H. Jantra, 112 S., 167 Farbabbildungen, kartoniert. ●●●

Erfolgstips für den Obstgarten
Gesunde Früchte durch richtige Sortenwahl und Pflege
(**0827**-9) Von F. Mühl, 184 S., 16 Farbtafeln, 33 Zeichnungen, kartoniert. ●●

Erfolgstips für den Gemüsegarten
Mit naturgemäßem Anbau zu höherem Ertrag. (**0674**-8) Von F. Mühl, 80 Seiten, 30 s/w-Fotos, 4 Zeichnungen, kartoniert. ●●

Obstgehölze sachgemäß schneiden
(**1127**-X) Von P. G. Wilhelm, 136 Seiten, 8 s/w-Abb., 367 Zeichnungen, kart.●●

Kompost im Hausgarten
herstellen und anwenden
(**1258**-6) Von H. Abels, J. Jöstingmeier, ca. 30 zweifarbige Zeichnungen, kart. ●

Der naturgemäße Zier- und Wohngarten
Anlegen · Gestalten · Pflegen
(**0748**-5) Von I. Gabriel, 128 S., 72 Farbfotos, 46 Farbzeichnungen, kartoniert. ●●

Natürlich gärtnern unter Glas und Folie
Anbauen und ernten rund ums Jahr
(**0722**-1) Von I. Gabriel, 128 S., 62 Farbfotos, 45 Farbzeichnungen, kartoniert. ●●

Nützliche Tiere im Garten
(**1472**-4) Von I. Polaschek, ca. 112 Seiten, ca. 120 Farbf., ca. 10 Farbzeichn., kartoniert. ●●

Schneckenbekämpfung
giftfrei und naturgemäß
(**1378**-7) Von B. Meyer, Y. Thalheim, 64 S., 25 s/w-Zeichnungen, 8 Farbtafeln, kart. ●●

Dekorative Kübelpflanzen
Auswahl und Plfege
(**1074**-5) Von H. Jantra, 112 S., 180 Farbfotos, 35 Farbzeichnungen, kartoniert. ●●

Blütenpracht auf Balkon und Terrasse
(**0928**-3) Von M. Haberer, 88 S., 139 Farbfotos, kartoniert. ●●

Moderne Gartengestaltung
(**1255**-1) Von K. Greiner, A. Weber, 128 S., mit Rasterbogen und Planelementen zum Ausschneiden, ca. 120 Farbfotos, ca. 20 vierfarbige Pläne, kartoniert. ●●●

Gestaltungsideen für
Schöne Gärten
(**4482**-8) Von H. Jantra, 168 S., 309 Farbfotos, 3 s/w-Fotos, , Pappband. ●●●●●

Der pflegeleichte Hausgarten
(**1170**-9) Von H. Jantra, 112 S., vierfarbige Abbildungen, kartoniert. ●●

Schöne Kräutergärten
(**1256**-X) Von H. Jantra, 112 S., vierfarbige Abbildungen, kartoniert. ●●

Kleingärten
Planen · Anlegen · Pflegen
(**1015**-X) Von H. Jantra, 88 S., 123 Farbfotos, 1 s/w-Foto, 14 Farbzeichnungen, , kart. ●●

Reihenhausgärten
Planen · Anlegen · Pflegen
(**1016**-8) Von H. Jantra, 104 S., 134 Farbfotos, 45 Farbzeichnungen, kartoniert. ●●

Kletterpflanzen
Mit Sonderteil Dachbegrünung
(**4546**-8) Von U. Mehl, K. Werk, 128 S., ca. 150 Farbfotos, farbige und s/w-Zeichnungen, Pappband. ●●●●●

Steingärten Wirkungsvoll gestalten und sachgerecht pflegen
(**4452**-6) Von A. Throll-Keller, 128 Seiten, 203 Farbfotos, 56 Farbzeichnungen, Pappband. ●●●●

Gartenteiche, Tümpel und Weiher
naturnah anlegen und pflegen
(**1073**-7) Von Dr. F. Liedl, H. Goos, 80 Seiten, 87 Farbfotos, 39 Farbzeichnungen, kart. ●●

Wasser im Garten
Von der Vogeltränke zum Naturteich · Natürliche Lebensräume selbst gestalten.
(**4230**-2) Von H. Hendel, P. Keßeler, 240 S., 315 Farbabb., 11 s/w-Fotos, Pappband. ●●●●●

Pflanzen und Tiere für den Gartenteich
(**1171**-7) Von W. Costa, 128 S., 169 Farbfotos, 40 Farbzeichnungen, 8 Bepflanzungspläne, kartoniert. ●●

Gestaltungsideen für den Wohngarten
Sitzplätze, Terrassen, Höfe und andere grüne Räume
(**4751**-7) Von H. Jantra, ca. 120 Seiten, ca. 100 Farbfotos und -zeichnungen, gebunden. ●●●●

Wintergärten
Das Erlebnis, mit der Natur zu wohnen. Planen, Bauen und Gestalten.
(**4256**-6) Von LOG ID, 136 S., 130 Farbfotos, 107 Zeichnungen, Pappband. ●●●●●

Rund ums Jahr erfolgreich gärtnern
Gewächshäuser
planen · bauen · einrichten · nutzen
(**4408**-9) Von Dr. G. Schoser, J. Wolff, 232 S., 368 Farbabb., 5 s/w-Fotos, Pappbd. ●●●●●

Das moderne Handbuch **Zimmerpflanzen**
(**4416**-X) Von H. Jantra, 304 S., 766 Farbfotos, 64 Farb- und 19 s/w-Zeichnungen, Pappband. ●●●●

365 Erfolgstips für schöne Zimmerpflanzen
(**0893**-7) Von H. Jantra, 144 S., 215 Farbfotos, kartoniert. ●●

Dekorative Blattpflanzen
Auswahl und Pflege
(**1128**-8) Von H. Jantra, 128 S., 198 Farbfotos, 20 Farbzeichnungen, kartoniert. ●●

Arbeitskalender für Zimmergärtner
(**1473**-2) Von H. Jantra, 112 Seiten, ca. 120 Farbfotos, kartoniert. ●●

Prof. Stelzers grüne Sprechstunde
Gesunde Zimmerpflanzen
Krankheiten erkennen und behandeln. Mit neuem Diagnosesystem.
(**4274**-4) Von Prof. Dr. G. Stelzer, 192 Seiten, 410 Farbfotos, 10 s/w-Zeichnungen, Pappband. ●●●●

Hydrokultur
Pflanzen ohne Erde – mühelos gepflegt.
(**0944**-5) Von H.-A. Rotter, 144 S., 167 Farbfotos, 13 Farbzeichnungen, kartoniert. ●●

Gesunde Pflanzen in
Hydrokultur
(**1257**-8) Von H.-A. Rotter, 80 Seiten, ca. 60 s/w-Zeichnungen, 8 Farbtafeln, kartoniert. ●

Bonsai Japanische Miniaturbäume und Miniaturlandschaften. Anzucht, Gestaltung und Pflege.
(**4091**-1) Von B. Lesniewicz, 160 S., 106 Farbfotos, 46 s/w-Fotos, 115 Zeichnungen, gebunden. ●●●●●

Kakteen
Auswahl · Pflege · Vermehrung
(**1429**-5) Von G. Andersohn, ca. 120 S., zahlr. Farbabbildungen, kartoniert. ●●●

Tiere

Grzimek Juniors **BUNTE TIERWELT**
(**4295**-7) Von Chr. Grzimek, 208 S., 308 Farbfotos, Pappband. ●●●●

Hunde
Rassen · Ausbildung · Pflege · Zucht
(**4118**-7) Von H. Bielfeld, 192 S., 222 Farb- und 73 s/w-Abb., Pappband. ●●●●

Das neue Hundebuch
Rassen · Aufzucht · Pflege (**0009**-X) Von W. Busack, überarbeitet von Dr. med. vet. A. H. Hacker und H. Bielfeld, 112 S., 8 Farbtafeln, 27 s/w-Fotos, 6 Zeichnungen, kartoniert. ●

Alles über Dackel, Teckel und Dachshunde
(**1079**-6) Von M. Wein-Gysae, 80 Seiten, 46 Farbfotos, 2 zweifarbige Zeichnungen, kartoniert. ●●

Hundeausbildung
Verhalten · Gehorsam · Ausbildung
(**0346**-3) Von R. Menzel, 88 S., 26 Fotos, kartoniert. ●

Grundausbildung für Gebrauchshunde
Schäferhund, Boxer, Rottweiler, Dobermann, Riesenschnauzer, Airedaleterrier, Hovawart und Bouvier.
(**0801**-5) Von M. Schmidt und W. Koch. 104 S., 8 Farbtafeln, 51 s/w-Fotos, 5 s/w-Zeichnungen, kartoniert. ●●

Der Hund in der Familie
(**1014**-1) Von J. Werner, 128 S., 106 Farbfotos, kartoniert. ●●

Der Deutsche Schäferhund
(**1091**-5) Von U. Förster, 112 S., 47 Farbzeichnungen, 2 s/w-Fotos, kartoniert. ●●

Der Deutsche Schäferhund
Aufzucht · Pflege und Ausbildung
(**0073**-1) Von A. Hacker, 104 S., 56 Abb., kart. ●

Alles über junge Hunde
(**0863**-5) Von Dr. med. vet. E. M. Bartenschlager, 64 S., 49 Farbfotos, 6 Zeichnungen, kartoniert. ●●

Richtige Hundeernährung
(**0811**-2) Von Dr. med. vet. E. M. Bartenschlager, 80 S., 51 Farbf., 4 Farbzeichn, kart. ●●

Hundekrankheiten
(**1077**-X) Von Dr. med. vet. R. Spangenberg, 96 S., 44 Farb- und 1 s/w-Foto, 22 Farbzeichnungen, kartoniert. ●●

Von Ajax bis Zamperl
Die beliebtesten Hunde-Namen
(**1174**-1) Von H.-J. Schließke, 96 Seiten, kart. ●

Die Katze in der Familie
(**1076**-1) Von U. Birr, 136 S., 112 Farbf., kart. ●●

Katzen
Rassen · Verhalten · Pflege · Zucht
(**4158**-6) Von B. Gerber, 176 S., 294 Farb- und 88 s/w-Fotos, Pappband. ●●●●

Das neue Katzenbuch
Rassen · Aufzucht · Pflege.
(**0427**-3) Von B. Eilert-Overbeck, 120 Seiten, 14 Farbfotos, 26 s/w-Fotos, kartoniert. ●

Katzenkrankheiten
erkennen und behandeln
(**1078**-8) Von Dr. med. vet. R. Spangenberg, 104 S., 40 Farbfotos und 11 Farbzeichnungen, kartoniert. ●●

Junge Katzen
(**0862**-7) Von Dr. med. vet. E. M. Bartenschlager, 72 S., 40 Farbfotos, 4 Farbzeichnungen, kartoniert. ●●

Pferde
(**4186**-1) Von H. Werner, 176 S., 196 Farb- und 50 s/w-Fotos, 100 Zeichnungen, Pappband. ●●●●

Reiten auf Gangpferden
Isländer, Pasos, Saddlehorses und andere Freizeitpferde
(**4716**-9) Von Dr. med. vet. H. Jung, ca. 112 S., zahlreiche Abbildungen, kartoniert. ●●●

Reiten im Bild
(**0415**-X) Von H. Werner, 128 S., 142 Farbfoyos, 107 Farbzeichnungen, kartoniert. ●●

Der Hobby-Imker
(**0978**-X) Von Dr. R. F. A. Moritz, 144 S., 106 zweifarbige Zeichnungen, kart. ●●

Geflügelhaltung als Hobby
(**0749**-3) Von M. Baumeister, H. Meyer, 184 S., 8 Farbtafeln, 47 s/w-Fotos, 15 zweifarbige Zeichnungen, kartoniert. ●●●

Sittiche und kleine Papageien
(**0864**-3) Von Dr. med. vet. E. M. Bartenschlager, 88 S., 84 Farbfotos, 9 Zeichnungen, kartoniert. ●●

Alles über Großsittiche
(**1320**-5) Von H. Bielfeld, 88 S., 88 Farbfotos, 3 Farbzeichnungen, kartoniert. ●●

Alles über Wellensittiche
(**1129**-6) Von H. Bielfeld, 64 S., 53 Farbfotos, 3 Zeichnungen, kartoniert. ●●

Alles über Kanarienvögel
(**0901**-1) Von H. Schnoor, 64 S., 58 Farbfotos und Zeichnungen, kartoniert. ●●

Nymphensittiche
Auswahl · Haltung · Pflege
(**1474**-0) Von F. Moll, ca. 64 Seiten, durchgehend vierfarbig, kartoniert. ●●

Beos
Haltung · Pflege · Zucht
(1475-9) Von M. Wagner, ca. 64 Seiten, durchgehend vierfarbig, kartoniert. ●●

Elternlose Jungvögel
Erste Hilfe · Aufzucht · Auswilderung
(**1319**-1) Von I. Polaschek, 80 S., 80 Farbfotos, 5 Farbzeichnungen, kartoniert. ●●

Diskusfische
Arten · Haltung · Pflege
(**1432**-5) Von H. Hirsch, 64 Seiten, 43 Farbfotos, kartoniert. ●●

Die Tiersprechstunde
Gesunde Fische im Süßwasseraquarium
(**1013**-3) Von H. J. Mayland, 96 S., 73 Farbfotos, 10 Zeichnungen, kartoniert. ●●

Alles über Zwerg- und Goldhamster
(**1012**-5) Von M. Mettler, 96 S., 96 Farbfotos, kartoniert. ●●

Alles über Chinchillas und Degus
(**1130**-X) Von M. Mettler, 96 S., 80 Farbfotos, 3 Zeichnungen, kartoniert. ●●

Alles über Meerschweinchen
(**0809**-0) Von Dr. med. vet. E. M. Bartenschlager, 72 S., 43 Farbfotos, 11 Farbzeichnungen, kartoniert. ●●

Alles über Zwergkaninchen
(**1075**-3) Von M. Mettler,. 64 S., 52 Farbfotos, kartoniert. ●●

Alles über Rennmäuse
(**1318**-3) Von M. Mettler, 80 S., 74 Vignetten, kartoniert. ●●

Sport und Fitneß

Neue Lehrmethoden der Judo-Praxis
(**0424**-9) Von P. Herrmann, 223 S., 475 Abb., kartoniert. ●●

Judo perfekt 1
(**1249**-7) Von K. Fuchs, 128 S., kartoniert. ●●

Judo perfekt 2
Wettkampftechniken im Stand
(**1461**-9) Von K. Fuchs, ca. 144Seiten, kartoniert. ●●

Fußwürfe
für Judo, Karate und Selbstverteidigung.
(**0439**-7) Von H. Nishioka, übers. von H. J. Heese, 96 S., 260 Abb., kartoniert. ●●

Karate 1
zur Selbstverteidigung
(**1312**-4) Von M. Nakayama, 96 Seiten, 315 s/w-Fotos, 5 Zeichn., kartoniert. ●●

Karate 2
zur Selbstverteidigung
(**1362**-0) Von M. Nakayama, 96 Seiten, 245 s/w-Fotos, kartoniert. ●●

Nakayamas Karate perfekt 1
Einführung.
(**0487**-7) Von M. Nakayama, 136 Seiten, 605 s/w-Fotos, kartoniert. ●●

Nakayamas Karate perfekt 2
Grundtechniken.
(**0512**-1) Von M. Nakayama, 136 Seiten, 354 s/w-Fotos, 53 Zeichnungen, kart. ●●

Nakayamas Karate perfekt 3
Kumite 1: Kampfübungen.
(**0538**-5) Von M. Nakayama, 128 Seiten, 424 s/w-Fotos, kartoniert. ●●

Nakayamas Karate perfekt 4
Kumite 2: Kampfübungen.
(**0547**-4) Von M. Nakayama, 128 Seiten, 394 s/w-Fotos, kartoniert. ●●

Nakayamas Karate perfekt 5
Kata 1: Heian, Tekki.
(**0571**-7) Von M. Nakayama, 144 Seiten, 1229 s/w-Fotos, kartoniert. ●●

Nakayamas Karate perfekt 6
Kata 2: Bassai-Dai, Kanku-Dai.
(**0600**-4) Von M. Nakayama, 144 Seiten, 1300 s/w-Fotos, 107 Zeichnungen, kart. ●●

Nakayamas Karate perfekt 7
Kata 3: Jitte, Hangetsu, Empi.
(**0618**-7) Von M. Nakayama, 144 Seiten, 1988 s/w-Fotos, 105 Zeichnungen, kart. ●●

Nakayamas Karate perfekt 8
Gankaku, Jion.
(**0650**-0) Von M. Nakayama, 144 Seiten, 1174 s/w-Fotos, 99 Zeichnungen, kart. ●●

Karate
(**2308**-1) Von A. Pflüger, 96 S., 134 Farbfotos, 4 s/w-Zeichnungen, kartoniert. ●●

Bo-Karate
Hanbo-Jitsu – die Techniken des Stockkampfes.
(**0447**-8) Von G. Stiebler, 176 S., 424 s/w-Fotos, 38 Zeichnungen, kartoniert. ●●

Karate 1
Einführung · Grundtechniken.
(**0227**-0) Von A. Pflüger, 144 S., 195 s/w-Fotos, 120 Zeichnungen, kartoniert. ●

Karate 2
Kombinationstechniken · Katas.
(**0239**-4) Von A. Pflüger, 176 S., 452 s/w-Fotos und Zeichnungen, kartoniert. ●●

Karate Kata 1
Heian 1–5, Tekki 1, Bassai-Dai.
(**0683**-7) Von W.-D. Wichmann, 164 Seiten, 703 s/w-Fotos, kartoniert. ●●

Karate Kata 2
Jion, Empi, Kanku-Dai, Hangetsu.
(**0723**-X) Von W.-D. Wichmann, 140 Seiten, 661 s/w-Fotos, 4 Zeichnungen, kart. ●●

Karate Kata 3
Bassai Sho, Kanku Sho, Nijushiho, Sochin.
(**1120**-2) Von W.-D. Wichmann, 144 Seiten, 598 s/w-Fotos, 4 Grafiken, kart. ●●

Dragon – der Drache
Die Bruce-Lee-Story
(**1415**-5) Von L. Lee, 192 S., 257 s/w-Fotos, kartoniert. ●●●

Bruce Lees Kampfstil 1
Grundtechniken
(**0473**-7) Von B. Lee, M. Uyehara, 109 Seiten, 220 Abbildungen, kartoniert. ●

Bruce Lees Kampfstil 2
Selbstverteidigungs-Techniken
(**0486**-9) Von B. Lee, M. Uyehara, 128 Seiten, 310 Abb., kartoniert. ●

Bruce Lees Kampfstil 3
Trainingslehre
(**0503**-2) Von B. Lee, M. Uyehara, 112 Seiten, 246 Abbildungen, kartoniert. ●

Bruce Lees Kampfstil 4
Kampftechniken
(**0532**-7) Von B. Lee, M. Uyehara, 104 Seiten, 211 Abbildungen, kartoniert. ●

Bruce Lee Kung-Fu
zur Selbstverteidigung
(**1399**-X) Von B. Lee, 104 Seiten, 120 s/w-Abbildungen, kartoniert. ●●

Chuck Norris
Meine Karatetechnik
Erfolgreich in Angriff und Abwehr
(**1460**-0) Von C. Norris, 128 Seiten, kartoniert. ●

Shaolin Kung-Fu 1
Grundlagen chinesischer Kampfkunst
(**1363**-9) Von C. D. Yao, R. Fassi, 124 Seiten, 207 s/w-Fotos, 30 s/w-Zeichn., kart. ●●●

Shaolin Kung-Fu 2
Kampftechniken für Angriff und Abwehr
(**1416**-3) Von C. D. Yao, R. Fassi, 144 Seiten, 581 s/w-Abb., kartoniert. ●●

Kung-Fu 1
Legende · Philosophie · Grundtechniken
(**0891**-0) Von Chr. Yim, 152 S., 401 s/w-Fotos, 2 s/w-Zeichnungen, kartoniert. ●●

Kung-Fu und Thai-Chi
Grundlagen und Bewegungsabläufe
(**0367**-6) Von B. Tegner, 182 Seiten, 370 s/w-Fotos, kartoniert. ●●

Kung Fu
Theorie und Praxis klassischer und moderner Stile
(**0376**-5) Von M. Pabst, 160 Seiten, 330 Abbildungen, kartoniert. ●●

Bruce Lees Jeet Kune Do
(**0440**-0) Von B. Lee, 192 S., mit 105 eigenhändigen Zeichnungen von B. Lee, kartoniert. ●●●

Shaolin-Kempo – Kung-Fu
Chinesisches Karate im Drachenstil.
(**0395**-1) Von R. Czerni, K. Konrad, 246 S., 723 Abbildungen, kartoniert. ●●

Kickboxen
Fitneßtraining und Wettkampfsport.
(**0795**-7) Von G. Lemmens, 96 S., 208 s/w-Fotos, 23 Zeichnungen, kartoniert. ●●

Ninja 1
Die Lehre der Schattenkämpfer.
(**0758**-2) Von S. K. Hayes, übers. von J. Schmit, 144 Seiten, 137 s/w-Fotos, kartoniert. ●●

Ninja 2
Die Wege zum Shoshin.
(**0763**-9) Von S. K. Hayes, übers. von J. Schmit, 160 S., 309 s/w-Fotos, 2 Zeichnungen, kartoniert. ●●

Ninja 3
Der Pfad des Togakure-Kämpfers.
(**0764**-7) Von S. K. Hayes, übers. von J. Schmit, 144 S., 197 s/w-Fotos, 2 Zeichnungen, kartoniert. ●●

Ninja 4
Das Vermächtnis der Schattenkämpfer.
(**0807**-4) Von S. K. Hayes, übers. von J. Schmit, 196 Seiten, 466 s/w-Fotos, kartoniert. ●●

Taekwondo perfekt 1
Die Formenschule bis zum Blaugurt.
(**0890**-2) Von K. Gil, Kim Chul-Hwan, 176 Seiten, 439 s/w-Fotos, 107 Zeichnungen, kartoniert. ●●

Taekwondo perfekt 2
Die Formenschule vom Blau- bis zum Schwarzgurt.
(**0976**-3) Von K. Gil, K. Chul-Hwan, 192 Seiten, 461 s/w-Fotos, 112 Zeichnungen, kartoniert. ●●

Taekwondo perfekt 3
(**1068**-0) Von K. Gil, K. Chul-Hwan, 200 S., 429 s/w-Fotos, kartoniert. ●●●

Taekwondo perfekt 4
(**1250**-0) Von K. Gil, 160 S., zahlr. s/w-Fotos und Schrittdiagramme, 17 Übungstafeln zum Herausnehmen, kart. ●●●

Ju-Jutsu 1
Grundtechniken · Moderne Selbstverteidigung.
(**0276**-9) Von W. Heim, F. J. Gresch, 164 S., 450 s/w-Fotos, 8 Zeichn., kartoniert. ●●

Ju-Jutsu 2
für Fortgeschrittene und Meister.
(**0378**-1) Von W. Heim, F. J. Gresch, 160 S., 798 s/w-Fotos, kartoniert. ●●

Ju-Jutsu 3
Spezial-, Gegen- und Weiterführungs-Techniken · Stockkampfkunst.
(**0485**-0) Von W. Heim, F. J. Gresch, 200 S., über 600 s/w-Fotos, kartoniert. ●●

Aikido
Lehren und Techniken des harmonischen Weges.
(**0537**-7) Von R. Brand, 280 Seiten, 697 Abbildungen, kartoniert. ●●

Hap Ki Do
Koreanische Selbstverteidigung nach dem Lehrsystem des Großmeisters.
(**0379**-X) Von Kim Sou Bong, 112 Seiten, 152 Abbildungen, kartoniert. ●●

Dynamische Tritte
Grundlagen für den Zweikampf.
(**0438**-9) Von C. Lee, 96 S., 398 s/w-Fotos, 10 Zeichnungen, kartoniert. ●●

Super-Tritte
(**1248**-9) Von W. Wallace, 136 S., kart. ●●

Selbstverteidigung
Abwehrtechniken für Sie und Ihn.
(**0853**-8) Von E. Deser, 96 S., 259 s/w-Fotos, kartoniert. ●

Die Faszination athletischer Körper
Bodybuilding
mit Weltmeister Ralf Möller.
(**4281**-7) Von R. Möller, 128 Seiten, 169 Farbfotos, 14 s/w-Fotos, 1 Farbzeichnung, Pappband. ●●●●

Ladyfitneß
Das neue Körperbewußtsein der Frau
Bodyshaping · Körperpflege · Ernährung · Entspannung
(**4433**-X) Von Prof. Dr. S. Starischka, B. Grabis, D. von Cramm, G. W. Kienitz, 128 S., 227 Farbfotos, Pappband. ●●●●

Bodybuilding für Frauen
Wege zu Ihrer Idealfigur
(**0661**-6) Von H. Schulz, 112 S., 84 s/w-Fotos, 4 Zeichnungen, kartoniert. ●

Bodybuilding
Anleitung zum Muskel- und Konditionstraining für sie und ihn
(**0604**-7) Von R. Smolana, 160 S., 171 s/w-Fotos, kartoniert. ●●

Bodybuilding
(**2314**-6) Von L. Spitz, 112 S., 203 Farbabbildungen, 10 Tabellen. ●●

Leistungsfähiger durch Krafttraining
Eine Anleitung für Fitness-Sportler, Trainer und Athleten.
(**0617**-9) Von W. Kieser, 96 S., 20 s/w-Fotos, 62 Zeichnungen, kartoniert. ●

Krafttraining
Wirbelsäulengerechte Übungen an und mit Geräten
(**1309**-4) Von A. Balk, 48 S., 8 Bildtafeln, Spiralbindung. ●●●

Muskeltraining mit Hanteln
Leistungssteigerung für Sport und Fitneß
(**0676**-4) Von H. Schulz, 104 S., 92 s/w-Fotos, 2 Zeichnungen, kartoniert. ●

Ausdauertraining
Einführung und Grundtechniken
(**1396**-5) Von G. Eyting, 32 S., 41 Farbfotos, 21 Farbzeichn., kartoniert. ●●●

Hanteltraining zu Hause
(**0800**-7) Von W. Kieser, 80 S., 71 s/w-Fotos, 4 Zeichnungen, kartoniert. ●

Optimale Ernährung
für Krafttraining und Bodybuilding.
(**0912**-7) Von B. Dahmen, 88 S., 8 Farbtafeln, 8 Zeichnungen, kartoniert. ●●

Aufwärmen
Übungen und Programme für Sport und Spiel
(**1311**-6) Von Dr. H. Wolff, 40 S., 8 Bildtafeln, Spiralbindung. ●●●

Fitneßtraining
Empfohlen vom Deutschen Sportbund
(**1245**-4) Von Marianne Schreiber, 32 Seiten, Spiralbindung mit Ausklapptafeln. ●●

Wirbelsäulengymnastik
Empfohlen vom Deutschen Sportbund
(**1246**-2) Von L. Keller, 40 Seiten, Spiralbindung mit Ausklapptafeln. ●●●

Aerobics
Low Impact, High-Impact, Step-Aerobic
(**1421**-X) Von M. Freytag-Baumgartner, 44 S., 3 Farbtafeln, 84 Farbfotos, 16 s/w-Fotos, Spiralbindung, kartoniert. ●●●

Stretching
Empfohlen vom Deutschen Sportbund
(**1247**-0) Von A. Balk, 40 Seiten, Spiralbindung mit Ausklapptafeln. ●●

Isometrisches Training
Übungen für Muskelkraft und Entspannung.
(**0529**-6) Von L. M. Kirsch, 104 S., 150 s/w-Fotos, kartoniert. ●●

Stretching
Mit Dehnungsgymnastik zu Entspannung, Geschmeidigkeit und Wohlbefinden.
(**0717**-5) Von H. Schulz, 80 S., 90 s/w-Fotos, kartoniert. ●

Stretching
(**2304**-9) Von B. Kurz, 96 S., 255 Farbfotos, kartoniert. ●●

Gesund und fit durch Gymnastik
(**0366**-8) Von H. Pilss-Samek, 88 Seiten, 130 Abbildungen, kartoniert. ●

Funktionelles Körpertraining
Grundlagen und Bewegungsprogramme
(**1367**-1) Von A. Balk, 40 S., 100 Farbfotos, kartoniert. ●●●

Spielerisch zur Kondition
Über 100 Trainingsspiele zur Verbesserung von Ausdauer, Schnelligkeit, Kraft und Beweglichkeit
(**1214**-4) Von U. Stumpp, 120 S., 30 Grafiken, kartoniert. ●●●

AOK-Videothek
Top-Form Gymnastik
Ein Bewegungsprogramm für pfundige Leute
(**6144**-7) VHS, ca. 30 Minuten, in Farbe. ●●●●*

Fit und frisch
Gymnastik für die ganze Familie
(**6501**-9) Von G. Sieber, 104 S., 306 Farbfotos, 5 Farbzeichnungen, kart., mit Audiokassette, Laufzeit 30 Min. ●●●

Sportjahr 93
Rekorde · Siege · Schicksale · Ergebnisse
Mit Sonderteil Leichtathletik-WM
(**4690**-1) 176 Seiten, 373 Farbfotos, Pappband. ●●●

Freeclimbing
Technik und Training
(**1251**-9) Von T. Strobl, 144 Seiten, durchgehend vierfarbig, kartoniert. ●●●

Fechten
Florett · Degen · Säbel.
(**0449**-4) Von E. Beck, 88 Seiten, 185 Fotos, 10 Zeichnungen, kartoniert. ●●

SportRegeln Volleyball
(**1368**-X) 88 S., 5 Farbtafeln, 19 s/w-Fotos, kartoniert. ●●

Fußball
(**2309**-X) Von H. Obermann, P. Walz, 112 Seiten, 47 Farbfotos, 18 Farb- und 25 s/w-Zeichnungen, kartoniert. ●●

Sepp Maier
Super-Torwart-Training
(**4451**-8) Von S. Maier, 168 S., 30 Farb- und 34 s/w-Fotos, 236 zweifarbige Zeichnungen, Pappband. ●●●●

Fußballtraining für Kinder und Jugendliche
Spiel- und Übungsformen zu Technik und Taktik
(**1463**-5) Von S. Asmus u. a., ca. 128 Seiten, durchgehend vierfarbig, kartoniert. ●●

SportRegeln
American Football
(**1165**-2) 136 S., 18 s/w-Fotos, kartoniert. ●

Streetball
Technik · Taktik · Spiel
(**1465**-1) Von J. Bezler und T. Paganetti, ca. 80 Seiten, durchgehend vierfarbig, kartoniert. ●●

Handball
Technik · Taktik · Regeln.
(**0426**-5) Von F. und P. Hattig, 128 Seiten, 91 s/w-Fotos, 121 Zeichnungen, kart. ●●

Handball
Grundlagen für Training und Spiel
(**2321**-9) Von H.-P. Oppermann, 120 Seiten, 39 Farbtafeln, 12 s/w-Fotos, 108 Farbzeichnungen, kartoniert. ●●

SportRegeln Handball
Die offiziellen Regeln
Wissenswertes von A bis Z
(**1099**-6) 88 Seiten, 32 s/w-Fotos, 14 Zeichnungen, kartoniert. ●

SportRegeln Rugby
Die offiziellen Regeln
Wissenswertes von A bis Z
(**1216**-0) 96 Seiten, zahlreiche zweifarbige Abbildungen, kartoniert. ●

Tennis
Technik · Taktik · Regeln.
(**0375**-7) Von W. u. S. Taferner, 112 Seiten, 81 Abbildungen., kartoniert. ●

SportRegeln Tennis
Die offiziellen Regeln
Wissenswertes von A bis Z
(**1097**-4) 88 S., 24 s/w-Fotos, 6 Zeichnungen, kartoniert. ●

Tischtennis-Technik
Der individuelle Weg zu erfolgreichem Spiel.
(**0775**-2) Von M. Perger, 144 Seiten, 296 Abbildungen, kartoniert. ●●

SportRegeln Tischtennis
Die offiziellen Regeln
Wissenswertes von A bis Z (**1252**-7) 96 S., zahlreiche zweifarbige Abb., kart. ●

Badminton
Technik · Taktik · Training.
(**0699**-3) Von K. Fuchs, L. Sologub, 168 S., 51 Abbildungen, kartoniert. ●●

SportRegeln
Badminton
(**1101**-6) 84 S., kartoniert. ●

Squash
(**2311**-1) Von P. Langhammer, R. Michna, 96 S., 86 Farbfotos, 13 Farbzeichn., kartoniert. ●●

Squash
Ausrüstung · Technik · Regeln
(**0539**-3) Von D. von Horn, H.-D. Stünitz, 96 S., 55 s/w-Fotos, 25 Zeichnungen, kart. ●

SportRegeln Squash
Wissenswertes von A bis Z
(**1100**-8) 64 S., 11 s/w-Fotos, 23 Zeichnungen, kartoniert. ●

Darts
Technik · Taktik · Spiel
(**1466**-X) Von R.W. Sohlbach, ca. 112 S., kart. ●●

Golf
Neue Wege zum erfolgreichen Spiel
(**4509**-3) Von O. Heuler, ca. 144 S., zahlr. Farbabbildungen, Pappband. ●●●●●

SportRegeln Golf
(**1315**-9) 96 S., 19 s/w-Fotos, kartoniert. ●

Golf
Ausrüstung und Technik.
(**0343**-9) Von J. C. Jessop, 96 S., 57 Abb., Anhang Golfregeln des DGV, kart. ●

Eishockey
Lauf- und Stocktechnik, Körperspiel, Taktik, Ausrüstung und Regeln.
(**0414**-1) Von J. Čapla, 264 S., 548 s/w-Fotos, 163 Zeichnungen, kartoniert. ●●●

SportRegeln
Eishockey
(**1098**-2) 116 Seiten, kartoniert. ●

Billard
Grundstöße · Viertelbillard und Freie Partie
(**1313**-2) Von Dr. H. Stingel, 112 Seiten, 196 Zeichnungen, kartoniert. ●●●

Grundlagen für Training und Spiel
Pool-Billard
(**2318**-9) Von B. Pejcic, R. Meyer, 96 S., durchgehend vierfarbig, kartoniert. ●●

Pool-Billard
(**0484**-2) Herausgegeben vom Deutschen Pool-Billard-Bund. Von M.Bach, K.-W. Kühn, 104 S., 64 Abbildungen, kartoniert. ●

FALKEN Video
Reiten
Von der ersten Stunde bis zum Ausritt
(**6097**-1) VHS, ca. 60 Min., in Farbe, mit Begleitheft. ●●●●*

Reiten
(**2322**-7) Von T. Eckholt, 128 S., durchgehend vierfarbig, kartoniert. ●●

Tanzstunde
Das Welttanzprogramm leicht gelernt
(**4409**-2) Von G. Hädrich, 164 S., 489 s/w-Fotos, 63 Zeichnungen, Pappband. ●●●

Wir lernen Tanzen
(**0200**-9) Von E. Fern, 152 S., 119 s/w-Fotos, 47 Zeichnungen, kartoniert. ●●

Anmutig und fit durch
Bauchtanz
(**0911**-9) Von Marta, 120 S., 229 Farbfotos, 6 s/w-Zeichnungen, kartoniert. ●●●

Segeln
(**1364**-X) Von H. Mönster u.a., ca. 128 Seiten, durchgehend vierfarbig, zahlr. Abbildungen, kartoniert. ●●●

Sporttauchen
Theorie und Praxis des Gerätetauchens
(**0647**-0) Von S. Müßig, 144 S., 8 Farbtafeln, 35 s/w-Fotos, 89 Zeichnungen, kart. ●●

Fit mit Sporttauchen
(**2320**-0) Von Dr. F. Naglschmid, 112 Seiten, 71 Farbfotos, 21 Zeichnungen, kart. ●●

Angelfischerei von Aal bis Zander
Fische · Geräte · Technik.
(**0324**-2) Von H. Oppel, 72 Seiten, 16 Farbtafeln, 49 s/w-Abb., kartoniert. ●●

Angeln
Kleine Fibel für den Sportfischer.
(**0198**-3) Von E. Bondick, 80 Seiten, 4 Farbtafeln, 116 Abbildungen, kartoniert. ●

Snowboarding
Ausrüstung · Fahrtechnik · Wettkämpfe
Videokassette (**6139**-0) VHS, ca. 45 Min., in Farbe. ●●●●*

Fibel für Kegelfreunde
Sport- und Freizeitkegeln · Bowling
(**0191**-6) Von G. Bocsai, 72 Seiten, 62 Abb., kartoniert ●

111spannende Kegelspiele
(**2031**-7) Von H. Regulski, 80 S., 53 Zeichnungen, kartoniert. ●

Mensch und Gesundheit

Der moderne Ratgeber
Wir werden Eltern
Schwangerschaft · Geburt · Erziehung des Kleinkindes.
(**4269**-8) Von B. Nees-Delaval, 376 Seiten, 335 2-farbige Abb., Pappband. ●●●●

Ich freue mich auf mein Baby
Ratgeber und Tagebuch für die Schwangerschaft
(**4711**-8) Von E. Portz-Schmitt, 184 S., 18 Farbfotos, 72 Farbzeichn., Pappband. ●●●●

Ich bekomme ein Baby
Wegweiser für Schwangerschaft und Geburt
(**1254**-3) Von B. Nees-Delaval, 144 Seiten, durchgehend zweifarbig, kartoniert. ●●

Wenn der Mensch zum Vater wird
Ein heiter-besinnlicher Ratgeber
(**4259**-0) Von D. Zimmer, 160 S., 20 Zeichnungen, Pappband. ●●●

AOK Bibliothek
Schwangerschaftsgymnastik und Geburtsvorbereitung
(**1423**-6) Von L. Keller, 112 S., 137 Farbfotos, 12 Farbzeichnungen, kartoniert. ●●●

Vorbereitung auf die Geburt und
Schwangerschaftsgymnastik
Atmung, Rückbildungsgymnastik,
(**0251**-3) Von S. Buchholz, 112 Seiten, 98 s/w-Fotos, kartoniert. ●

AOK-Bibliothek
Rückbildungsgymnastik
Informationen, Tips und Übungen
(**1470**-8) Von L. Keller, ca. 112 Seiten, zahlreiche Farbfotos und Farbillustrationen, kartoniert. ●●●*

AOK-Videothek
FALKEN Video
Rückbildungsgymnastik
Informationen, Tips und Übungen
(**6176**-5) Laufzeit ca. 30 Minuten. ●●●●*

Die Kunst des Stillens
nach neuesten Erkenntnissen
(**0701**-9) Von Prof. Dr. med. E. Schmidt, S. Brunn, 112 S., 20 Fotos und Zeichnungen, kartoniert. ●

Der große FALKEN BabyKurs
Pflege · Ernährung · Entwicklung · Erziehung
(**4739**-8) Von K. Schutt, ca. 352 Seiten, ca. 400 Farbfotos, gebunden. ●●●

Das Babybuch
Pflege · Ernährung · Entwicklung
(**0531**-8) Von A. Burkert, 96 Seiten, 76 zweifarbige Zeichnungen, 22 s/w-Zeichnungen, kartoniert. ●●

Babyfitneß
Massage, Spiele, Gymnastik und Schwimmen für Kinder im 1. Lebensjahr
(**1034**-6) Von G. Zeiß, 112 Seiten, 179 zweifarbige Illustrationen,, kartoniert. ●●

Wenn Kinder krank werden
Medizinischer Ratgeber für Eltern
(**4240**-X) Von B. Nees-Delaval, 232 Seiten, 163 Zeichnungen, Pappband. ●●●

Keinen Mann um jeden Preis
Das neue Selbstverständnis der Frau in der Partnerbeziehung
(**4440**-2) Von Shere Hite, Kate Colleran, 208 Seiten, Pappband. ●●●

Total verknallt ... und keine Ahnung?
Alles über Liebe, Sex und Zärtlichkeit
(**1024**-9) Von H. Bruckner, R. Rathgeber, 104 S., 38 Abbildungen, kartoniert. ●●

Streicheleinheiten für Körper und Seele
Partnermassage
(**4444**-5) Von Chr. Unseld-Baumanns, 136 S., 145 Farbfotos, Pappband. ●●●●

Partner gesucht
Die besten Tips und Strategien fürs Kennenlernen
(**1481**-3) Von Dr. C. Harmsen, 128 Seiten, kartoniert. ●●

freundin Ratgeber
Glück braucht Mut
Die Psycho-Logik des Jens Corssen
(**1176**-8) Von J. Corssen, B. Schmidt, 160 S., kartoniert. ●●

freundin Ratgeber
Die faire Trennung
Wie man mit Anstand auseinandergeht
(**1477**-5) Von I. Weber, ca. 144 S., kart. ●●

Angst und Panik
Ursachen · Symptome · Therapie
(**1422**-8) Von Prof. Dr. H.-R. Lückert, 176 S., kartoniert. ●●●

Wörterbuch der Medizin
(**4535**-2) 400 Seiten, 229 Farbfotos, Pappband. ●●●●

Bildatlas des menschlichen Körpers
(**4177**-2) Von G. Pogliani, V. Vannini, 112 Seiten, 402 Farbabbildungen, 28 s/w-Fotos, Pappband. ●●●●

Richtig essen bei
Nahrungsmittelallergien
(**4745**-2) Von Dr. med. C. Thiel, A. Ilies, 128 S., ca. 90 Farbf., gebunden. ●●●

Nahrungsmittelallergien
So ernähren Sie sich richtig!
(**0913**-5) Von Priv.-Doz. Dr. med. Dr. med. habil. J. von Mayenburg, Prof. Dr. med. Dr. phil. S. Borelli, E. Polster, 136 S., kart. ●●

Neurodermitis
Ursachen · Ganzheitliche Behandlung · Selbsthilfe
(**1218**-7) Von Prof. Dr. med. Dr. phil. S. Borelli, 144 S., kartoniert. ●●

Bluthochdruck
Risikofaktoren · Vorbeugung · Behandlung
(**1125**-3) Von Prof. Dr. med. D. Klaus, R. Unsorg, G. Leibold, 152 S., 25 Farbfotos, 22 Farbzeichnungen, kartoniert. ●●●

Arteriosklerose
Risikofaktoren/Vorbeugung/Therapie
Richtige Ernährung bei erhöhtem Cholesterinspiegel.
(**1020**-6) Von Prof. Dr. med. G. Assmann, Dr. troph. U. Wahrburg, 192 S., 84 farb. Abb., 4 s/w-Zeichnungen, kartoniert. ●●●

Asthma
Pseudokrupp, Bronchitis und Lungenemphysem
Krankheitsbilder · Diagnose · Therapie
(**1126**-1) Von Prof. Dr. med. W. Schmidt, S. Ertelt, 152 S., 110 zweif. Zeichn., kart. ●●●

Risiko Herzinfarkt
Empfohlen von der Deutschen Herzstiftung
(**1217**-9) Von C. Halhuber, M. J. Halhuber, 152 S., 38 Farb- und 8 s/w-Zeichnungen, kartoniert. ●●●

So arbeitet das Immunsystem
Funktionsweise · Störungen · Natürliche Stärkung
(**1253**-5) Von V. Friebel, J. Ledvina, A. Roßmeier, 168 S., 18 Farbtafeln, 38 zweifarbige Zeichnungen, kartoniert. ●●●

Diabetes
Krankheitsbild, Therapie, Kontrollen, Schwangerschaft, Sport, Urlaub, Alltagsprobleme. Neueste Erkenntnisse der Diabetesforschung. (**0895**-3) Von Dr. med. H. J. Krönke, 120 S., 4 Farbtafeln, 14 s/w-Fotos, 13 s/w-Zeichnungen, kartoniert. ●

AOK-Bibliothek
Gesunde Haut
Ratgeber für Pflege und Gesundheit
(**1468**-6) Von Dr. med. J. Müller und Dr. med. K.-U. Schmidt, ca. 112 Seiten, zahlr. Abbildungen, durchgehend vierfarbig, kart. ●●●

Naturkosmetik
Die Grundlagen gesunder und natürlicher Hautpflege.
(**1080**-X) Von N. E. Haas, 120 Seiten, 63 Farbabbildungen, kartoniert. ●●

Die sanfte Art des Heilens
Homöopathie
Praktische Anwendung und Arzneimittellehre
(**4418**-X) Von J. H. P. Kreuter, 216 S., 49 Zeichnungen, Pappband. ●●●

Aromatherapie
Gesundheit und Entspannung durch ätherische Öle.
(**1131**-8) Von K. Schutt, 96 S., 40 zweifarbige Abbildungen, kartoniert. ●●

Heilatmen
Ein Weg zu Lebenskraft und innerer Harmonie
(**1047**-8) Von K. Schutt, 112 S., 57 zweifarbige Abbildungen, kartoniert. ●●

Bewährte Naturheilverfahren bei
Herz-Kreislauf-Erkrankungen
(**1084**-2) Von Dr. med. O. Wolff, G. Leibold, 104 Seiten, kartoniert. ●

Risiko Herzinfarkt
(**1217**-9) Von Dr. C. Halhuber, Prof. Dr. M. J. Halhuber, 160 S., durchgehend zweifarbig, kartoniert. ●●●

Krebsangst und Krebs behandeln
Mit einem Vorwort von Prof. Dr. med. Friedrich Douwes.
(**0839**-2) Von G. Leibold, 104 Seiten, kartoniert. ●

Bewährte Naturheilverfahren bei
Krebs
(**1082**-6) Hrsg. H.-R. Heiligtag, 88 Seiten, kartoniert. ●

Heilen mit Blütenenergien
nach Dr. Bach
(**1141**-5) Von J. Wenzel, ca. 96 S., kartoniert. ●

Bewährte Naturheilverfahren bei
Migräne und Schlafstörungen
(**1081**-8) Von G. Leibold, Dr. med. H. Chr. Scheiner, 112 Seiten, kartoniert. ●

Gesunder Schlaf
Schlafstörungen ohne Medikamente erfolgreich behandeln.
(**1036**-2) Von D. H. Alke, 88 S., 22 s/w-Abb., mit Audiokassette, kartoniert. ●●●

Natürliche Behandlungsmethoden bei
Rückenschmerzen
Massage · Gymnastik · Entspannung
(**4447**-X) Von Prof. Dr. med. H. Hess, K. Eder, H.-J. Montag, K. Schutt, 152 S., 168 Farbabbildungen, Pappband. ●●●

TELE-Rückenschule
Wohlbefinden durch bewußte Körpererfahrung
(**1310**-8) Von K. Haak, 64 S., 19 Farb-, 24 s/w-Fotos, 24 Zeichnungen, 2 Ausklapptafeln, mit Audiokassette, kartoniert. ●●●●

TELE-Rückenschule
Wohlbefinden durch bewußte Körpererfahrung
Videokassette (**6108**-0) VHS, ca. 60 Min., in Farbe, mit Broschüre. ●●●●*

Rheuma behandeln und lindern
Mit einem Vorwort von Dr. med. Max-Otto Bruker.
(**0836**-8) Von G. Leibold, 96 Seiten, kartoniert. ●

Besser sehen durch Augentraining
Ein Gesundheitsprogramm zur Verbesserung des Sehvermögens.
(**0914**-3) Von K. Schutt, B. Rumpler, 96 S., 32 s/w-Zeichnungen, kartoniert. ●●

So arbeitet das
Immunsystem
(**1253**-5) Von V. Friebel, I. Ledvina, A. Roßmeier, 192 Seiten, durchgehend zweifarbig, kartoniert. ●●●

Allergien behandeln und lindern
Mit einem Vorwort von Prof. Dr. med. Axel Stemmann.
(**0840**-6) Von G. Leibold, 96 Seiten, 4 Zeichnungen, kartoniert. ●

Enzyme
Vitalstoffe für die Gesundheit
(**0677**-2) Von G. Leibold, 96 S., kartoniert. ●

Besser leben durch Fasten
(**0841**-4) Von G. Leibold, 96 S., kartoniert. ●

Massagetechniken und Heilanzeigen
Reflexzonentherapie
(**4404**-6) Von G. Leibold, 128 Seiten, 53 Farbzeichnungen, Pappband. ●●●

Akupressur zur Eigenbehandlung
(**0417**-6) Von G. Leibold, 112 S., 78 Abb., kartoniert.●

Shiatsu-Massage
Harmonisierung der Energieströme im Körper
(**0615**-2) Von G. Leibold, 196 S., 180 Abb., kartoniert. ●●●

Fußsohlenmassage
Heilanzeigen · Technik · Selbsthilfe
(**0714**-0) Von G. Leibold, 96 S., 38 Zeichnungen, kartoniert. ●

Entspannung und Schmerzlinderung durch
Massage
(**0750**-7) Von B. Rumpler, K. Schutt, 112 S., 116 zweifarbige Zeichnungen, kartoniert. ●

Gesundheit und Entspannung durch
Massage
(**1317**-5) Von K. Schutt, 168 S., 126 Farbfotos., 61 Farbzeichnungen, kartoniert. ●●●

Gesundheit für Körper und Seele
Entspannung
(**1471**-6) Von K. Schutt, ca. 80 Seiten, durchgehend zweifarbig, kartoniert, Audiokassette ca. 60 Minuten Laufzeit. ●●●●

Entspannung
(**0834**-1) Von Dr. Med. Chr. Schenk, 88 S., 29 Zeichnungen, kartoniert. ●

Autogenes Training
Ein Programm zur Streßbewältigung
(**1278**-0) Von Dr. P. Kruse, B. Pavlekovic, K. Haak, 112 S., durchgehend zweifarbig, kartoniert. ●●●

Erfolg und Lebensfreude durch
Autogenes Training und Psychokybernetik
(**1035**-4) Von D. H. Alke, 80 Seiten, 2 s/w-Zeichnungen, mit Audiokassette, kartoniert. ●●●

Chinesisches Schattenboxen
Tai-Ji-Quan
für geistige und körperliche Harmonie
(**0850**-3) Von F.T. Lie, 120 S., 221 s/w-Fotos, 9 s/w-Zeichnungen, Beilage: 1 s/w-Poster mit zahlreichen Abbildungen, kartoniert. ●●

AOK-Bibliothek
Qi-Gong im Alltag
Chinesische Atem- und Bewegungsübungen
(**1316**-7) Von L. U. Schoefer, ca. 80 Seiten, durchgehend vierfarbig, zahlreiche Fotos, kartoniert. ●●

AOK-Bibliothek
Qi-Gong im Alltag
Chinesische Atem- und Bewegungsübungen
(**1427**-9) Von L. U. Schoefer, ca. 80 Seiten, durchgehend vierfarbig, zahlreiche Fotos, kartoniert, mit Audiokassette. ●●●●

AOK-Videothek
Qi-Gong im Alltag
Chinesische Atem- und Bewegungsübungen
(**6179**-X) Von L. U. Schoefer, ca. 60 Minuten Laufzeit. ●●●●

Yoga für jeden
(**1277**-2) Von K. Zebroff, 144 Seiten, Spiralbindung, durchgehend vierfarbig, kartoniert. ●●●

Yoga
Weg zur Harmonie
(**4417**-8) Von A. Harf, W. von Rohr, 176 S., 171 Farbf., 12 s/w-Zeichn., Pappband. ●●●●

Yoga gegen Haltungsschäden und Rückenschmerzen
(**0394**-3) Von A. Raab, 104 S., 215 Abb., kart. ●

AOK-Bibliothek
Radwandern
für die Gesundheit
(**1369**-8) Von S. Kälberer, J.–U. Knoll, 128 S., 126 Farbfotos, kartoniert. ●●●

AOK-Bilbliothek
Osteoporose
Vorbeugen · Diagnose · Behandlung
(**1371**-X) Von A. Baumgarten, 96 S., 74 Farbfotos, 17 Farbzeichn., kartoniert. ●●●

AOK-Bibliothek
Erkältungskrankheiten
Vorbeugung und Behandlung
(**1372**-8) Von G. Leibold, 112 S., 74 Farbfotos, 7 Farbzeichn., kartoniert. ●●●

AOK-Bibliothek
Krankenpflege zu Hause
Anleitungen, Tips und Informationen
(**1373**-6) Von S. Hof, 104 S., 68 Farbfotos, 32 Farbzeichn., kartoniert. ●●●

PfundsKur Kochbuch
(**4726**-6) Von F. Metzler, 112 S., 81 Farbfotos, Pappband. ●●●

Fit ohne Fett
Die neue PfundsKur
(**1370**-1) Von Prof. Dr. V. Pudel, 128 Seiten, kartoniert. ●

Die aktuelle
Ballaststofftabelle
(**1288**-8) Von Dr. H. Oberritter, 80 Seiten, kartoniert. ●

Neue Rezepte für **Diabetiker-Diät**
Vollwertig · abwechslungsreich · kalorienarm
(**0418**-4) Von M. Oehlrich, 96 S., 8 Farbtafeln, kartoniert. ●

Diät bei Herzkrankheiten und Bluthochdruck
Rezeptteil von B. Zöllner
(**3202**-1) Von Prof. Dr. med. H. Rottka, 92 S., 4 Farbtafeln, kartoniert. ●●

Diät bei Erkrankungen der Nieren, Harnwege und bei Dialysebehandlung
Rezeptteil von B. Zöllner.
(**3203**-X) Von Prof. Dr. med. Dr. h. c. H. J. Sarre und Prof. Dr. med. R. Kluthe, 96 S., 33 Farbfotos, 1 s/w-Zeichnung, kartoniert. ●●

Diät bei Gicht und Harnsäuresteinen
Rezeptteil von B. Zöllner.
(**3205**-6) Von Prof. Dr. med. N. Zöllner, 112 S., 35 Farbtafeln, kartoniert. ●●

Diät bei Zuckerkrankheit
Rezeptteil von B. Zöllner (**3206**-4) Von Prof. Dr. med. P. Dieterle, 112 S., 42 Farbfotos, 4 vierfarbige Vignetten, 1 s/w-Zeichnung, kartoniert. ●●

Diät bei erhöhtem Cholesterinspiegel und anderen Fettstoffwechselstörungen
Rezeptteil von B. Zöllner.
(**3208**-0) Von Prof. Dr. med. G. Wolfram, 102 S., 32 Farbfotos, kartoniert. ●●

Ballaststoffreiche Kost bei Funktionsstörungen des Darms
Rezeptteil von B. Zöllner.
(**3212**-9) Von Prof. Dr. med. H. Kasper, 96 Seiten, 34 Farbfotos, 1 s/w-Foto, kartoniert. ●●

Diät bei Krankheiten des Magens und Zwölffingerdarms
Rezeptteil von B. Zöllner
(**3201**-3) Von Prof. Dr. med. H. Kaess, 96 Seiten, 35 Farbfotos, 1 s/w-Zeichnung, kartoniert. ●●

Diät bei Krankheiten der Gallenblase, Leber und Bauchspeicheldrüse
Rezeptteil von B. Zöllner.
(**3207**-2) Von Prof. Dr. med. H. Kasper, 88 Seiten, 35 Farbfotos, 1 s/w-Zeichnung, , kartoniert. ●●

Video

Hobby Aquarellmalen
Landschaft und Stilleben
(**6022**-X) VHS, 40 Min., in Farbe, mit Begleitheft. ●●●●*

Hobby Ölmalerei
Landschaft und Stilleben
(**6025**-4) VHS, 40 Min., in Farbe, mit Begleitheft. ●●●●*

Seidenmalerei
leicht gemacht
(**6173**-0) VHS, ca. 30 Min., in Farbe ●●●●*

Basteln mit Kindern
(**6041**-6) VHS, 60 Min., in Farbe, mit Vorlagen in Originalgröße, mit Begleitheft. ●●●*

Die Modelleisenbahn
Anlagenbau in Modultechnik
(**6028**-9) VHS, 30 Min., in Farbe. ●●●●*

Golf
(**6053**-X) VHS, 60 Min., in Farbe, mit Begleitheft. ●●●●●*

Reiten
(**6097**-1) VHS, ca. 60 Min., in Farbe, mit Begleitbroschüre. ●●●●*

Karate
Einführung und Grundtechniken
(**6037**-8) VHS, ca. 45 Min., in Farbe, mit Begleitbroschüre. ●●●●*

Skigymnastik perfekt
(**6052**-1) VHS, ca. 60 Min., in Farbe, mit Begleitbroschüre. ●●●●●*

Snowboarding
(**6139**-0) VHS, ca. 45 Min., in Farbe, mit Broschüre.●●●●*

Pflanzenjournal
Blumen- und Pflanzenpflege im Jahreslauf
(**6036**-X) VHS, 30 Minuten, mit Begleitheft. ●●●●*

Schnitt und Pflege
von Bäumen und Sträuchern
(**6050**-5) VHS, 45 Minuten, in Farbe, mit Begleitheft. ●●●●*

Erfolgreiche Streßbewältigung
Autogenes Training
Video 1: Einführung und Kurs
Video 2: Übungen
(**6132**-3) VHS, jeweils ca. 60 Minuten, in Farbe. ●●●●●*

Aktfotografie
Gestaltung/Technik/Spezialeffekte
Interpretationen zu einem unerschöpflichen Thema
(**6001**-7) VHS, 60 Min., in Farbe, mit Begleitheft. ●●●●●*

Videografieren perfekt
Profitricks für Aufnahmetechnik und Nachbearbeitung
(**6042**-4) VHS, (**6044**-4) Video 8, 60 Min., in Farbe, mit Begleitheft. ●●●●●*

Besser Videofilmen
(**6172**-2) VHS, ca. 60 Minuten, in Farbe. ●●●●●*

Top-Form Gymnastik
Ein Bewegungsprogramm für pfundige Leute
(**6144**-7) VHS, ca. 30 Minuten, in Farbe. ●●●●*

Fitt ohne Fett
PfundsKur Video
(**6142**-0) VHS, ca. 40 Min., in Farbe.●●●●*

Streicheleinheiten für Körper und Seele
Partnermassage
(**6051**-3) VHS, 45 Min., in Farbe, mit Begleitheft. ●●●●●*

Tele Partner Massage
Zärtliche Entspannung zu zweit
(**6131**-5) VHS, ca. 60 Minuten, in Farbe. ●●●●*

Sinnliche Stunden
(**6099**-8) VHS, ca. 60 Min., in Farbe, mit Begleitbroschüre. ●●●●●*

Nie wieder rauchen
(**6100**-5) VHS, ca. 45 Min., in Farbe, mit Begleitbroschüre. ●●●●*

New York
(**6151**-X) VHS, ca. 60 Min., in Farbe. ●●●●*

Kalifornien
(**6152**-8) VHS, ca. 60 Min., in Farbe. ●●●●*

USA Südwest
(**6153**-6) VHS, ca. 60 Min., in Farbe. ●●●●*

Florida
(**6154**-4) VHS, ca. 60 Min., in Farbe. ●●●●*

Hawaii
(**6164**-1) VHS, ca. 60 Min., in Farbe. ●●●●*

Irland
(**6167**-6) VHS, ca. 60 Min., in Farbe. ●●●●*

Norwegen
(**6161**-7) VHS, ca. 60 Min., in Farbe. ●●●●*

Kanarische Inseln
(**6162**-5) VHS, ca. 60 Min., in Farbe. ●●●●*

Mallorca
(**6143**-9) VHS, ca. 60 Min., in Farbe. ●●●●*

Toscana
(**6148**-X) VHS, ca. 60 Min., in Farbe. ●●●●*

Rom
(**6145**-5) VHS, ca. 60 Min., in Farbe. ●●●●*

Venedig
(**6146**-3) VHS, ca. 60 Min., in Farbe. ●●●●*

Florenz
(**6147**-1) VHS, ca. 60 Min., in Farbe. ●●●●*

Paris
(**6157**-9) VHS, ca. 60 Min., in Farbe. ●●●●*

Wien
(**6158**-7) VHS, ca. 60 Min., in Farbe. ●●●●*

London
(**6159**-5) VHS, ca. 60 Min., in Farbe. ●●●●*

Prag
(**6165**-X) VHS, ca. 60 Min., in Farbe. ●●●●*

Griechische Inseln
(**6166**-8) VHS, ca. 60 Min., in Farbe. ●●●●*

Kuba
(**6150**-1) VHS, ca. 60 Min., in Farbe. ●●●●*

Dominikanische Republik
(**6163**-3) VHS, ca. 60 Min., in Farbe. ●●●●*

Malediven
(**6156**-0) VHS, ca. 60 Min., in Farbe. ●●●●*

Bali
(**6149**-8) VHS, ca. 60 Min., in Farbe. ●●●●*

Thailand
(**6155**-2) VHS, ca. 60 Min., in Farbe. ●●●●*

Hongkong
(**6160**-9) VHS, ca. 60 Min., in Farbe. ●●●●*

Berlin
(**6177**-3) Laufzeit ca. 60 Minuten. ●●●●*

Tunesien
(**6174**-9) Laufzeit ca. 60 Minuten. ●●●●*

Kanada
(**6178**-1) Laufzeit ca. 60 Minuten. ●●●●*

Bestellschein

Erfüllungsort und Gerichtsstand für Vollkaufleute ist der jeweilige Sitz der Lieferfirma. Für alle übrigen Kunden gilt dieser Gerichtsstand für das Mahnverfahren. Falls durch besondere Umstände Preisänderungen notwendig werden, erfolgt Auftragserledigung zu dem bei der Lieferung gültigen Preis.

Ich bestelle hiermit aus dem Falken-Verlag GmbH, Postfach 1120, D-65521 Niedernhausen/Ts., durch die Buchhandlung:

Ex.

Ex.

Ex.

Ex.

Name: Datum:

Straße:

Ort: Unterschrift:

Die hier vorgestellten Bücher, Videokassetten und Software sind in folgende Preisgruppen unterteilt:

● Preisgruppe bis DM 10,–/S 79,–/SFr 11,–
●● Preisgruppe über DM 10,– bis DM 20,– S 80,– bis S 160,– SFr 10,– bis SFr 21,–
●●● Preisgruppe über DM 20,– bis DM 30,– S 161,– bis S 240,– SFr 21,– bis SFr 30,–
●●●● Preisgruppe über DM 30,– bis DM 50,– S 241,– bis S 400,– SFr 30,– bis SFr 50,–
●●●●● Preisgruppe über DM 50,–/S 401,–/SFr 50,–
* (unverbindliche Preisempfehlung)

Die Preise entsprechen dem Status beim Druck dieses Verzeichnisses (s. Seite 1) – Änderungen, im besonderen der Preise, vorbehalten –

Falken-Verlag GmbH · Postfach 1120 FALKEN **D-65521 Niedernhausen/Ts. · Tel.: 0 61 27 / 70 20**